This is the sort of sight that brings one back to Southeast Asia, despite all the discomfort, inconvenience and sickness. A rose-pink sky behind the clouds and a range of sawtooth mountains. On the plain below the mountains, mist and smoke haze, hanging white above the ground. The green vegetation dark in the pre-sunrise minutes and a laterite road glowing in surreal—almost 'Day-Glo'—orange running parallel with the rail track. The whole world except for the mist suffused for this moment with every shade of pink and orange, even the buffaloes by the road.

Written after watching dawn break over southern Thailand while travelling on the overnight express from Bangkok to Hat Yai. 12 April 1980.

'Pol Pot's government solved the leprosy problem: they killed all the lepers.'

Dr Ly Po, Head of Battambang province's Health Service, in conversation, Cambodia, 28 August 1981

Publications by Milton Osborne

Books

The French Presence in Cochinchina and Cambodia: Rule and Response (1859-1905), 1969; reprinted with introduction 1997.

Region of Revolt: Focus on Southeast Asia, 1970; revised expanded edition 1971

Politics and Power in Cambodia: The Sihanouk Years, 1973

River Road to China: The Mekong River Expedition, 1866-1873, 1975; new edition 1996

Southeast Asia: An Introductory History, 1979; 12th edition 2016, translated into Japanese, Korean, Thai, Khmer and Chinese languages.

Before Kampuchea: Preludes to Tragedy, 1979; reprinted with Postscript 1984

Sihanouk: Prince of Light, Prince of Darkness, 1994; translated into Japanese and Czech languages.

The Mekong: Turbulent Past, Uncertain Future, 2000; updated edition 2006

Exploring Southeast Asia: A Traveller's History of the Region, 2002

Phnom Penh: A Cultural and Literary History, 2008

Research Monographs

Singapore and Malaysia, 1964

Strategic Hamlets in South Vietnam: A Survey and a Comparison, 1965

River at Risk: The Mekong and the Water Politics of Southeast Asia, 2004

The Paramount Power; China and the Countries of Southeast Asia, 2006

The Mekong: River Under Threat, 2009

PRAISE FOR MILTON OSBORNE

"A fascinating, first-person journey through s ome of t he m ost important periods of Southeast Asian history in the 20th century. A compelling mix of memoir and history, full of wit and personality and sorrow."

-- Joshua Kurlantzick, Senior Fellow for Southeast Asia at the Council on Foreign Relations (CFR) in New York.

Starting with Sihanouk's Cambodia and Graham Greene's Vietnam— an elegant memoir by Australia's best-known Southeast Asia specialist. Writing of his life as a diplomat and academic, and of his extraordinary work for the United Nations, Osborne provides portraits of key figures in the turbulent 1960s and 1970s—Australians as well as Cambodians and Vietnamese— and reminds us just how different and dangerous the ASEAN region was in that dark period.

-- Anthony Milner, Australian National University, Professorial Fellow University of Melbourne, a Director of Asialink.

"An engaging memoir of travel, inquiry, and wartime peril in Southeast Asia, written by one of the foremost authorities on the region."

-- From John Burgess, author of *Temple in the Clouds: Faith and Conflict at Preah Vihear,* and a former *Washington Post* foreign correspondent.

"This book reaffirms Milton Osborne as a leading historian and analyst of Southeast Asia in general and of Cambodia and Vietnam in particular. Like his definitive biography of Norodom Sihanouk, the elusive "God-King" of Cambodia, and his books on the water politics of The Mekong River this memoir is of international importance."

-- From Sir Leslie Fielding, a former British diplomat, EU Commission Director-General, and Vice-Chancellor of Sussex University.

For Fiona, again

Published in 2018 by Connor Court Publishing Pty Ltd

Connor Court Publishing Pty Ltd
PO Box 7257
Redland Bay QLD 4165

sales@connorcourt.com
www.connorcourtpublishing.com.au

Phone 0497 900 685

ISBN: 9781925501803

Front Cover Design: Maria Giordano. Front cover photo: exhumed skulls at Choeung Ek, 'The Killing Fields,' which were still being dug up in August 1981, © Milton Osborne (private collection).

Photos in the book belong to © Milton Osborne (private collection).

Printed in Australia.

Contents

Prologue

How it started

What follows in this book is an account of my initially unexpected and subsequently prolonged association with Southeast Asia, and with Cambodia and Vietnam in particular. The association began in 1959, when I was posted to the Australian embassy in Phnom Penh. But although Southeast Asia remains very much part of my life today this book's material ends in 1981 when, after twenty years away from government service I returned to work in the Office of National Assessments. My posting to Cambodia was preceded by a brief introduction to expatriate life in Papua New Guinea that was important for my later research concerning French colonial policy in Cambodia and Vietnam as a graduate student at Cornell. There are two Epilogues dating from the years after 1981: one dealing with my search for information about the execution in Cambodia by the Khmer Rouge of my friend Monsignor Paulus Tep Im Sotha, and the second reproducing my obituary of Norodom Sihanouk, a looming presence throughout the years I cover. The book does not canvass another aspect of my involvement in Southeast Asia—the more than three years I spent based in Singapore between 1975 and 1979. That may be a task for another time.

The material in the book is episodic in character, but I'm sufficiently immodest to think that the periods I discuss remain subjects of continuing historical and even contemporary political interest. Most of what appears in this book has not appeared in my previous writings. This is particularly so in relation to Vietnam and to the time I spent in Paris where I went to carry out research in the colonial archives dealing with Cambodia and Vietnam.

I first began this book it with my daughter in mind and my realisation of how very little there is in print dealing with my own father's life, the grandfather she never knew. There is, it's true, an entry for George Davenport Osborne in the *Australian Dictionary of Biography* and the obituaries at the time of his death in 1955, at the early age of fifty-five, give some details of his professional career as a university-based geologist. There are, too, his academic papers, most importantly a substantial monograph dealing with the Upper Hunter region of New South Wales. (*The Structural Evolution of the Hunter-Manning-Myall Province*, New South Wales, Royal Society of New South Wales, Monograph No.1, 1950) This considerable achievement, the culmination of his life's work in that region, had a direct connection with his deep regard for his mentor at the University of Sydney, T.W. Edgeworth David. For it was in the Hunter region, under Edgeworth David's tutelage, that he determined on his career. But these materials provide little insight into his personality.

If I ever tried to write about his life it would be a difficult task, not because of any lack of anecdotes—I remember many—but rather because nowhere are there extended accounts of his life in Australia and overseas of the kind found in journals or diaries, or in a store of

10

surviving letters. The *Dictionary's* account does not tell you he was a more than competent horseman, as he had to be as he undertook his field work in the 1920s and 1930s, when, in an age before GPS devices and Google Earth, he did his own mapping, carrying a plane table on his back and both a theodolite and an aneroid barometer to record his findings. It does not tell a reader that he was an excellent raconteur, though it does record that he could be a marvellously engaging lecturer, particularly in the field, if not always fully prepared for lecture room presentations. And while the *ADB* entry makes clear his love of music, it does not record the fact that as a small child I knew no greater pleasure than hearing him play the pipe organ in the University of Sydney's Great Hall, a "command performance" for me that always ended with a stirring rendition of "Gaudeamus Igitur". Nor does it tell of how he wept at the manner in which Eugene Goosens, the then permanent conductor of the Sydney Symphony Orchestra, was hounded from Australia in the 1950s for the importing of "pornography" that would scarcely raise an eyebrow today.

Any account of his life would record his talent for friendship, a talent reflected in the passage of an extraordinary range of individuals through our home, from federal cabinet ministers to Jesuit priests from the Seismograph Observatory at Riverview. Just as he always treated my brother and me with respect, so he gave as much of himself in his evening lectures to technical college students as he did to the highest of high flyers among his honours students at the university. It may sound old-fashioned now, but I look back in envy at the groups of students he led in songs both in the drawing room at Turramurra and around a campfire on geology excursions in the country.

In writing about him I would also have to offer thanks to both my parents for the love of travel they inculcated in me. Here was where his skill as a story teller came to the fore with accounts of their staying with Count Bernadotte in Sweden, and lacking formal evening dress to the distress of the household staff, marching side by side with hilarious retelling of encounters with the Irish, for his specialist interest in Serpentine rocks took him to Ireland as well as to New Zealand. Nearly falling to his death when climbing Mount Egmont (Mount Taranaki) in the latter country became the basis for another story that I never ceased to want repeated. In my parents' household I grew up knowing that travel was a normal pursuit, not something to be hoped for in the distant future. In this respect my mother's, Gwynneth Janet Osborne's, account of accepting an invitation to accompany friends driving from Cambridge to John O'Groats for a funeral "just for the ride" seemed an entirely sensible way of behaving.

* * *

But the original inspiration for this book has not led me to write about my personality. It is most certainly not an *apologia pro vita mea*; quite to the contrary. I don't think that book will ever be written. And if some who know me might describe my personal life as chequered, I have no illusions that this is of much interest to anyone but those who were directly part of it. Rather, as was the case when I have previously written about Cambodia and Vietnam, I hope that some of my personal experiences shed light on bigger issues—though I readily admit the account I give of my time in Paris contains much that is essentially personal in nature.

Fundamentally, it is a book about Cambodia and Vietnam, countries that have been a cause for fascination, happiness and deep despair.

Dropping a catch

I had begun university studies with the hope of becoming a barrister and so started a combined Arts-Law course at the University of Sydney. My father's death, when I was in my second year of studies, brought a change of plan and eventually, on graduation, the opportunity to join the Australian Department of External Affairs (today's Department of Foreign Affairs and Trade) at the beginning of 1958. Without any firm expectation about where I might serve overseas I certainly hoped it would be somewhere both interesting and important—London, Washington, Tokyo or Jakarta. The possibility that it could be Phnom Penh, Cambodia's capital city, never entered my mind. I knew where that city was, but very little more. And even today there is, at least for me, a question mark over just why I should have ended being posted there.

My first year as a trainee diplomat in Canberra was, well, in the French term, *mouvementé*, marked first by being arrested with one of my colleagues, Gregory Clark, for trying to pull a signpost from the ground while certainly the worse for wear in terms of alcohol consumed. We both weathered this experience with remarkably little difficulty as the department showed remarkable forbearance over this event, dismissing it, accurately, as "undergraduatish". But then, in what I have always thought was a second strike, I failed dismally to take a catch off the bowling of the head of the department, the formidable Arthur Tange, in a social cricket match—he was knighted and became Sir Arthur the following year.

Nothing was said at the time to link my failure in the field and my posting shortly afterwards, and the fact that I had some competence in French certainly played some part, surely the major part, in my being posted to Phnom Penh. But I could not dismiss from my mind the possibility that being sent to one of Australia's most out-of-the-way diplomatic posts was at least partially related to my fielding lapse. More than twenty years later I felt bold enough at a social gathering to ask Sir Arthur if my supposition was correct. Still the formidable figure that I had known before, even though he was by then retired, he fixed me with his trademark unblinking stare and, for at least thirty seconds said nothing. Then, and I believe there was even a grin, he said, "Made a career of it, didn't you!"

And, it has be to be said, Arthur Tange was right, though it took a little while for me to accept that this was how matters were to be. To write that spending over two years in Phnom Penh before I turned twenty-six was "life changing" sounds all too like an exercise in pop psychology, but it's true. To live in Cambodia in the early 1960s was to enter a world so different from anything I had previously experienced it was inevitable that it struck deep responses, not that these were always positive. And not even the experience of nearly dying from a severe case of amoebic dysentery that hospitalised me in Thailand for almost a month—"lost a couple like you last month," I was told on admission to the Bangkok Nursing Home—could dim the impact of that long-ago period in Cambodia.

If ever there was a "golden age" for Prince Sihanouk, the unchallenged leader of Cambodia at this time, this was it. Cambodia, and most particularly Phnom Penh, was a remarkable blend of Asian exoticism and the remnants of *la France d'outre-mer*. It was a country where I made friends, only to lose them to the Khmer Rouge two decades later. And if Phnom Penh was once arguably the most charming city in Southeast Asia it was also a jumping off point to the incomparable temples of Angkor, for Saigon with its echoes of Graham Greene's *The Quiet American*, and for Bangkok's pervasive whiff of sin. This was a heady mix to imbibe, and having done so to the full, then and later, I continue to return after years of studying, despairing and hoping there might be a better future for the country and its people than the economically booming but deeply corrupt and authoritarian regime that currently exists.

Vietnam was different, a country alien to Cambodia that held a different interest for me. Although I never felt as engaged nor made the close friendships that marked my time in Cambodia, Vietnam before the communist victory of 1975 exercised its own demanding fascination. In part this was because of what that country meant in terms of sharply divided international opinion. And in part because, again in an unplanned fashion, I saw so much of what was happening on the fringes of the war.

Writing of another time and another place in his book, *Bush Whacking and other tales from Malaya*, the largely-forgotten writer and colonial administrator, Sir Hugh Clifford, conjures up the appeal of Asia in one of his short stories, in which he is the principal protagonist. In the story he describes how, one has to presume in England, he met an old man who had once served as a colonial official in India. Responding to a question from the old man as to where he had served overseas, Clifford's protagonist replies, "In the East ..." This reply brings an emotional and lengthy response from his older interlocutor, which includes the words, "Youth and Asia were both ours for a space and in leaving Asia we left our Youth behind . . . Yet She [Asia] too gave us something—memories: memories of Asia and of Youth—eternal memories that will be with us to the end".

Read now this passage seems overblown and very nineteenth-century in tone, though in fact it was written in 1929. And Clifford might be regarded by some as a quintessentially unattractive example of a colonialist, given that he once wrote of how British rule in Malaya brought the inhabitants of that country "into the daylight of personal freedom such as white men prize above most mundane things". And yet I sense an underlying element of truth to what Clifford wrote, not least in relation to the grip that past sights and experiences in Cambodia and Vietnam have on my memory. It is a grip that has much to do with the exoticism of the locations and the people who lived in them; in Cambodia's case to have been in a country where the monarchy still mattered; and in both Cambodia and Vietnam to have lived through the dramatic contrasts of the seasons, the excitement of the time when these sights were seen and where these experiences occurred—some dramatic, all too many tragic. It involves memories of repeated early morning starts to the day to reach a distant destination and the sight of occasional majestic sunsets—far fewer than my romantic image of "the tropics" had conjured up before I went to live in Cambodia. And it surely also a grip that gains force through my age when the experiences took place: only twenty-two when I first went to Cambodia in 1959 to spend over two years there, and still only twenty-nine when I returned again in 1966.

In the book the material dealing with Papua New Guinea, my first period of living in Phnom Penh and the time I spent in Paris in 1965 and 1966, relies on scattered notes, letters and clippings. But from the time I went back to Cambodia and Vietnam in 1966, and subsequently, what I have written draws directly on the detailed journals I have kept over the years to the end of 1981. (An exception is the account I give of my time working as a consultant to the United Nations High Commissioner for Refugees in relation to the Cambodian refugee problem in 1980 and 1981. For those periods I have an accumulation of working notes, the lengthy (unpublished) reports I prepared for UNHCR and some published material rather than a daily journal proper.) In writing my journals I did not follow in the footsteps of Samuel Pepys and complete my entries at the end of the day. Rather, whenever possible, I typed them or wrote them up in long hand when circumstances required it early each morning. I found this delay meant that I had sorted out in my mind what seemed worth recording. Even now I retain a an affectionate memory for the reliability of my long-vanished but trusty Olivetti portable with its metal carrying case that I used to make my entries. It's an affection I don't think will ever quite be transferred to my laptop and my iPad.

What follows, then, is selective in scope, spanning just twenty-five years as I seek to describe what it was like to live through some aspects of those years. Not all of those years were universally grim in character. There were moments of amusement as well as of despair, with the latter emotion sadly more than balancing out the former. Indeed, for both Cambodia and Vietnam the story I have to tell is one of ever-growing worry about the consequences of war and defeat. Yet I can only count myself fortunate to have been on the margins of history during the years

I describe, a location which was not always comfortable but which was never less than interesting. And while what I have written has grown far beyond its original conception, it may still be seen as an extended letter to my daughter.

Milton Osborne, Sydney, 2018

1

Before Cambodia

Papua New Guinea 1956-57

Colonialists All

Briefly, between my third and fourth years as a university student, I found what it was like to be an Australian colonialist, observing the rules of separation between white Australians and the people of Papua and New Guinea, and looking the part in the everyday dress of the *mastas*: white shirt, white shorts and long white socks. I was dressed like this because I had seized the opportunity offered to students by the Australian government to spend the 1956-57 university long vacation in Papua New Guinea; pay your fare to Port Moresby and we will provide you with two or three months of employment was the deal. I didn't in fact have all of the money needed to pay my fare of £50, but with generous help from my late father's closest friend, the mining engineer John Proud, I was able to meet the cost of the airfare and fly slowly from Sydney to Port Moresby in a DC3.

The scheme's aim was to induce students, once they had graduated, to join the Papua and New Guinea Administration. I don't know what the success rate was for the scheme, but it certainly didn't work in my case. Still, negative though my reaction was at one level, I don't regret the three weeks I spent in the Administration's headquarters in Port Moresby and the nearly two months in Rabaul, in Eastern New Britain. For my experience not only showed me how easy it was to slip into colonial ways. It has continued to provide a necessary corrective to present-day views of the nature of our colonial venture, when the passage of time has lent a warm, rosy glow to memories of the years when Australia ruled Papua New Guinea.

For the reality was one of inequality sanctioned by law, however much individuals worked for the benefit of the local people and despite the admirable courage and devotion shown by intrepid patrol officers, the *kiaps*, as they performed their often difficult and sometimes dangerous tasks. This fundamental inequality did not mean that everything Australians did in Papua New Guinea was "bad", even if some of it most certainly was. To the contrary, and most obviously in terms of medical advances, the limitation of tribal conflict, and to some degree developments linked to education, much of Australia did as the colonial power in PNG was worthy of approval, and even admiration. But even the best was achieved within an overarching pattern of relationships that was unequal. And my recognition of that fact was important to the research I carried out years later in relation to the French colonial control of Cambodia and Vietnam. No matter how it operates and however well intentioned, colonialism is fundamentally about inequality.

This does not mean that the men and women who played their roles in all colonial situations should be universally condemned. Indeed, I have repeatedly written in admiring terms about Francis Garnier, who by any measure was an archetypical French colonialist—the very *beau idéal* for the colonialists of nineteenth-century French Indochina for his role in exploring the Mekong River, and less attractively for his attempt to seize control of northern Vietnam in 1873. But what I have admired was his courage and his intellect, not his worldview, which he once summarised by saying that "Countries without colonies are dead countries, like beehives from which no bees swarm." Like many others I have read with interest and pleasure of the derring-do of the Nicholsons and Lawrences at the time of the British *Raj* in India, just as I have enjoyed the novels of John Masters and admired Philip Mason's evocation of life as a servant of the *Raj*. It was not a case of my short time in Papua New Guinea turning me into a post-colonial killjoy, simply the fact that it alerted me to the need to separate out the multiple elements of colonial relationships, and to realise its failings when, much later, I wrote about French colonialism in nineteenth-century Cambodia and Vietnam.

No Natives or Dogs Allowed

To say that I was "shocked" by what I found during my brief colonial interlude is true, but in need of much qualification. This was over sixty years ago and the idea that (white) Australians in Papua New Guinea should have a beach, in the capital, Port Moresby, with a sign reading, "European Swimming Area, No Natives or Dogs Allowed," was not as surprising to me then as it appears now, even if it should have been. And the fact that locals were banned from drinking alcohol seemed to be part of "an established order". But there were two instances, when I was, indeed, shocked without qualification. They were very different in character but both are imprinted on my memory. The first was the greeting I received from the District Commissioner of East New Britain, Noel Foley, when I became his "gopher" in Rabaul. "Welcome Osborne," he said as I entered his office. Then, without any transition that I could discern, he continued by saying with apparent regret, "You'll find that things aren't like they used to be, when you could take the coons behind a shed and beat them with a piece of two by four." He was not, it was quite clear, joking. Yet this greeting came from a man whom I would subsequently observe genuinely wanted the best for the "natives", always so long as Australians were in charge and deciding what that "best" should be.

The other particularly shocking experience had a more immediately personal character. When I was sent to Rabaul I met up with two contemporaries from Wesley College, my residential college at the University of Sydney, both medical students. They, too, had seized on the opportunity for vacation employment in an exotic location. And there was another medical student from Wesley in Rabaul, Edwin Lee, an outstanding athlete and rugby player who had been educated in a Sydney private school and was ethnically Chinese. He was in Rabaul on holiday with his parents and we other three Wesleyans linked up with him, were entertained by his parents, and then revealed our ignorance of PNG mores. We invited Edwin to join us at the local swimming pool. He ruefully told us that he could not come with us. Like most other long-term ethnic Chinese resident in New Guinea at that time he was not an Australian citizen, but rather an "Australian Protected Person", a step down the status ladder. As such, he was not permitted to use "white only" facilities like Rabaul's public swimming pool.

The rank absurdity of this situation revealed how, even with the best intentions, PNG operated what was effectively an apartheid system; not, it's true, apartheid with all the awfulness of that system in South Africa, but a system of legally sanctioned racial separation nonetheless. If the ethnic Chinese of Rabaul did not quite enjoy the same rights as white Australians, the division between the latter and local people in both Papua and New Guinea—one a long-term colony, though the word was not used officially, the other a Mandated United Nations territory -- was even sharper.

All this took place in an ambience that I now realise was familiar elsewhere in colonial societies, an underlying ambience of uncertainty and suppressed boredom. The uncertainty was not of the type that was found in some other European colonies, in Vietnam, for instance, where fear of revolt was never far distant in the minds of French colonialists. But there was still a concern that a "trusted native" might suddenly turn on those he served, while boredom for some could only be assuaged by binge drinking on a notable scale. This last was particularly to be found among the younger copra planters, mostly Australian though there were other nationalities among them, including some Dutch who had worked in Indonesia before it gained independence. For many of these men their weekends passed in a haze of alcohol, ending in New Britain on a Sunday night with their "driver boys" carting them off back to their plantations, barely conscious, from the Kokopo Country Club. All in all there was a hollowness to much of life in expatriate circles and for some, at least, it was accompanied by a besetting boredom. If it was not quite the renowned *cafard* of French colonies, it was something close to it.

But this was not the only ambience. I have already written that Noel Foley wanted the best for the "natives" under his charge, and that qualification is one that applied to almost all the Australians at this time. Certainly it needs to be recorded in relation to the missionaries, both Catholic and Protestant, who "knew" they had a better creed to offer their parishioners than the traditional beliefs these people had held before the coming of the white men. In New Britain there was fierce competition between the missionaries of the Catholic Church and the Methodists for converts in what were known among people in the Australian administration as "holy wars". On occasion the rivalries led to bloody physical confrontations between the most dedicated supporters of the rival religious groups as they sought to "convert" rivals or to establish a presence where one or other of the missionary groups was already entrenched. At the time I was in Rabaul there were also tensions within the Catholic Church, due to the fact that the Bishop for the diocese was a Pole, or at least of Polish descent. He presided over a team of clerics who seemed to be almost entirely Australian-Irish in background. I was shown, probably improperly but very interestingly, a letter written by one of these priests, which had been intercepted by the administration, dealing with inter-faith rivalries. Once this issue had been dealt with, the letter concluded in a striking fashion, "As for the Pole," the priestly author of the letter wrote, "he can shove his crozier up his arse, Yours in Christ . . ."

And it would be wrong not to note the outstanding and knowledgeable men and women whom I met in New Guinea, and none more so than two Australian officials I met in Rabaul, Max Orken and Jack Emmanuel, the District and Assistant District Officers for East New Britain based in Rabaul. In Jack Emmanuel's case that knowledge and commitment did not spare him from being killed in New Britain's Gazelle Peninsula, in 1971, in an event linked to the rise of the Mataungan Association with its claims for independence and reforms linked to land usage and ownership. The issue of land ownership was a matter already causing difficulties for the administration when I was in Rabaul at the beginning of 1957. Simplifying greatly, the indigenous Tolai people of the Gazelle Peninsula deeply resented the situation in which land they regarded as their own had been alienated by the colonial powers, first the Germans and then the Australians. In 1957 this resentment was present and recognised, but it is a sad comment on the limitations of the Australian governments over succeeding years that they had failed to find a way to solve the problem that finally reached a climax in Jack Emmanuel's death. He was by this time a "special duties" officer with the rank of District Commissioner specifically engaged in efforts to solve the land issues of the region. Because he had frequently risked his life in these efforts he was awarded a posthumous George Cross.

New Year's Eve in Port Moresby

Capturing the flavour of the times that I have been writing about is not easy. Not only was it so long ago. It was, as I hope I have clearly suggested, a period infused with attitudes that most people would be hesitant to admit to holding now. Shortly after I returned to Australia from my time in Papua and New Guinea, I wrote an account of New Year's Eve 1956 in Port Moresby. It drew on notes I made at the time and I have never previously published it. It should certainly be classified as the juvenilia of a 20 year-old, but, very lightly edited to provide context, it captures something of that long-ago period -- and the terms in the account, such as "natives" and "half caste" are those of the time. It's a reflection of the passage of time that I need to mention that a "sing-sing" was and is a term used to describe traditional PNG dancing and chanting; the "Rigos" mentioned in the text are inhabitants from a region of eastern Papua, in this case working in Port Moresby away from their home villages; while *taubada* and *sinabada* were respectful terms for white men and women in the Police Motu lingua franca of Papua. The hotel mentioned in the first paragraph was the Boroko Hotel located some five or six kilometres from the centre of Port Moresby where we short-term student visitors to the territory were accommodated.

"Yes, we'll stay open as long as there's customers . . ." the hotel manager was expansive. The Christmas night celebrations had been a great success. There had been eight courses, as much drink as they'd wanted and, it was his own idea, a "sing-sing" by the Rigos, who made up the majority of his staff.

"Yes, I know we should close the bar at eleven, but hell it's New Year's Eve and besides we kept it open longer on Christmas night, and you remember who was there." (He was referring to the presence of several very senior officials who had paid no attention to the breach of closing hours.)

And on Christmas night's showing it did seem that the hotel would be a centre of New Year's Eve celebration. At 5.30 there were plenty of drinkers fuelling up for the night. We (half a dozen university students) sat there too and drank a little, experiencing the separation that strangers feel in a community that is just too large to absorb them into its celebrations.

But the drinkers moved away, one by one, and by dinner only a few remained, probably those who were unable to move after this day put a cap on their five-day drunk. So we sat at dinner and debated what we could do to celebrate New Year's Eve. We could get drunk. This had palled in the five days of nothing else to do. Besides, in the heat you lost too much liquid perspiring. Someone had told us there would be a "sing-sing" in Hanuabada, that sprawling overcrowded native village on the outskirts of Port Moresby. The next problem was how to get there.

We waited for a bus but in our impatience started thumbing lifts from the passing cars and trucks. For a quarter of an hour none stopped and then an old, rattling truck pulled up. So off we went into Port Moresby driven by a grey-haired elderly half caste. We bought him a drink in town. We could do this legally; he had a licence.

Then from Port Moresby proper to Hanuabada we travelled by bus past the Administration's headquarters at Konedobu and the Administrator's home, to the giant native village stretching out on piles into the bay and smelling of all of the accumulated scents of its inhabitants. Leaving the bus we found ourselves among hundreds of natives who were wandering aimlessly along. They seemed to have no purpose. Tonight they knew the white *taubadas* and *sinabadas* were enjoying themselves, but it was hard for them to know why. Christmas they could understand. It had been explained to them by the missionaries. But it was difficult to see why tonight had brought all the drinking and celebration in the Airways Mess and the RSL Club.

At first we could find no "sing-sing". And we wandered, so far as we could see, the only whites among these people who have had contact so long with the European way of life and yet remained in so many ways apart from the Europeans. Then we found something that made our wandering worthwhile. An isolated group of "foreign" natives were having a "sing-sing". Taller than the natives about Port Moresby, these men were from the western area of Papua close to the border with Netherlands New Guinea. They sang and danced in a formation that was almost military both in its form and its precision. There were twenty-four of them, tall and graceful, with rattles on their hands and feet. They probably once used seashells as rattles but now they were bottle tops. They took their time from two drums and joined in choruses dictated by a leading singer.

We stood and watched, standing only for a little while as the other bystanders with the innate courtesy of Papuans offered us stools from a nearby hut. So we sat like Elizabethan grandees with their stools on the stage itself so as not to miss the slightest thing. We said the conventional things to each other . . . how good it would have been to have had a tape recorder or a camera with a flashlight attachment. But mostly we watched, fascinated by the movements of the dancers and the marvellous chanting.

But the "sing-sing" stopped and there was little else to do but go back. And we, quite as much outside the general celebrations as the natives and finding a bus this time, went back towards the hotel, past the Airways Mess, past the "Europeans Only" swimming area and the RSL. Past the Four Mile Toilers Club to the hotel, where we found the bar deserted and being closed with three-quarters of an hour still to go to midnight.

"No, we backed the wrong horse this time," said the disgruntled hotel manager. "Should have known better, I suppose. Those dancers always get them in." So it was bottles up to one of the rooms to wait for midnight.

And when midnight came the hotel boys knew that this was something that ought to be celebrated. They beat their drums and ran sticks along the corrugations of the galvanised iron of the boy houses. This was soon stopped. Why should they be allowed to make any noise? What should have been a big night had flopped and all the manager wanted now was to get to sleep. He wanted none of that damn nonsense.

Members of the Royal Ballet performing in 1959 during a visit by President Sukarno of Indonesia. The dancer on the left is Prince Sihanouk's daughter, Princess Bopha Devi. Author was in attendence.

Author attending a press conference for the Thai Foreign Minister Thanat Khoman, Phnom Penh, 1959 (seated first on the left, second row).

2

Cambodia, 1959-61 – Vietnam, 1962-63

I arrived in Phnom Penh on 6 April 1959, still aged twenty-two, to begin my first extended period of living overseas as an adult. That this experience took place in such an exotic setting has played its part in fixing the events of the time and the individuals I encountered firmly in my mind. To note that Cambodia in 1959-61, the years I spent *en poste* as a junior diplomat in the Australian embassy in Phnom Penh, was very different from the Cambodia of today is a truism, but one that deserves emphasis. It was a country off the beaten track where much of government business was transacted in French, a partial reason for my being sent there. And its capital was much, much smaller than today's sprawling city, where high-rise buildings are becoming a major feature of the built environment.

Sihanouk's Cambodia

Most importantly, it was Prince Norodom Sihanouk's Cambodia. It is impossible to exaggerate the pervasive presence of this man in the Cambodia of the time. At the height of his powers his word was law for almost all his subjects. He was the impresario, composer, conductor and principal player of the Cambodian "state orchestra". Over and again he showed his charismatic capability to capture a crowd, as I saw during the official visit to Cambodia of the then President of Indonesia, Sukarno, in May 1959. In addition to the routine engagements of a state dinner and a performance in the royal palace by the court dancers, Sukarno addressed a large gathering on the *Men* ground, the open space in front of the National Museum. This was, and still is, a location rich in symbolism as it is used for important royal cremation ceremonies—such, indeed was the case, for the solemn ceremonies at the cremation of Sihanouk's father, King Suramarit, in August 1960 and as it has been more recently for Sihanouk himself, in February 2013. As I watched with a scattering of other foreign diplomats the occasion, became a starring act for both Sukarno and Sihanouk. Sukarno orated in English, a language unknown to almost all in the crowd, while Sihanouk, in a bravura performance, translated extemporaneously into Khmer. As Sukarno denounced "imperialism" with ever growing passion, Sihanouk matched him with his voice rising in volume and in pitch, until Sukarno ended is speech in a ringing eulogy of Sihanouk. As Sihanouk began to translate he was overcome with apparent embarrassment and gave way to characteristic giggles. But there was no question that he had the crowd with him as they cheered both to the echo and looked on their Prince with undisguised and emotional admiration.

The exotic was almost constantly present, with Sihanouk so often an essential element, in this long-ago Cambodia. It was Sihanouk who led a band of princes at *soirées dansantes* within the palace to which diplomats were invited; who looked benevolently on as we scrabbled in the dust to plant trees in an effort to revegetate exhausted land; and who, on occasions very different to the shared oration with Sukarno, could whip himself into a towering rage, his voice rising ever sharper in pitch, as he denounced the perfidious neighbours to the east and west, South Vietnam and Thailand. But the exotic could be seen in less regal aspects of the city and the country; in the noisy funerals of the Chinese community and the *Fête des Génies*—sometimes called the "Procession of the Twenty-Five Spirits"—a ritual procession honoured in the past by both the Chinese and Vietnamese communities and marked by mediums in trances slashing their tongues with knives and piercing their cheeks with lances—the procession took place in the middle of the first lunar month of the Chinese calendar.

And then there were the elephants, not just the palace beasts that processed along Okkna Chhun Street (now better known as Street 240) close to the embassy each morning on their way to graze in the fields on the city's outskirts. I was later delighted to find that among the traditional punishments for adultery handed down by Cambodian authorities was the requirement that the guilty parties should expiate their guilt by harvesting grass for the royal elephants. This was because in pursuing their passions the miscreants would have flattened the grass on which royal elephants would have fed. Separate from the royal beasts there were other elephants brought into the city to take part in celebrations or to play a role in moving heavy materials. And, most grandly of all, there were the elephants that formed an essential part of the funeral procession of King Suramarit in August 1960. In my memory there were several dozens of them, but a photograph I took at the time suggests a much smaller number, and I have now found in my notes that there were a total of thirty. The most important bore gilded howdahs with members of the court ballet in their costumes riding in them, a sight of truly oriental fantasy. Many years later I found a French official's nineteenth-century account of the Cambodia court returning to the palace in a procession with no fewer than two hundred elephants and leaving "an unforgettable enchanted picture". He and I shared the same reaction.

Exoticism could also impinge quite directly on daily life, as I found when I had to arrange an exorcism. Quite without warning the two embassy drivers announced that they could not park the mission's cars in the chancery driveway because a malevolent spirit had taken up residence in the tree whose branches hung over it. Consultation with the drivers made clear that this problem would only be solved by the performance of an exorcism, and for that I needed to recruit the help of Buddhist monks—and not any Buddhist monks, but those from the Wat Botum Vaddei, the headquarters of the Thommayut sect. The upshot was that I found myself in discussion with the *wat's* abbott, over the procedure that would be followed and, in a most delicate fashion, the size of the donation the embassy would have to make once the exorcism had taken place. To my considerable relief, and even more so to the drivers', the exorcism, which involved lengthy chanting in *Pali*, worked and the spirit went off to work its evil elsewhere.

Diplomats and other expatriate species

The diplomatic corps, of which I was a minor member, formed part of Sihanouk's court. We paraded at his beck and call in our formal, shiny-white sharkskin cloth suits: short and tall, light and dark-skinned. When we were all together the group conjured up the image of a convention of rather seedy Italian ice cream sellers. Of course there were variations within the group beyond this overall image. There were the red-faced Russians who seemed constantly troubled by Cambodia's climate, the more so if they had had the opportunity to down several drinks at a daytime reception. Some among the representatives of the large American embassy did not hide their dislike of having to be present at events marked by Sihanouk's voicing criticism of their country in one of his lengthy speeches. This comment most certainly did not apply to David Chandler whom I first met in 1960 when he, like me, was sent as a third secretary to the American embassy. He has remained a friend ever since, and has gone on to become the most important historian of modern Cambodia. As for the Chinese, they appeared to have been schooled to match the stereotype of "the inscrutable Oriental". But I have written too little of the individuals who made up this assorted group and the other people who stand out in my memory from that period.

Thinking about them now, I have to wonder whether it would still be possible to find such an assorted group of interesting, sometimes offbeat, and even sinister people that I encountered when I first went to Phnom Penh. No doubt the fact that I was still so young meant that the impression they made on me was heightened by my naiveté. But there is no denying that after growing up in Australia, and with only three months spent in Papua New Guinea previously exposing me to an expatriate world as an adult, I was unprepared for this distinctly different society into which I was suddenly translated. Perhaps if I had read Lawrence Durrell's *Esprit de Corps* before going to Phnom Penh, rather than afterwards, the experience might not have been so surprising.

It's fair to say that the Australian embassy was, by comparison with many of the other diplomatic missions in Phnom Penh, a haven of rationality, if not totally devoid of occasional bickering. The fact that my ambassador wrote his drafts with a quill pen seemed little more than an instance of harmless eccentricity. And I found I could live with the openly expressed resentment of the embassy's secretary-typist who had been used to my predecessor's being a bachelor. This had meant she had been able to attend official functions as his "companion", something made easy by the fact that invitations were marked by a Gallic quality of requesting the presence of "Monsieur so and so and Madame". Now this option was no longer possible. With a married third secretary in the mission this meant that she missed out on many a boring reception, but she was resentful nonetheless.

As for the small number of Australians involved in aid projects under the Colombo Plan who came under the embassy's care, their gripes and personal idiosyncrasies did not seem beyond the norm for people doing a difficult and, in their mind, sometimes thankless job. I did, it's true, find dealing repeatedly with the irate creditors of one of these "experts", as they were known, called for more than normal diplomatic skills. But all in all the "Australian community" seemed to be able to rub along without too much difficulty or scandal. This was despite the circumstances in which the mail from Australia was irregular and in the case of parcels frequently purloined at the post office; Radio Australia was almost impossible to receive; and basic shopping was either so limited or expensive in Phnom Penh's shops that everyone had to import their groceries by sea from Hong Kong. And this was living at the personal level. When it came to official matters, there were times when the "safehand bag" took thirty days to reach the embassy from Canberra. If one couldn't put up with a degree of inconvenience and isolation, Phnom Penh was not a place to be despite the exoticism of its setting and the welcome availability of domestic help.

Exoticism among diplomats was to be found elsewhere than among the Australians, and not surprisingly in the French embassy. At a time, more than fifty years ago, when France had only recently given up its colonial presence in *notre Indochine*, Paris saw its best interests served by maintaining a large embassy in Phnom Penh mainly staffed by officials who had served there before the country gained independence in 1953. With Norodom Sihanouk as Cambodia's dominant politician and former king a Francophile, this made great sense, for overall Cambodia's separation from French "protection" had been surprisingly amicable. Despite the rebuffs that Sihanouk received from French politicians in the course of his manoeuvring to achieve his country's independence, Cambodia never experienced the bitter, armed confrontations with the colonial power that took place in neighbouring Vietnam. Indeed, Sihanouk himself has recorded how, on Independence Day in November 1953, the commander of French forces in Cambodia, General de Langlade said to him, "Sire, you have whipped me." To which Sihanouk had replied, "But no, general, I have followed as best I can the excellent lessons in tactics that you gave me at Saumur"—the French army's cavalry school where Sihanouk had been a student on two occasions.

It was still the case in 1959 that the French ambassador was given a position of honour in advance of the rest of the diplomatic corps at all state ceremonies, and Ambassador Pierre Gorce, took this position as of right. French gossips maintained that at other times Ambassador Gorce had a penchant for travelling around Phnom Penh by *cyclopousse*, the local bicycle rickshaw, chatting to the local prostitutes. But, the gossips hastened to say, the diminutive but steely-eyed Madame Gorce ensured that no more than chatting was involved. One of Ambassador Gorce's staff, Claude Epevrier, had been Sihanouk's private secretary in the years leading up to independence. At another level Sihanouk's doctor was a French military officer, Colonel Armand Riche, who was attached to the embassy. And consular matters were handled by Claude Copin, who had lived through the Second World War period in what had still been French Indochina. A lover of food and wine he was so taken with the gift of a bottle of wine from the Hunter Valley which I gave him that he arranged to have Australian oysters airfreighted in from Hong Kong to eat with it. But none of these men, however important they were in keeping the flame of French interests alight, matched the flamboyant, and to my immature mind the stereotypical, French style of the embassy's deputy head of mission, Pierre Mathivet de la Ville de Mirmont.

He was tall, handsome and debonair. Gossip surrounded him, fuelled by the nature of his personal life that saw him rotating two immensely attractive *Parisiennes* through Phnom Penh, whom he happily introduced as his "first and second wives". He kept a baboon at his house and, though I could never verify the truth of the suggestion made with vigour by some in the French community, there were those who suggested the baboon also shared Mathivet's bed. None of this detracted from his diplomatic skills and he was as respected among Cambodians as he was among his diplomatic colleagues for his clear grasp on the realities of local politics.

Yet if the French embassy was home to an exotic such as Mathivet, few if any of the other diplomatic missions could boast a personality more powerful than the wife of the British ambassador, Muriel, wife of Frederick (Freddy) Garner. Both were old Asia hands, having lived in China before the Second World War and both having spent that war in Japanese internment camps. Freddy Garner spoke English with a slight Spanish accent, the result of having spent his early years in Costa Rica, where his father owned a plantation. He was a fluent Mandarin speaker, a fact that he mentioned with the observation that having learnt his Chinese in Hunan he was one of the few foreigners who could understand Mao Zedong's speeches with ease. He was always approachable, a fact of great importance to me when I found myself alone at the embassy for periods as chargé d'affaires. His amiability meant I did not hesitate to ask him questions that might normally have seemed out of place in a conversation between an ambassador and a very junior diplomat from another mission. I once, for instance, asked him what it was like being interned by the Japanese. With only a hint of a smile he responded by saying that it "wasn't too bad for someone who had been educated at Rugby". And what's more, he told me, he had been on the garbage detail, which meant he ate better than many of his fellow internees. On another occasion I asked a question to which I received an unexpected and sobering answer, as I enquired about the most important differences he saw between living in contemporary Asia and how it had been for expatriates before the war? I had expected a response that referred to refrigerators and air conditioners. Instead he spoke of how tropical diseases had carried off people with terrifying speed. You met them in the morning and they were dying by the end of the day.

39

If Freddy Garner exuded competence and quiet but firm charm within the British embassy his wife, Muriel, was ready to show that she had power and knew how to wield it. She was a very grand lady, an intimate of Elizabeth the Queen Mother, which meant that when Princess Alexandra of Kent visited Phnom Penh Muriel Garner had no compunction in indicating that this princess's presence was rather a nuisance. She fulminated against Alexandra's arriving late for a reception at the British residence. And then, when she did arrive and further delayed meeting the assembled throng by wanting to use the lavatory, Muriel loudly announced the fact by calling for the staff to, "Put up the screens. Princess wants to make pee-pee". As for the gifts Alexandra had brought to dispense in the course of her visit, these were in Muriel Garner's eyes so awful that she had to draw on her own stock of possessions to replace them.

Recounted in this way, Muriel Garner sounds a dubiously sympathetic character, and that's unfair, or so at least I found in personal dealings with both her and her husband. And, in any event I and many others were ready to forgive her almost anything as, on one notable occasion, she administered what has to have been the ultimate "perfect squelch". This involved the behaviour of Bill Waterson, a junior member of the British embassy's staff—junior in status but probably in his mid-forties in age. Invited to his house for a drink shortly after arriving in Phnom Penh I found that he entertained his guests by showing a film he had shot on a previous posting in India; the film showed turtles feeding on partially decomposed bodies floating down a river; I think it was the Ganges. Along with this less than attractive preoccupation, he had a disconcerting habit of telling all and sundry of a problem he had with some form of skin disease on his legs. In gathering after social gathering, and there were an inordinate number of them in Phnom Penh, Bill W would pull up his trouser leg and launch into repeated litany of, "Look at me scabs," in a glottal-stop-ridden north London accent. For most of us this meant he was a man to be avoided if at all possible. For Muriel Garner his behaviour was such that she decreed he was not be invited to any social function hosted by British Embassy members at which she was going to be present. This worked, and was generally sympathetically accepted, but there was one occasion at which her edict could not be applied: the Queen's Birthday reception at the British embassy residence.

So, in 1959, we were all gathered in a large reception room at the British residence when Bill hitched up his trouser leg and launched into his familiar 'request' that people should look at his scabs. Across the room Muriel Garner saw what was happening. With the commanding presence that was very much part of her nature she brought the room to silence with an imperious sweep of her arm that ended pointing at the unfortunate Bill. And then in her cut glass accent she delivered five devastating words, "Poor man, syphilis you know." In the silence that followed the unfortunate Waterson disappeared. One moment he was there and the next he was gone like some figure in a pantomime who disappears through the floor in a flash of light. All that was missing was a roll of drums, a clash of cymbals and a puff of black smoke.

The 'anciens de l'Indochine'

Away from the diplomatic corps there were plenty of other characters in the Phnom Penh of fifty years ago: Jean of the eponymous Bar Jean, who appeared to have been transported, along with many of his customers, directly from the waterfront of Marseilles to its location beside the Tonle Sap River. Years later I was to find him in Saigon, after Sihanouk had been deposed in 1970, managing a restaurant that seemed to have the same character as his Phnom Penh bar despite its changed location. He was a quintessential Indochinese old hand having first come to the region in 1937. His only competition, at least for French expatriates, was the Zigzag bar run by a lugubrious ex-Foreign Legionnaire, Albert Vandekherkove, who, late in the evening would signal his intention to close by playing a record of "Le Boudin," the Legion's marching song. And, of course, there was Monsieur Mignon of La Taverne, my favourite restaurant in the city, located across the square from what was then the central post office, and one which probably had looked very much the same in the 1930s, when he had come to Cambodia, as it did in the 1960s. Monsieur Mignon's kitchen showed me that the simplest dishes when well prepared were as satisfying as fancier offerings—La Taverne's tomato soup was a revelation and its pepper steaks, with the sauce using Cambodia's wonderfully aromatic pepper; both live in my memory.

I'm not sure if I fully understood the origins of the term "carpetbagger", when I first lived in Phnom Penh, but there is no doubt that in its modern usage it applied to some of the characters who drifted through the city, always on the point of striking a deal and seemingly able to survive while never actually concluding one. Ted Amour was one of these, an Englishman with a North Country accent who seemed vaguely disreputable and was certainly shunned by the members of his country's embassy. If it was impossible to avoid him one had to be prepared to hear of plans for some commercial venture that was bound to bring fortunes to those who invested in it. To my surprise he was still offering his dubious roads to riches to anyone who would listen when I returned to Phnom Penh in 1966.

Getting to know Cambodians

Meeting Cambodians was easy. It was part of the job. Coming to know them other than superficially was not. But by great good fortune I came to know Prince Sisowath Phandaravong, or Ratsody as he was known by his nickname, a friend and guide to his country with whom I maintained contact until very recently, when his health declined. Unlike so many others I knew he survived the Khmer Rouge period by being absent from the country when Pol Pot's forces marched into Phnom Penh in April 1975. His survival contrasts with the death of almost all his close relatives, including his parents, a half-brother and a brother-in-law, who fought on opposite sides of the tragic civil war.

Amazingly enough, for a very junior diplomat in the Phnom Penh of the early 1960s, senior Cambodian officials and even ministers showed themselves ready to deal with me both with politeness and humanity: Son Sann the courtly economics minister who was a graduate of one of the *grandes écoles* in Paris and Sihanouk's chief adviser on financial and economic issues and whom I was to meet again twenty years later as the unlikely leader of an insurgent group ranged against the Vietnamese occupying Cambodia; the bluff Nhiek Tioulong, who filled many ministerial roles and was regarded as one of the few among Sihanouk's associates who would dare to contradict the prince; Sonn Voeunsai who, as Cambodian ambassador in Paris in 1966, remembered me from my time in the embassy and facilitated my receiving a visa to go to Phnom Penh at a time when Cambodia was little inclined to receive foreign scholars; Sarin Chhak at the Ministry of Foreign Affairs, both diplomat and historian, who was later to be of great assistance to me in Paris, where he was rector of the Maison du Cambodge in the Cité Universitaire and who acted as a helpful guide to the French archives. He was living in Phnom Penh when the Khmer Rouge took the city in 1975 and appears to have survived until almost the end of the Pol Pot regime before vanishing. According to some reports he was taken into captivity by the Vietnamese and was never heard of again.

And then there was Kou Roun. I wrote at the beginning of this chapter that there were sinister people to be encountered when I first went to Phnom Penh, and it was and it is Kou Roun whom I particularly had in mind. As Sihanouk's Minister for Security he presided over the secret police and was the man who, we now know, was responsible for overseeing the secret assassinations and beatings of those regarded as opponents to Sihanouk's regime. We also now know that Kou Roun and his brutish associates acted with the full knowledge and authority of Sihanouk, however much the prince tried to distance himself from this fact in his writings and statements. In appearance Kou Roun looked a thug, and his manner and style of speech went with that appearance. I once asked him about the policies the regime had adopted towards the minority hill people who lived in the northeast of the country. "We Khmerise them," he said, meaning as I later discovered that many of these people were forced against their will into fixed settlements and so to abandon their formerly nomadic way of life. Failure to comply in their new settlements meant beatings, or worse.

Only occasionally did Kou Roun's heavy-handed suppression of dissent come to the notice of the foreign community. Such was the case with the assault he organised against Khieu Samphan, then a little-known journalist, later a key figure in Pol Pot's Khmer Rouge regime and who was finally put on trial for crimes against humanity in a special United Nations-backed court in Phnom Penh. Returning from Paris, where he completed a doctoral thesis in the Faculty of Law and Economic Sciences, and imbued with left-wing ideas, Samphan was the moving force behind a weekly newspaper published in Phnom Penh, *L'Observateur*. Skilfully written, but clearly critical of Sihanouk's regime without ever quite stepping over the mark of personal lèse-majesté, the prince bitterly resented Khieu Samphan's articles in the newspaper. So it was that in July 1960 as Khieu Samphan was leaving the offices of his newspaper he was surrounded by *cyclopousse* riders, beaten and debagged, and then photographed standing naked in the street. Given that other dissidents were shot or "disappeared", Khieu Samphan was lucky to survive. Only a year earlier the editor of the left-wing newspaper *Pracheachon*, Nop Bophan, had been shot and killed outside his office. But survive Khieu Samphan did for another seven years in the hot house of Phnom Penh politics before fleeing into the *maquis* in 1967 to join Pol Pot and the developing Cambodian Communist Party.

Early Days in the Vietnam War, 1962-63

It says much about the awfulness of Cambodia's experience under Pol Pot and the lingering war that followed his regime's overthrow at the beginning of 1979, that memories of what happened there have survived so strongly as an issue in the public mind, a situation summed most obviously in the pervasive understanding of the term, "the Killing Fields". For those who worked and fought in Vietnam in the 1960s and 1970s memories are, of course, still sharp, but I'm not sure this is the case more generally as Vietnam at war has become a subject to forget. So when I record my experiences in the sixties and at the beginning of the seventies I recognise I am dealing with a period that has slipped out of the consciousness of even many thoughtful people—veterans of the war fought in Vietnam notably excepted. As what follows makes very clear, it is still very much part of my own memory.

Saigon, modern Ho Chi Minh City, has always loomed large in my mind, right from the start of my posting to Phnom Penh in April 1959. Overnighting there on the way to Phnom Penh and then making short visits in the course of my posting, Saigon in the early 1960s seemed so much more a sophisticated city than "provincial" Phnom Penh. The French had referred to it as the "Pearl of the Orient" and consciously sought to construct its public buildings to rival those in Singapore and Hong Kong. If Phnom Penh in the sixties had a rather austere charm, Saigon, in contrast, managed to combine a louche reputation, so sharply portrayed in Graham Greene's *The Quiet American*, with an almost truly metropolitan air along its main shopping street running from the Saigon River up to the Catholic cathedral.

It was on this street in the 1960s that a visitor found the city's two venerable hotels, the Majestic, which overlooked the river where the street began, and the Continental Palace, which was positioned by the square in front of the Opera House, half way along the street. Both hotels continue to operate today even with the competition they face from newer and more glamorous newcomers; the Majestic considerably renovated, the Continental remarkably unchanged except for the regrettable removal of its famed terrace. While France was still in charge the street had been the rue Catinat, a less than subtle affirmation of French sovereignty since the name was taken from the French warship that had participated in the invasion of southern Vietnam in 1859. Yet that name was still being used in 1960, and not just by old colonial hands but also by members of the southern Vietnamese bourgeoisie. Indeed the street has been an index of where power lay in Saigon. It was officially renamed *Tu Do* (Freedom) Street after independence in 1954. Nowadays, and after the communist victory of 1975 uniting the whole of Vietnam, it has been renamed again as *Dong Khoi* (General Uprising) Street. Since it is common nowadays to see the street crammed with expensive European cars, including on one recent occasion a late model Rolls Royce, I have to wonder what the remaining communist ideologues think has happened to their revolution.

Intimations of a darker future

Saigon was not just fascinating for its already-fictionalised past dominated by Graham Greene's novel, its restaurants, cafes and shops —there were jewellers, tailors, bootmakers, lacquer and ceramic shops, to mention only a few of the offerings—there was, additionally, a harder side to life in the city that was already apparent at that time. As foreigners we lived in a largely untroubled Phnom Penh in the late 1950s and early 1960s. Of course, we were aware of the aborted coup mounted by Sihanouk's former ally, Dap Chhuon, in February 1959 and an attempt to blow up Sihanouk later the same year by way of a bomb smuggled into the palace—the latter did indeed kill a member of the royal family, Prince Vakravan, and is now known to have been organised by Ngo Dinh Nhu, President Diem of Vietnam's brother. Yet these events seemed overshadowed buy an awareness of the extent to which the security situation in South Vietnam was steadily deteriorating in a fashion more deeply serious than events in Cambodia.

Though much of South Vietnam appeared apparently untroubled by insurgency safety on the main roads was already becoming a concern. When I drove from Phnom Penh to Saigon in April 1960 to go on mid-term leave, this was the last officially sanctioned car trip by an Australian diplomat between the two cities for many years. Then, in November 1960, immediately after making a short visit to Saigon, I flew back to Phnom Penh to hear the news that dissident army units were besieging the presidential palace and demanding the resignation of President Ngo Dinh Diem, the South Vietnamese leader. The news arrived in the course of the French embassy's Armistice Day reception and the hosts and the senior Cambodians present, who both despised Diem in their different ways, greeted the apparent fall of Diem with delight. As it was, he survived, only to face another, and this time successful, coup and to lose his life three years later.

That fatal coup was still more than eleven months away when, I arrived in Saigon the day before Christmas Eve 1962. No longer a junior diplomat I was instead a prospective graduate student waiting to learn if I would be accepted to study in Cornell's Southeast Asia Program. In anticipation I had come to Saigon to begin research in the colonial archives the French had left behind when they quit Vietnam in 1954. I found there was much of interest in those archives, but it was soon overshadowed by the febrile political and military atmosphere of the time. The developing guerrilla war waged by Vietnamese communist forces, by then known universally as the Viet Cong (a catch-all term for the communist insurgents), was not being halted by the Saigon military. Concurrently, the hopes that had been placed in the Strategic Hamlets Program—a program of resettling large numbers of rural peasants modelled loosely on the 'New Villages' of the Malayan Emergency period—were increasingly recognised as misplaced. It was clear despite the free and easy atmosphere that prevailed in Saigon that matters were very different from my last visit in 1960.

The Battle of Ap Bac

Into this mix came the shattering events that became known as the Battle of Ap Bac on 2 January 1963. By comparison with later main force engagements in the Vietnam War it was not a major affair, but symbolically it was of great importance. It marked the beginning of an increasingly rapid deterioration of security that finally brought full-scale American military involvement. By comparison with later years, at the beginning of 1963 there were still a relatively limited number of American troops in Vietnam, just over 16,000. But the size of the American military commitment had been growing from late 1961 as "advisers" and helicopter pilots were deployed to assist the South Vietnamese forces, the ARVN, in their operations against the growing guerrilla challenge to the Saigon government.

Learning that there was a concentration of Viet Cong troops in the Mekong delta village of Ap Bac, some sixty kilometres southwest of Saigon, the commander of South Vietnam's Fourth Army Corps ordered troops from the Seventh division to attack the communists. The government troops, estimated to outnumber the enemy by a factor of ten, were assisted by an American helicopter unit. Yet the engagement that took place on 2 January 1963 became a debacle, marked by gross failures of leadership and command on the South Vietnamese side. Five of the fifteen American helicopters were put out of action and three American were killed. On the South Vietnamese side losses were much higher, more than sixty killed and more than a hundred wounded. The true number of communist casualties was never known as they withdrew under cover of darkness.

News of the battle hit Saigon like a storm. While all I met, Vietnamese and foreigners alike, asked how the South Vietnamese and American losses could have happened, this did not seem a question being asked at the highest levels of the American embassy and its military mission in Saigon. In fact, the American Commander-in-Chief for the Pacific, Admiral Harry D. Felt, who arrived in Saigon shortly after the battle, lauded what had occurred as a South Vietnamese victory. Ap Bac, and the growing evidence that the Strategic Hamlet Program was falling apart, foreshadowed the way in which the war was viewed over the following years. On the one hand there were repeated official claims of success while on the other the doubters, particularly among the American journalists in Vietnam, were more often than not proved to be correct in qualifying or totally dismissing these claims.

I can't pretend that in 1963 I had concluded the war against the communists would ultimately be lost. To the contrary, if by 1966 I had begun to think that the war was un-winnable, it was not until some time in 1970 that I became finally convinced there was no hope for anything better than a negotiated settlement to the conflict, and possibly not even that. For I had no doubt that the Vietnamese communists would simply not settle for anything less than control of the whole territory of Vietnam. As someone who had studied the history of French involvement in Vietnam and the events of 1954 when Vietnam achieved divided independence, I was well aware of the frailty of the Diem regime and of the dynamism and ruthlessness of the Vietnamese communists with their claim to represent the country's true nationalist identity.

But whatever hindsight now tells us about the ultimate fate of South Vietnam and the triumph of the communists, the issue was less clear-cut in the period I'm describing, unless one was ideologically committed one way or the other. So rather than being certain about the likely future success of the communists, I had concluded something rather different: that what was happening in Vietnam posed a terrible moral dilemma. This may sound far too grand a way to describe how I felt, and some might see such a position as lacking in intellectual rigour. But I came to realise, and never forgot, that when people in Australia and the United States came to talk easily of how "the West" should not support "the corrupt South Vietnamese regime," whether they were talking about Diem or his various successors, they were not thinking about what this meant for those in that country's population who feared what a communist victory would mean. And central to this personal conclusion were the thoughts and fears of a minor civil servant named Duong Sanh, whom I first met in 1963. He was the chief librarian of the National Library, and some of his staff referred to him as its director, but he was in reality a fairly low level South Vietnamese official. Later, I was to meet and spend considerable time with much more senior figures, including two of the generals who led the coup that overthrew Ngo Dinh Diem, Tran Van Don and Ton That Dinh, but Duong Sanh's concerns crystallised for me the problem of making easy judgments about Vietnam.

Duong Sanh had been born in the colonial era and was in his mid-40s when I first met him. Shorter than most of his compatriots, his slight frame seemed even less substantial by his tendency to stoop as he faced the world with a perpetually worried frown. A Catholic who feared communism, by 1966 he had reached the point of wanting "peace at any price" as he deplored the moral decay he saw all around him. But even before this, in 1963, he presented me with a picture of the security situation in the south that was very different from the official view of the governments supporting the Diem regime. He spoke of the extent to which the Viet Cong operated within Saigon itself, levying taxes and propagandising clandestinely; of the corruption of Ngo Dinh Diem's administration, not on the part of the president himself but of those close to him in his family and entourage; and of the way he and tens of thousands of others with some education wondered how they could leave Vietnam if the communists came to power.

I was to meet and talk with Duong Sanh repeatedly over my later visits to Saigon into 1971 as he continued to be a disturbing reference point for my thoughts about the war. Was the war worth fighting for people like him? What would be his fate if the communists won? By comparison with his rural compatriots he was hardly a typical South Vietnamese, if the peasantry was taken as a guide to national identity. Indeed, it could be said that he was *dépaysé* like the other South Vietnamese who had grown up and been educated while the French were still the colonial power. But did this mean his ultimate fate was unimportant? And did concern for the Duong Sanhs of South Vietnam weigh sufficiently heavily in any judgments about the war and the way in which it was fought to overcome other doubts about the role of America and its allies, including Australia? I had no easy answer to these questions, but I never thought that the issue was as clear-cut as the vehement opponents of the war claimed was the case. If right did not lie firmly on the side of the South Vietnamese, I did not conclude that it lay, in contrast, absolutely in the hands of those who ruled in Hanoi. This was never a popular position to hold, with either the supporters or the opponents of the war, but at least I held it on the basis of seeing what was happening on the ground. Of course, what I thought about the war in Vietnam did not matter for its ultimate outcome. That was determined by two essential factors, the unswerving goal of the Vietnamese communists to gain control of the whole of the country no matter what the cost in men and treasure and the Nixon administration's wish to find a way to put the war behind them in response to the deep divisions that it had caused in the United States. Nothing sums up the administration's policy better than Kissinger's concept of "an elegant bugout," which was, though it is not nearly widely enough recognised today, a thinly disguised American abandonment of its Vietnamese protégé regime in Saigon.

As I recount later, I met Duong Sanh many times in Saigon in the years that followed but finally he did manage to leave that city before the war ended and the communists won, and I last saw him in Paris in 1973, working in the Bibliothèque Nationale, where he had found employment bringing books to the more privileged persons who were readers in the great library.

3

Searching for Indochina in France, 1965-66

After leaving Saigon at the end of January 1963, I did not visit either Vietnam or Cambodia again for another three years. In August 1963 I had become a graduate student at Cornell University. Then in 1965, and after completing my requisite course work and "plundering" the rich holdings on Southeast Asia in Cornell's Olin Library, I had begun to think that I could transform my fascination with Cambodia and Vietnam into a worthwhile subject for a PhD dissertation. But to do this I needed to carry out research in the French archives in Paris and then to see what I might find in archival records the French had left behind in Phnom Penh and Saigon.

My embassy posting in Phnom Penh, and the time I had spent in Saigon had left me with a deep impression of the impact French colonialism had had in both Cambodia and Vietnam. It seemed to me that the first fifty years of the French colonial presence—from the 1860s to the first decade of the twentieth century—had played a key part in shaping later developments; that the way the French had governed the two countries in the nineteenth century mattered in the twentieth. The French had left a king on the throne in Cambodia and it was clear that

Prince Sihanouk's contemporary role as his country's leader benefited greatly from the powerful symbolism that went with his having been king before his abdication in his father's favour in 1955. In Vietnam, in contrast, the French had undermined the monarchy and in the case of southern Vietnam abolished the traditional administration. This, surely, had something to do with the rise of a range of nationalist responses, including a response that blended nationalism with communism.

And it was not only in the field of government that French influence had been so readily apparent. In those now-distant days of the fifties and sixties French was the language used by the elite, their children were sent to schools that taught in French, in both Phnom Penh and Saigon, and the chance to study in France itself was the prize of prizes. Just ten years before I had come to know the countries that had formed part of French Indochina, Pol Pot, had gone to study in France, as did a number of those around the same time who later headed the infamous Khmer Rouge regime. But many others of his compatriots had studied in France had done so without coming to believe that a savage version of Marx and Lenin's ideas was the answer to Cambodia's ills.

In Vietnam's case, France and French education had had an even more important impact, and though I was not setting out to chronicle the rise of the Vietnamese Communist Party I was struck by the extent to which French ideas and French education had played a role in the life of so many of its stalwarts—and this was despite the often draconian measures taken by the French against those Vietnamese who challenged their rule. How, for example, could one ignore the observation attributed to Ho Chi Minh that "in Paris my soul can breathe". And if there may be doubt about the authenticity of this comment there is no doubt about the impact French education had on those Vietnamese who were talented enough or well-connected enough to attend the *lycées* or the university in Hanoi established in Vietnam by the colonial power—the famed victor of the Battle of Dien Bien Phu, General Vo Nguyen Giap, was one of these and it was in these institutions that he became acquainted with his military hero, Napoleon Bonaparte. Less dramatically, the pervasive presence of French-style bread in the form of *baguettes* was another sign of the French influence throughout both Cambodia and Vietnam, even in the most distant provinces. Indeed, when Princess Pengpas Yukanthor, the doyenne of Cambodian culinary experts, was asked in the 1950s to list some of her country's most important dishes several of them involved the use of "French" bread.

I had some sense of what records still existed to be consulted in Saigon as a result of the month I had spent there in 1963, but only a vague sense of what might exist in Phnom Penh. Paris, on the other hand, beckoned as a certain rich source of materials about the colonial period and it was there I went at the end of August 1965 with plans to travel on to carry out research in Cambodia and Vietnam later. And the day after I arrived, still uncertain as to where I would live, or indeed for how long, I went to open a bank account.

Banking, 'comme il faut'

I headed for the head office of the Chase Manhattan Bank (the forerunner of today's J.P. Morgan Chase), for it was to this major bank that the Tompkins County Trust Company of Ithaca, New York, had remitted the sum of $1,000, my travelling scholarship stipend for the next six months; it's no longer sited there, but in 1965 the head office of the bank was in an austere section of the rue Cambon. This street runs from the rue de Rivoli to the Boulevard Madeleine, but it is not until it crosses the rue Saint-Honoré that it gives in to any hint of frivolity. And it was to this imposing address that I went, hesitantly, on my first full day in Paris in the expectation that I would be able to open a bank account but knowing nothing of banking practices in France.

Opening a bank account was scarcely something new for me. I had had cheque accounts as a student in Sydney, then in Canberra, Cambodia and Hong Kong before moving to Ithaca and opening my account there. But I certainly had never before been greeted, as I was when I came to the door of Chase Manhattan's grand banking chamber, by such an imposing figure. He may have only been the doorman but he was clad in a full morning suit. Pretending not to notice that I was not wearing a suit—I *was* wearing a navy blazer and a collar and tie—he led me, after I had explained the purpose of my visit, to another gentleman, an assistant manager who was no less elegant in appearance, though in his case he was dressed in the darkest of well-cut business suits. Identifying myself by my passport, a phone call established that my one thousand dollars had indeed been received. "I would like," I then said, "to open a cheque account with your bank which I would operate for the period I am going to be in Paris carrying out research."

My memory of the conversation that took place over the next few minutes is slightly hazy to begin with, but becomes sharper towards its end. I don't think there was any hint of concern in my elegant interlocutor's response as he said that the bank would be happy to open an account for me. But when I next said that with the account opened I would be withdrawing one hundred francs, the mood of our encounter changed. It was not that the elegantly clad gentleman was rude, far from it. He was just very firm as he said, "I am afraid that will not be possible. Chase Manhattan Paris will only maintain accounts with a minimum balance equivalent to one thousand dollars."

This was, to say the least, a stopper. I had never been in Paris before and I feared that if Chase Manhattan would not open an account for me there was no reason to think any other bank would do so. I had no idea where I was going to live for the next eight or nine months and I certainly did not wish to take the risk of carrying a large sum of money around in my pockets. What to do? Just every now and then a thought comes to mind that provides an unexpected but effective answer to a problem. And this was one of those times as I realised I had an ace up my sleeve named Rockefeller, the family closely associated with Chase Manhattan for many decades. Speaking very carefully and making as sure as I possibly could that my French was correct, I said, "I wonder what Mr Nelson Rockefeller, the Governor of New York and a member of the Cornell University Board of Trustees, would think of my not being able to open an account with Chase Manhattan?"

There was a pause that probably did not last as long as my memory suggests. And then, in a gracious retreat, the assistant manager with whom I was talking said, to my great relief, "We will be pleased to open an account for you." And they did, treating my measly deposit with the same care as the other accounts in the bank, and finally embarrassing me when, after I thought I had closed my account more than a year later, by pursuing me in the nicest way to notify me that I still had a credit of nearly one hundred dollars in my account waiting to be withdrawn.

Exploring the archives and eating yesterday's baguettes

Just as Rick told Ilsa in "Casablanca", any of us who have had the good fortune to live in Paris for any length of time can repeat his declaration, or was it more of an apology in the circumstances, that "We'll always have Paris." Given the number of memoirs, in so many forms, by so many people famous and otherwise, it seems risky to venture into the field, but perhaps the justification is that each person's Paris really is distinctive, even if there are widely shared experiences. So I may be forgiven for writing that I knew I was not alone in finding, initially, that Parisians are indeed frequently brusque in manner. I have read many explanations for this characteristic, ranging from their dislike of "outlanders", whether French provincials or foreigners, to the congested nature of life within the city. Whatever may be the case, my "epiphany" was the realisation that Parisians were just as brusque in their dealings with each other as they were with me. What's more, there were sudden and unexpected signs that at some levels I had become, if not a Parisian, at least part of the city's human landscape. So I was delighted when the man at the newspaper *kiosque* near the colonial archives handed me a copy of *Le Monde* each evening without my asking for it. Now that made me feel I had at least partially arrived. So, too, did being able to respond to the surprising number French visitors to the capital who asked me for directions. They knew I was not French, but I was answering them in their language and knew the streets of inner Paris well through my frequent walking to save money. And above all else, I alone can recount the experiences I had with my landlady at the Pension Littré, Madame Vanoit, or later with the scholarly and generous antiquarian bookseller, Ian Feldman?

Somewhat to my surprise I found that there was a wider range of archives to consult than I had initially anticipated. The most rewarding archives were those of the former Ministry of the Colonies in the rue Oudinot, with its somewhat down-at-heel reading room, and the colour scheme of the paint along its corridors exactly the same as I had seen in the former French colonial offices in Phnom Penh. But I found much that was useful in the other archival *dépôts* in the French capital—those at the headquarters of the National Archives in the elegant Hôtel de Soubise; at the Quai d'Orsay, the Foreign Ministry, where the chairs were upholstered in leather as befitted that grand institution; and those of both the Army and the Navy, with the latter distinguished by the fact that when I worked there a sailor brought me a cup of tea at four in the afternoon. Had I been embarking on this research some years later my main base for research would not have been in Paris but in Aix-en-Provence, to which location the colonial archives were later moved—a charming city, it's true, but not with the same appeal as Paris. So I was lucky. And lucky in more ways than one, since in the mid-1960s research in the colonial archives that dealt with Cambodia and Vietnam was an essentially solitary affair as French graduate students were still for the most part not addressing this period of history. For them, and for France as a whole, memories of defeat at Dien Bien Phu in 1954, followed by the anguish of the Algerian War, in which so many troops who had fought in Vietnam were also engaged, were still too sharp a memory. As a result I was given a degree of special attention by the *Directrice*, Mademoiselle Meunier, eventually to the point where she allowed me to continue working in a separate room over the otherwise firmly closed lunchtime hours between twelve and two. Here, at least, I was accepted.

Working in the colonial archives and using a rather grubby card catalogue that had clearly existed for many decades, I selected the dossiers I wanted to examine, never quite knowing what would be brought to me from the stacks by the reading room clerk. He was a former soldier from one of France's African colonies south of the Sahara, who made no effort to hide his disdain for the "privileged" types who could spend their time poring over documents rather than "doing something useful". He took great pleasure in shooing us out of the reading room at noon. When he returned to open the doors at two in the afternoon it was clear he had downed more than one glass of rough red in the interim. His disdain for us readers and our research was broadly reciprocated and I once heard one of my fellow French *chercheurs* describe him, in a fashion that had little to do with either *egalité* or *fraternité*, as *ce macaque*.

More often than not excitement triumphed over disappointment when the dossiers reached my table. How could it be otherwise when I found I was looking at letters from the King of Cambodia to the French *Résident* in Phnom Penh, written on gold-coloured silk and hung about with massive wax seals; or the lengthy account of this same king's half-brother's effort to sell the king down the river, or at very least into exile, if only the French would make sure that he, Prince Sisowath, could take the throne occupied by Norodom. The accounts of what had appeared to have been a minor revolt against French control of Cambodia in the 1880s, in terms of what I had previously read, now it became clear from documents in the archives was a major rebellion that exacted a high cost in French casualties. And, as an evocation of the macabre, there was the reference to French officials in Vietnam, racked by dysentery, sentencing to death rebels against their rule while sitting on their *chaises percées*. It was only many years later that I read a summary of Jacques Derrida's views that archives could be "dangerous, glorious, insidious and inebriating" and capable of imposing order when, in fact, none existed. Derrida's point is clear, but as I found interest, pleasure and satisfaction in my discoveries it was the "glorious" part of this comment that resonates for me.

The Pension Littré

But as I made my notes in the archives, I still had not found a place to live on a permanent basis. My first mistake was to think it would be possible to find a room in a modest hotel somewhere in the Latin Quarter and so to emulate Elliot Paul, whose wonderful evocation of interwar Paris, *A Narrow Street*, had been recommended to me by my mother when it became clear I would be doing research in the City of Light. My second mistake was to have gone through the procedure of obtaining a student visa before leaving the United States. These two mistakes built on each other since, as I quickly found, there were no hotels that were ready to accept the presence a long-term guest, and the fact of holding a student visa meant that I had to report to the local police commissariat each time I moved hotels; in one ghastly week I moved no less than five times. At least I only had to carry one suitcase and my trusty Olivetti portable typewriter on these moves. Looking back, this really was what it means to be travelling light. But light though my luggage was, time was passing with the weather in late September growing colder and my frequent efforts to find a lodging taking up time that could have been much better used for research.

Salvation came in the form of the Pension Littré after a French acquaintance suggested that a pension might be the answer to my problems. Effectively, a many-roomed boarding house with a central dining room, the pension was accommodated in a building on the corner of the rue de Fleurus and the rue Jean Bart that had once been home of the notable nineteenth-century French lexicographer, Emile Littré. So it wasn't the heart of the Latin Quarter, but the narrow streets of that *quartier* were within easy walking distance; I could see the trees if the Luxembourg Gardens if I leaned out of my window; and there was at least some connection with the Paris of famous expatriates in the interwar years as the house where Gertrude Stein and Alice B. Toklas had lived in the rue de Fleurus was close by. And, more importantly than any other consideration, being given a place in the Pension Littré meant I met and was educated in French politics by *la patronne*, Madame Vanoit.

She must have been in her mid to late-fifties, handsome and very direct in her manner. It became clear fairly early in my call on her to seek a place in her pension that she was predisposed to offer me a room and she even forgave my occasional stumbles in her language. But it was only at the end of our conversation that it became clear why I was, apparently, welcome. Just as I was about to thank her and leave, she said, "And you may use the shower whenever you want. Since as an Australian you are a sort of *Anglo-Saxon*, and I shall always remember *les tommies* with whom I fought in the war."

The full implications of all this took a little time to understand. Being allowed to use the pension's shower whenever I wished was indeed a privilege, since the other *pensionnaires* were only allowed one free shower a week; after that they had to pay extra. And Americans, it became clear, did not receive the same dispensation, since two Bennington College students spending an academic year in Paris and living in the pension were not accorded Anglo-Saxon status. As it was, the nature of Madame Vanoit's time with *les tommies* was only slowly revealed, but eventually in bits and pieces I learnt most of the story of her chequered life. She had, indeed, fought in the Second World War, first as a *résistante—une vraie résistante* as she emphasised showing me her medals—and then after Normandy with one of the allied teams that parachuted into France behind enemy lines. But before this she had fought on the Republican side in the Spanish Civil War. What made this the more remarkable was the fact that by the time I met her she had embraced the far right of French domestic politics and was preparing to vote for Jean-Louis Tixier-Vignacour in the December 1965 presidential elections. After the Second World War she had married a French colonel who was killed in Indochina and this, apparently, led to her decisive switch in political affiliations from left to right. Here was another link to the former French presence in Indochina that never seemed too far away in Paris.

It was nearly three months after I had been living in the Pension Littré that Madame Vanoit again made crystal clear the importance she placed on her association with the British in the Second World War. It was in early December when the first round of the French presidential election took place and when, as I have noted, she was supporting the far right candidate, Tixier-Vignancour. He had no hope of winning and the real race was between the incumbent, Charles de Gaulle, and François Mitterand of the French Socialist Party. When the results of first round of voting were announced Mitterand gained enough support to force de Gaulle into a run-off electoral race. At this point Madame Vanoit broke out champagne for all living in the pension. This was an act of surprising generosity from a businesswoman who had a Gallic eye for value—her *homme à tout faire*, André, was despatched late each afternoon to buy our next day's breakfast baguettes when they were marked down in price just before the *boulangerie* closed. Indeed, the only cross words she ever spoke to me was when I paid my first month's bill by cheque. This indiscretion became the occasion for a lengthy lecture on the advantages of settling one's bills in cash, whenever possible, since to do so meant that the state was, properly, removed from the monetary equation. But her gesture of dispensing champagne to her *pensonnaires* was even more striking since throughout the previous weeks Madame Vanoit had been fulminating against Mitterand as little more than "a communist".

So, as we sipped her champagne, I felt I now knew her well enough to ask her why she had acted in this way. "But don't you see," she said briskly to me, "I'm not celebrating the votes given to Mitterand. I'm celebrating de Gaulle being *mis en ballotage*. I will never forgive him for the way he has acted against the British who stood out against Hitler *and* gave him refuge, which he has never properly acknowledged." There was a fine Cartesian logic to this, but I stopped short of asking her about her decision to vote for Tixier-Vignancour, who had been an enthusiastic supporter of Pétain during the early Vichy period in the Second World War and was jailed for eighteen months for this collaboration when the war ended. After all, it was people like Tixier against whom Madame Vanoit and her colleagues in the Resistance had fought and died.

Au Bouquiniste Oriental

None of the archives and libraries that dominated my life during the week was open on Saturdays or Sundays, which meant these were days to devote to museums, galleries and historical sites. And to my surprise I found that there was much that I could do without having to pay for the pleasure. The Louvre was free from ten in the morning until noon every Sunday, and in the 1960s this meant I could be one of only a handful of visitors to that great museum through the winter months— nowadays it is only free on one Sunday each month and the queue to take advantage of this dispensation stretches back hundreds of metres from the Pyramid. Perhaps more surprisingly, I found that some of the grandest private art galleries on the Right Bank were perfectly happy to have a non-paying visitor admire their remarkable holdings of the finest art. And just off the Boulevard Saint-Germain in the rue de Seine, not far from my pension, I found that the staff at Paul Prouté et Fils (now Paul Prouté S.A.) were ready to let me spend hours looking through the folios holding their rich collections of engravings and lithographs. As a very small response to their kindness I eventually bought, for a surprisingly modest price, a tiny Goya engraving from his "Incongruities" series: "The Prisoner bound by his chains." Goya's own comment on this series of three "Prisoner" engravings was that, "The punishment is worse than the crime."

But just as importantly these were times for wandering through the streets of the city, above all in the Latin Quarter, without any particular purpose. I didn't think I had coined a new way to describe this activity when I told myself that I was walking through history, but cliché or not, it was how I felt. It was also a time to match fictional figures to their Parisian surroundings. So a painfully prolonged visit to the Préfecture de la Seine on the Ile de la Cité to verify the status of my student visa at least gave me the opportunity to imagine Maigret smoking his pipe as he walked along the Quai des Orfèvres. And as I walked past the Conciergierie on my way to the headquarters of the National Archives housed in the Hôtel de Soubise, in the rue des Francs-Bourgeois, I thought of Sydney Carton on his way to the guillotine.

So it was, on one Saturday afternoon of pleasantly aimless wanderings, that I turned left off the rue St-André-des-Arts into the rue Séguier, which leads down to the Seine, and found myself looking through the dusty window of Au Bouquiniste Oriental, one of the many antiquarian bookshops clustered around the eastern end of this ancient street. From outside I could see that there were books everywhere, on shelves, on tables and piled in heaps on the floor. This impression of an apparently chaotic lack of order was reinforced when I hesitantly entered, wondering if among the shop's stock there might be anything relating to the former French Indochina that I could afford. And so I met the remarkable Ian Feldman, or "Mr Feldman" as I always addressed him once we decided that we would converse in English.

I never knew Ian Feldman's precise age. Almost thirty myself, I thought of him as an old man and everything about him suggested someone in his middle to late sixties. By birth he was Armenian, but he had moved from place to place during the interwar period, including living for long periods in both England and France, and briefly in Egypt. A non-practising Jew, he was fluent in several European languages and extraordinarily knowledgeable about books relating to the "Orient", which for him included the Middle East as well as what I thought of as "Asia". He had spent much of the 1930s in England and, thankfully, all of the Second World War years. For, as he observed more than once to me, the French have many admirable qualities, such as their readiness to accept "flotsam such as me" living among them. But their hospitable nature deserted them under Vichy and the German occupation. Always involved with books, he had been on the edge of London's literary and antiquarian book scene in the thirties, rubbing shoulders with such figures as Christina Foyle, of the famous bookshop in Charing Cross Road, and famous dealers from Maggs and Bernard Quaritch.

Quizzing me about my reasons for being in Paris, he asked me how much I knew of the exploration of the Indochinese region and in particular of the French Mekong River expedition that took place in the 1860s. When I told him that I knew a little but wanted to learn more he started searching through the volumes that seemed stacked without any order. Within minutes he handed me Francis Garnier's one-volume account of the expedition, published posthumously in 1885, a copy of the *Tour du Monde* magazine, which contained the first account of Henri Mouhot's travels in 1860 that brought European attention to the ruined temples of Angkor, and two beautifully bound off-prints of articles

Garnier had written after the Mekong expedition concluded in 1868. Not only were these books I had to have, but ones that provided the start to my long-term interest in the expedition and which led, finally, to the publication of my book about it: *River Road to China*. In a mark of the generosity that was Feldman's personal hallmark he allowed me to arrange to pay for my now treasured possessions by instalments.

This was the start of a friendship with Ian Feldman that lasted for nearly ten years, until the sad day when I returned to Paris in the early 1980s, after an absence of some six or seven years, to find his shop was closed and no one was able to tell me if he was still alive. He was not only a guide to often obscure publications dealing with the countries of the former French Indochina, his remarkable stock of books and prints introduced me to an antiquarian world about which I knew almost nothing. Did I know about Napoleon Bonaparte's Egyptian campaign? Well here, he showed me proudly, were the twenty-seven volumes of the *Description de l'Egypte* that Napoleon had commissioned. And had I ever seen the evocative lithographs of the Middle East by the Scottish artist David Roberts? Well here were some them, too. And a presentation for my inspection of these and other treasures was followed by a complaint that he repeated over and again. Once these items were sold how would he ever find replacements for them?

Ian Feldman was an entertaining raconteur and not averse to sharp commentary on some of his competitors and others who had crossed his path. He recommended that I should call on Georges Taboulet, a prolific chronicler of the former French colonies in Indochina, but he warned me to be prepared to meet an unreconstructed *colon* of the old school—

as indeed Taboulet proved to be. Aged seventy-seven when I met him, he had responded promptly to my request to call on him and received me in his apartment, in a dimly lit study lined with books and with a miniature portrait bust of the explorer of the Mekong River, Francis Garnier, on his desk. During the colonial period Taboulet had been in charge of the education system (the *Instruction Publique*) throughout French Indochina and he made clear to me his conviction that the policies over which he had presided were a quintessential example of France's commitment to the pursuit of her *mission civilistrice* for the populations of French Indochina. There was no sense in what he had to say that any aspect of France's role was open to critical examination. Once he had made clear this view he proved to be full of information on issues of detail, in particular the promotion of the French language, and I saw little point in suggesting that there were other ways of looking at the education policies that had been instituted in Vietnam and Cambodia. After all, Taboulet's most important publication, a monumental two-volume annotated compilation of documents relating to French Indochina, had the title, *La Geste française en Indochine* (The Heroic Story of France in Indochina), published in 1955-56. And in his Preface Taboulet had written of " . . . the great and generous civilising action [that France] had undertaken for more than a century" in Indochina.

Almost dining at the Tour d'Argent

Many of Ian Feldman's anecdotes were retailed to me over the lunches or dinners to which he would invite me from time to time. It took me a little while to understand at least part of the underlying basis of this welcome hospitality, for it was indeed a very acceptable alternative to the repetitive culinary offerings of the pension. To some extent the varied meals we had together were the generous act of a man able and willing to offer them to a graduate student who, while not poor, was short of money—there is a real difference between these two states. But after a while it also became apparent that he was a man whose two sons were a cause for repeated concern. It became clear that one had spent time in prison for some kind of financial scam, while the other seemed set to follow in the same path. In short, and while this was never put into so many words, I was to some small extent a surrogate child; roughly the same age as his sons, not tainted by past or incipient criminality, interested in the books that were Feldman's life both as a business and as a vocation. And if I added a measure of warmth to his life, he was one of the few people in Paris with whom I could talk easily. Philippe Devillers, the French academic and author whom I had met at Cornell, was a helpful guide to the Paris university world, particularly Sciences-Po, and my fellow *pensionnaires* were never less than friendly. But at a time when loneliness was never too far absent, Ian Feldman was a welcome companion.

Over the eight or so months I saw him regularly in 1965 and 1966 we dined together at least half a dozen times, probably a couple more than that. I don't remember every occasion, but a few stand out in my memory; the long-established Polidor *brasserie* in the rue Monsieur-le-Prince and Chez Maître Paul in the same street with its food from Gascony in the southwest; a now-vanished restaurant serving Alsatian food in the Place Saint-André-des-Arts, which rekindled my memories of *steak au poivre* in Phnom Penh's La Taverne from years before. And one evening we ate at an Armenian restaurant, which I remember chiefly for the haze of the cigarette-generated fug that filled its room. But most of all I remember the day I almost dined at the Tour d'Argent—well, for a moment it seemed that was what I was going to experience.

I had called to talk to Ian Feldman at his shop on a Saturday in early March to tell him that I would be leaving Paris for Cambodia early the following month. I knew I would never be fully sure that I had found all that might be useful for my research in the Paris archives and libraries, but I had enough material to take the next step by going to look in the unexplored archives of the colonial period that remained in Phnom Penh and Saigon. Moreover, there was both a time and a monetary limit to how long I could stay overseas before returning to Cornell to write my dissertation. "Well," Feldman said, "we must have one more meal together. Meet me here next Wednesday and we will have a final lunch to mark your time in Paris." And so I gratefully came to Au Bouquiniste Oriental shortly after midday as he suggested on the Wednesday.

Walking with Ian Feldman was a fairly slow affair. He had a gammy leg so that although he was perfectly able to move about the city he did so at a gentle pace, a fact that gave me plenty of time to wonder where we were going, since unlike other occasions he had not told me our destination. Leaving his shop, on a day of bright sunshine that gave final confirmation that spring was not far distant, we turned right on to the Quai des Grands Augustins at the foot of the rue Séguier and then continued at a stately pace along the Seine. After crossing the beginning of the Boulevard Saint-Michel opposite the Ile de la Cité, we continued along the Quai Montebello to the Quai de Tournelle. By this stage I really dared to think the unthinkable about our destination, for we were drawing ever closer to that pinnacle of Paris restaurants, the Tour d'Argent. Could it really be that this generous man was going to crown my Parisian culinary experiences with lunch at a three-starred temple to food and wine? It really began to seem possible until, just before the intersection of the quai and the rue Cardinal Lemoine, and so the entrance to the Tour d'Argent, we stopped and entered the Rotisserie de Beaujolais. But I had no reason to be other than very grateful for what was a marvellous lunch that ended with a glass of *marc* to follow the generously dispensed Beaujolais wine that was and is the restaurant's speciality. I have still not been to the Tour d'Argent. But I have returned many times to the *rotisserie* where I always think of Ian Feldman, the kindly guide to rare books who made my time in Paris so much more pleasurable than it might otherwise have been the case and taught me so much about the books written with France's colonies in Asia as their subject.

Vous êtes condamné à la mort

"Walking through history" on a Saturday could bring a welcome surprise, such as finding Ian Feldman's Au Bouquiniste Oriental, but few surprises could match the one I experienced on 6 November 1965, when I saw a man sentenced to death. And like the best, or possibly in this case the worst surprises, the events that led to my having this experience were banal in the extreme.

I had been invited to visit the University of Hull at end of November to present a paper on the research I was undertaking in Paris, and so on this Saturday I had set off from the Pension Littré shortly after midday to buy a ticket for the boat train to England. To my frustration when I reached Thomas Cook's office near the Madeleine I found it was closed. I then decided that I would go to a bookshop on the Boulevard Saint-Michel where I had previously noted a couple of books about Vietnam were on sale at much reduced prices. This should have been a simple course of action: leave Thomas Cook's and take the Métro from the Concorde station to Chatelet and change there to travel on another line to the Saint-Michel station. What I had not factored in was the maze of tunnels that link the Chatelet station, where I disembarked, to no fewer than three other Métro lines, and so six separate station platforms. I was disoriented as I tramped through what have to be some of the longest *correspondance* tunnels in the whole Paris system. Finally, I admitted defeat and took the first stairs I could find to the streets above to walk across the Seine to the Ile de la Cité and then to the Boulevard Saint-Michel. So far, so normal, I was just another foreigner still not fully attuned to the complexities of the Métro despite using it almost every other day.

I never reached the bookshop since my change of travel plans led me to do something I had meant to do for some time, to visit Sainte Chapelle and the Conciergerie, both on the island that had been the centre of the city in medieval times. Nowadays visiting Sainte Chapelle, Louis IX's remarkable thirteenth-century foundation built to house relics of Christ's crucifixion, means joining a lengthy queue at almost any time of the year. But in 1965 I was able to enter immediately and stand in wonder in this remarkable pavilion of stained glass. And then, as I set off to visit the Conciergerie close by I found myself crossing the courtyard in front of the Law Courts, the Palais de Justice, where there was a crowd of lawyers in their robes and many Republican Guards carrying sub-machine guns. Clearly something was happening that had provoked more than usual interest. Inquisitive as ever, and without anyone asking me where I was going—unimaginable nowadays in an age of security inspections—I followed the movement of others into the corridors of the building and so entered a crowded courtroom and found a place to stand. It was only then, as I took account of the presence of Republican Guards, once again with their sub-machine guns, and a bench of five judges, two of whom were in military uniform in contrast to the cardinal red robes of the other three, that I realised where I was. I had come by chance to the Court of State Security where Jacques Vasseur was on trial for his crimes in the city of Angers during the years of German occupation.

I had read about the trial both in *Le Monde* and in *The New York Times*. Over some weeks *Le Monde* had been recording the testimony by witness after witness accusing Vasseur of assisting the Germans in arresting members of the Resistance, being present at torture sessions and, according to some witnesses, administering torture himself. According to press reports, Vasseur had been responsible for the arrest and torture of as many as 430 people, the deportation of 310, and the death of 230, of whom 52 had been shot in France itself. It was a trial, *The New York Times* observed, that was casting a shadow that the French nation would just as soon not see. The accuracy of this comment was not as clear in 1965 as it later became, for at the time of Vasseur's trial much of France was still in a state of wilful amnesia so far as the period of occupation was concerned. There was an awareness of collaboration with the Nazi occupiers, but this was matched by a hope that the purges that immediately followed the end of the war had brought a close to that particular and unhappy national chapter. But now, here was Vasseur, a man who had been sentenced to death in his absence in 1944 before the end of the war but who had managed to escape justice for nearly eighteen years. For almost all of that time he had been hiding in the attic of his mother's apartment. Vasseur, his crimes and the readiness of other French citizens to work closely with the German occupiers were issues that many, indeed most, French did not want to think about. This was before the publication of Robert Paxton's ground-breaking book on collaboration, *Vichy France: Old Guard and New Order*, and the release of Marcel Ophüls' film "Le Chagrin et la Pitié", both of which did so much to open up discussion of the wartime years. It was before the realisation that men such as René Bousquet and Maurice Papon, who had continued to hold high positions in government service after the war, had played guilty roles in the deportation of Jews from France, and in Bousquet's case had subsequently been protected for many years by François Mitterand.

I knew very little then of life in France during the Second World War as I watched and listened to Vasseur's defence counsel plead for his client, though I knew from Madame Vanoit at my pension that there were *vrais résistants* and *résistants de la dernière heure*. Like most foreigners I had no deep appreciation of the extent to which the occupation period was an unexamined subject and of the extent to which Gaullist propaganda had sought to draw a veil over the period, not least of how the General himself had done everything possible to minimise an awareness of the role played by Madame Vanoit's *tommies* in aiding the Resistance. But because of press coverage I knew the essentials of the case against Jacques Vasseur. He was a student in his early twenties at the time of the German defeat of France with a good knowledge of the victors' language. This led to his accepting employment as an interpreter, a role that was rapidly transformed into the post of heading, in the city of Angers, what came to be known as the "French Gestapo"—the political police of the French administration that functioned under German control.

Now I heard these facts given a particular slant in the closing address of Vasseur's defence counsel. Even for a foreign outsider the pleas sounded hollow as the counsel argued that witnesses could not be certain of their identification of Vasseur after eighteen years. Why, he argued, many of us cannot remember the details of a traffic accident three months ago. Then he changed tack. Even if Vasseur had done some of the things of which he was accused these occurred in wartime and one cannot judge a man too harshly in peacetime for what took place in the war. Vasseur, the counsel continued, is not mad, but he is schizoid and the judges should take this into account in their deliberations. This defence was delivered in a manner that was highly theatrical with the counsel's voice ranging from a shout to barely a whisper. And throughout his defence counsel's address the prisoner sat, handcuffed to two guards, with his head sunk on his chest, pale and insignificant against the majesty of the setting, the robes of the judges and counsels, and the seriousness of the charges. When the defence counsel had finished his plea there was only a brief pause before the president of the court read the charges against Vasseur, at speed and in a thick regional accent so that I, at least, could scarcely understand half of what he was saying. What was clear to me was that there were four charges against Vasseur and he was being tried on each of these.

The moment the president had ceased reading the charges the judges departed and the spectators around me started loudly discussing the likely outcome of the trial. There seemed to be no unanimity of opinion, other than the expectation that Vasseur would be sentenced to a long jail term. When the judges returned the verdicts were delivered at a rush: on the first count, guilty; on the second, not guilty—a sigh from the spectators; on the third count, guilty; and on the fourth count, guilty. Then, after a rapid rush of legal language, came the verdict. "Vasseur, Jacques, vous êtes condamné à la mort." There was utter silence as the judges quickly withdrew and Vasseur, almost collapsing, was dragged from the court by his handcuffs. As I stood among the silent spectators it took me more than a moment to realise just what I had seen, a man condemned to death. It is something I never wish to see again. I had formed the view many years before that the death penalty should never be imposed, but this event provided an affirmation that went beyond the theoretical and hypothetical views I had previously developed. Walking into the brisk November air under a leaden sky did little to soften the shock of what I had seen and heard.

* * *

Vasseur was not executed as President de Gaulle commuted his sentence to life imprisonment and President Pompidou later reduced the sentence to twenty years in prison. He lived to be released in 1984 and married a German woman with whom he had corresponded while in prison. Much later, in 2008, Vasseur became the subject of a novel by Dominiqe Jamet, *Un Traître*, where his life forms the narrative of a figure who evokes Vasseur, but under a different name as Delau—a different name, but one that is the novelist's sly pointer to his character's real-life identity. For "Delau", or "De l'eau", literally "of water", picks up the German word for "water," "wasser". And "wasser" would be written *phonetically* in French as "Vasseur".

The novel aside, Vasseur is scarcely remembered today, unlike Paul Touvier, the collaborator who worked with Klaus Barbie in Lyon and who was controversially pardoned by President Pompidou and only finally brought to trial in 1994 after decades of being protected by Catholic priests and religious orders who still had sympathy for the Vichy period. He, also, was the inspiration for a novel, Brian Moore's *The Statement*, where the fictional former collaborator, Pierre Brossard, is depicted as having a life similar to Touvier's.

Was it a surprise that Vasseur should have escaped execution? Probably not, for by the time he was sentenced there was little of the passion for retribution that had been present at the time of the *épuration*, the purge of collaborators which took place at the time of liberation in 1944 and following the end of the war in 1945. Nevertheless, his sentence came at the time when the death penalty was still in operation—it was not abolished until 1981, and the last execution, by the guillotine, took place in 1977.

The Missions Etrangères

As February drew to a close and as I increasingly sensed that I had found the bulk of the interesting material I had been looking for in the various French government archives, there was one remaining archival holding I hoped to examine, that of the French Catholic missionary order founded in the seventeenth century that had long been active in Cambodia and Vietnam, the Société des Missions Etrangères with its headquarters in the rue du Bac. I had passed this collection of buildings regularly as I walked from the Pension Littré, passing along the rue de Babylone to reach the colonial archives located at the corner of the rue Oudinot and the Boulevard des Invalides. Even before I had left Cornell I had heard that the priests of the Missions Etrangères were hesitant to allow access to their records; there had been some contretemps about their missionary activities when France had been fighting the First Indochina War, but I thought that by emphasising my interest was limited to the nineteenth century this might improve my chances of being allowed to see at least some of their archives. So one March morning I presented myself at their headquarters and walked into an austere building suggestive of high purpose and frugal living.

Might I seek permission to examine the Order's records in relation to Cambodia and Vietnam? The answer was "yes" and I was ushered into a nearly bare room, furnished with a table and two chairs, and with a simple crucifix the only object to make clear this was a building dedicated to religion. Here I was received by an elderly priest whose demeanour was a match for the less than welcoming surroundings. After I had explained my interests he quickly made clear that I would not be allowed access to the Order's written archives, and that there could be discussion about this decision. But I could, he told me, examine the Order's *Lettres Communes*, an in-house printed newsletter, which was published annually and gave summaries of the activities of its priests overseas, sometimes in the words of the bishops in change of particular dioceses. I thanked the archivist, thinking that this arrangement was, at least, better than nothing.

It was, in fact, a great deal better than I anticipated for the records in the series of *Lettres Communes* were frequently surprisingly frank, not least in terms of the difficulties members of the Order encountered in their missionary activity, particularly in Cambodia. Although the newsletter recorded a measure of success in Vietnam, once France had established a colonial presence in southern Vietnam, Cambodia continued to be a disappointment. Even before France extended its control over Cambodia in 1863, Bishop Miche recorded an assessment that summarised the difficulty for missionaries working in the profoundly Buddhist country. The only way to gain converts, Miche recorded, was through buying the freedom of debt slaves, and that method was "long and very costly". Like Madame Vanoit, Bishop Miche had a well-developed Gallic sense of value.

4

Cambodia 1966

If returning to Cambodia in 1966 had the air of a homecoming it was a homecoming in which I was returning to familiar territory in a very different guise. No longer sheltered by diplomatic status, however junior, I was uncertain of just what I would find, if anything, in the archives left behind when the French departed from Cambodia after independence had been granted in 1953. I certainly had no sense on arrival that I was coming to a Cambodia in which politics had taken on a new character by comparison with what I had observed between 1959 and 1961.

For what I witnessed in Cambodia in 1966 was the beginning of a slow decline of Sihanouk's power symbolised, most notably that year, by his obsessive preoccupation with film-making when other issues weighed heavily on the governance of the state, not least the intensification of the war next door in Vietnam. This decline took place in an atmosphere marked by the pervasive presence of corruption at all levels of Cambodian society. And while it would be wrong to suggest that in 1966 Cambodia was already set on the path that would see Sihanouk toppled from office and the awful triumph of the Khmer Rouge, it was entirely possible to recognise that he was a weaker leader than had been the case previously. The clearest evidence of this was his decision not to be personally involved in selecting candidates for the national assembly for the elections that took place in September 1966. We will never know the full range of reasons led to this decision. He had every reason to be tired physically, and just as importantly both the right and left of Cambodian politics had shown a readiness to speak in ways that would previously have been regarded as close to lèse-majesté. If anything, it was the left that caused him the greatest annoyance. Moreover, and though he did not admit at the time, the visit to Cambodia by Sihanouk's great idol, General Charles de Gaulle, at the end of August had not led to any real change in the international crisis created by the ongoing war in Vietnam.

So although my time in Cambodia in 1966 was very much shorter than the more than two years of my embassy posting it made at least as deep an impression as had that earlier period. The fact that it was a period of heightened political controversy and disputation made the whole experience sharper, particularly as I had the opportunity to speak to Cambodians who were now ready to speak with remarkable frankness to me about contemporary political issues in a way that had never been possible when I was serving in the country as a diplomat.

Away from Phnom Penh

Both in my diplomatic posting and in later visits to Cambodia I developed a deep sense of attachment to the city of Phnom Penh. This was before its tragic history of abandonment under the Khmer Rouge regime in the 1970s and its fate, now, as it increasingly falls victim to the contemporary vogue for "development", with a resultant building boom marked by the construction of multiple high-rise buildings. But there is much about Cambodia away from its capital that remains strong in my memory. I think, for instance, of the quiet but intense pleasure of travelling down the Mekong, from Kratie to Kompong Cham, on a slow river ferry, when that great river was in flood in September 1966, an experience that was a welcome contrast to the febrile political atmosphere then pervasive in Phnom Penh. It was a journey begun very early in the morning, that magical time of the day when it is possible for a little while to imagine that the heat of the day will be held at bay. As I noted then:

> The boat left at dawn and as we moved out from the dock at Kratie the sky was streaked with pink. From then on we sailed through a perfect sunny day with the light bouncing off the water and the vegetation along the river a brilliant green in the sun. All along the banks there was clear evidence of how high the water is. Many houses were fully or partly flooded, and at times where the water of the river ended and the water of the flooded paddies began was impossible to judge. There were all manner of water birds along the route, pelicans, waders of various sorts, cormorants.

> The boat zigzagged from bank to bank always stopping at a landing even if there was only a single passenger to be collected. Many of these riverine villages looked extremely prosperous, with freshly painted *wats* and substantial houses. There were settlements of Chams, a minority group with historical links to Vietnam who are followers of Islam, as well as those of Cambodians and the inevitable Chinese and Vietnamese minorities. We passed the paper factory installed by the Chinese some years ago. It looked

run-down, although it is not very old. A few Chinese technicians, unmistakable in their blue wide-bottomed trousers, were standing near the wharf when we docked at the settlement by the factory.

And I recorded an early morning drive from Phnom Penh to Kompong Cham at the beginning of the rainy season in June:

> The trip to Kompong Cham takes one through a prosperous rice-growing area; great alluvial plains stretch back into the distance, and now the country is beginning to be covered with wide sheets of water. All is green, the deeper green of the countryside refreshed by the coming of the rains, and the bright green of the rice shoots. The relief comes in the blue of the sky and the flowers which Cambodians plant about their houses. There is lilac coloured bougainvillea, and a whole series of flowering trees, the "flamboyants", and yellows and reds from other trees. The sense of fecundity, now that the rainy season has begun is profound. Cattle and water buffalo crowd the road, only just missing being mowed down by the high-loaded buses which jolt past. The rain has brought life, and the people and animals are showing that life in such an observable way.

That particular journey was made to visit Alastair and Frances Chisolm who lived just outside the town of Kompong Cham in circumstances, in 1966, that recalled life in tropical outposts as depicted by Somerset Maugham many years earlier. Alastair worked for the Cambodian branch of British Tobacco:

> . . . They are only 124 kilometres from Phnom Penh, but that distance is sufficient to remove them from almost all the

amenities of the capital, to leave them without a fully qualified doctor readily at hand—the nearest one is at a rubber plantation over an hour away across the Mekong—and to make them two of the five or six permanent members of the Kompong Cham European community. Quite clearly, this is not real isolation. But it has elements of a much stricter isolation. Frances Chisolm is kept busy by one year-old twins, but for the rest of the time she has no one to talk to except her husband. Alastair's social contacts have to be with his colleagues or with the rival tobacco firm. They travel to Phnom Penh about once a month, but life must be lonely, for it is loneliness accentuated by the lack of local newspapers, lack of a radio station, other than short wave, and the feeling which one cannot avoid of knowing that one is isolated in a foreign land . . .

Talk is what the Chisolms miss most—and talk there was, almost non-stop from the time we arrived until 2 am Sunday morning . . .

The next day offered the vision of another kind of isolation, the deliberate holding at arms-length of local society in which a large group of expatriates lived in, but largely apart from Cambodia. This was a visit to Chup, then the largest rubber plantation in the world. It was a very different world from that depicted in the film 'Indochine', but sharply reminiscent of Pierre Boulle's little-known novel, *Sacrilege in Malaya* :

. . . Its expatriate staff number over one hundred and fifty. The rich red soils of the area are ideal for rubber production. I have never found rubber plantations particularly attractive. There is a lowering, sombre quality to the acres upon acres of closely planted rubber trees, marching away in their precise rows, shutting out the sun so that the roads that run through the plantations are constantly in shadow.

And with Chup there is the added quality of its being a tropical company town. Hierarchy is everything, junior members of the personnel should not be seen too often at the club; the club is exclusively for Chup personnel and their guests; there are certain calls to be made on one's senior colleagues; everything one buys comes from the well-stocked company commissary . . . The swimming pool is superior to any other in Cambodia, except perhaps the new pool at the national stadium.

But isolation was not just an issue for expatriates. Cambodian officials posted to locations distant from the capital felt their own removal from the country's policy hub deeply, and in some cases their additional "expatriation" from a long-ago and warmly remembered time as students in France. This was how it seemed at dinner in Kratie, the night before the ferry trip down the Mekong described earlier:

> . . . we had an appointment for dinner with the Chief of the Forestry Service for the region. (He had been at the dinner given by Governor Ok Nall the night before.) The governor was there, as was the local army doctor and one other member of the governor's staff. It really was an excellent dinner, presented with a menu and even Bourbon among the choice of pre-dinner drinks! And the conversation was better than the night before. I think everyone was more relaxed. There was a definite sense of this being An Occasion for the Cambodians—visitors from the

outside, educated company after having to put up with the locals. Some time was spent by the Cambodians in reminiscences of student days in Paris. The chief forester has a matchbox cover from the Café de la Paix . . .

Dining with Wilfred

There has surely never been a more controversial Australian journalist than Wilfred Burchett, who was born in 1911 and died in 1983. I had first heard his name when I had joined the then Department of External Affairs to become a member of the Australian foreign service. So that even before my posting to Phnom Penh in 1959, Burchett's life was a matter of great interest and quite frequent discussion among my senior colleagues. And for students of Cambodia, indeed of all of the countries of the former French Indochina, by the 1960s his was a familiar name for his books dealing with the region, probably most importantly, *Mekong Upstream*, first published in 1957. The book was, for the time, one of the first in English to offer a detailed account of post-Second World War political developments in Cambodia and Laos, as well as often striking descriptive writing about those countries. And it is a book that leaves no doubt about Burchett's commitment to a left-wing view of the world as, equally, did his book published a little earlier, *North of the Seventeenth Parallel*, dealing with North Vietnam. On the basis of his writings I certainly had come to think of him as a 'communist,' though not attaching party membership to that description.

His name was more generally familiar to Australians for other reasons. Having established himself as a hard-working foreign correspondent during the Second World War, including writing about the Chindit leader Orde Wingate. His scoop in visiting Hiroshima after its destruction by the atomic bomb, and only a day after Japan's formal surrender, made his name famous. But following Burchett's acting as a journalist reporting on the Korean War from the North Korean side of that conflict and playing a highly dubious—some would say contemptible—role in relation to prisoners of war held in North Korea, he lost his passport in mysterious circumstances and the Australian government of the day refused to issue him with a new one. This refusal, his political affiliations and disputed actions in Korea aside, always seemed to me to be a reprehensible position. And it is clear that it was a position opposed by many of the most senior members of the Australian diplomatic service. Indeed, throughout the long period when Burchett was not able to return to Australia because of having no passport many Australian diplomats overseas maintained discreet but generally amiable relations with Burchett.

There is, however, another aspect to the long-running debate about Burchett and his political sympathies, a debate quite separate from his actions in Korea. His claim throughout his life was that he was independent" and that his choice to report from the "other side" of conflicts, first in Korea and later in Vietnam, was the choice of a journalist not of an ideologue, despite his readiness to acknowledge his commitment to "socialist" values. The indisputable evidence has been available, at very least since 2008 if not before, to show that Burchett was not "independent". To the contrary, he was a secret member of the Australian Communist Party and an unreconstructed Stalinist throughout his life whose writings from Eastern Europe in the 1950s were shameless apologies for Stalin's policies. Why does this matter? It does to me since it casts a new light on to the statements Burchett made about developments in both Vietnam and Cambodia when I met him in Phnom Penh both in 1966 and 1968.

My first meeting with Burchett in Phnom Penh in 1966 was brief, in mid-May and in the company of Donald Lancaster, Sihanouk's English–language secretary and a former British diplomat. I had met Lancaster shortly after arriving in Cambodia in April and he had proved to be a helpful guide to contemporary Cambodia and an amiable acquaintance. Indeed, he lent me the use of his apartment for nearly two months when he went on leave, so providing me with a standard of accommodation greatly superior to my un-airconditioned room in the Hôtel le Royal. Meeting Burchett while chatting to Lancaster was a reflection of this period in Phnom Penh when the small number of expatriate Europeans who worked for or with Sihanouk often met each other on a casual social basis. Men such as Lancaster, and Charles Meyer and Jean Barré, who were more or less full-time employees of Sihanouk, along with other less well-known individuals, including Pierre Fuchs and Loïc Evan, occupied various positions in the prince's secretariat. Burchett was not formally among this number, but as a *quid pro quo* for being able to live in Phnom Penh and pursue his journalistic career he occasionally undertook specific tasks for Sihanouk. So it was not surprising that I should have met him while talking to Lancaster. My first reaction, as I recorded at the time was, "I suspect he is rather shrewd. He likes his gin." He certainly exuded bonhomie, with a frequent grin and an impression of energy that belied his rather tubby appearance.

Nearly a month later he invited me to dinner, and with considerable curiosity and a measure of apprehension I accepted on 13 June:

> . . . His less than sympathetic Bulgarian wife retired early with stomach trouble. This after such gems of progressive comment as "one would expect the French and the Dutch to know about tropical medicine because of their imperialist colonialist activities," when I remarked that the local doctors were not of high calibre. Her retirement left Burchett and me alone for nearly three hours to talk, during which he drank a great deal of whisky and pressed much upon me . . .

What a strange and sad man. He obviously dotes on his children and would dearly like to have the opportunity to regain Australian citizenship. It is difficult to know what his wife wants for them, and I sense the marriage—this is his second—is not overwhelmingly successful. At intervals through the evening he spoke of Australia with an intense longing and nostalgia. He comes from East Gippsland and he clearly misses the country in an emotional sense.

Between these references to Australia he discoursed on Cambodia, China and Vietnam. He made comments about the current situation very similar to those made by Charles Meyer. Burchett quite obviously deplores the current situation in which the Prince seems to be more concerned with film-making than with the country's economic crisis. Equally clear is the fact that for the moment Cambodia provides a convenient pied-à-terre for his journalistic activities, and not a great deal more. He resents the time he loses having to do English translations of articles for the Prince's journals . . .

. . . there was no doubt about his feelings on Vietnam. Unstinted admiration for both the Northern government and the National Liberation Front. When he spoke of the Front there was very little which has not already appeared in his books. He gave a few personal details which I do not recall being there— for instance during the entire time of his visit in South Vietnam the Front provided him with the services of one of their most qualified doctors . . . He praised the discipline, the patriotism and the ingenuity of the Front. There was never any doubt in as to his view on the eventual outcome of the struggle.

Burchett's account of Vietnam is of the same order as his book —all praise for the communists. It is hard to sort the wheat from the chaff. Just as it is hard to know whether he is a party member or just an enthusiastic propagandist journalist for the communist cause.

But whatever else is clear or unclear, one fact does emerge, Burchett is making a great deal of money from his books, and now from his televison films. He has sold 30,000 copies of "Vietnam: Inside story of a guerrilla war" in the States alone. And his television film on the north has been shown all over Europe and now in America. He has another film that will be released at the end of the northern summer, in Europe. And his main concern at the moment is whether to allow Gallimard, the Paris publishers, to have worldwide rights to his latest book.

Burchett in 1966 was the man Western journalists—or at least those few permitted to enter Cambodia—were steered to see by Charles Meyer, Sihanouk's French, left-wing adviser, and it was only later that I learnt Burchett had been dogmatic in denying, misleadingly, to these visitors, including I.F. Stone, of *I.F. Stone's Weekly*, who came to Cambodia in April 1966, and Harrison Salisbury of *The New York Times*, who visited Phnom Penh in June, that there were any North Vietnamese or National Liberation Front troops enjoying sanctuary on Cambodian soil. He gave the same message to those journalists who were allowed into Cambodia to cover the visit by General de Gaulle in August 1966. He also, insistently, peddled the misleading propaganda line that the NLF was a totally separate movement from the communist government in Hanoi. And I heard him myself making comments on these issues to visiting Australians in 1968. He, almost better than anyone else, knew the falsity of these statements.

In later years his refusal to recognise the nature of the Khmer Rouge regime until the last year of its terrible reign over Cambodia was another example of Burchett's inability to separate his ideological commitments from the reality of the facts before him. Indeed, when I met him by chance in the rue de Rennes in Paris in 1973, he was then full of praise for the forces fighting against the Lon Nol regime in Phnom Penh under the supposed leadership of Norodom Sihanouk.

Cambodian valedictory

Graduate students don't write valedictory despatches in the manner of departing ambassadors, but I did summarise my feelings about Cambodia in a letter written just before I left Phnom Penh in late September 1966.

I wrote of the "changed atmosphere in the country. There is discontent, and there is a surprising amount of speculation about the possibilities of change in the direction of the country." But this speculation was not accompanied by any unanimity about any alternatives to Sihanouk . . . And I described him as being in charge, still, as "he remains in the saddle, perhaps with his feet no longer in the stirrup irons". I noted the discontent of the commercial community, the lack of jobs for those graduating from high schools and universities and reached the conclusion that the army appeared to be the only institution capable of taking over if, in some fashion, Sihanouk departed. In a concluding paragraph of my letter I wrote:

> If one wants one word to summarise, I would pick "fluid". *Au fond* all situations are fluid, but is the infinitely greater degree of fluidity which I find most striking. Elite discontent with the regime may continue for some time, but there is no doubt in my mind that it has reached stage 1 in a move toward change. (I am simplifying enormously in suggesting there are two stages to a change in a regime—the first when the desire for change becomes manifest, and the second when some action is taken to effect change.) I do not believe that this was the case five years ago.

Royal elephants parade in King Suramarit's funeral procession, Phnom Penh, August 1960.

Sharing a drink with Prince Sisowath Phadaravong (Rat-sody), my oldest Cambodian friend, and still thin from my bout of amoebic dysentery. He inscribed on the back of the original, '*A mon cher Osborne. En souvenir to votre agréable compagnie lors de l'Anniversaire de la Reine Elisabeth d' Angleterre. Phanda-ravong. Bein cordialement. Phnom Penh, le 4/7/61.*'

5

Vietnam at War 1966

After a break of nearly three and a half years, I returned to Saigon late in the afternoon of 30 June 1966 and stayed for a month. In contrast to my earlier visit, and as I had been doing in Cambodia, I kept a daily journal, making this entry the following day as I reacted to seeing the city again:

On this first full day in Saigon it was staggering the number of American troops on the streets. . . . They are everywhere—and not as in 1963 out of uniform. Jeeps and army trucks choke the roads. All the government buildings are protected at their entrances by sandbags, as are all the American army billets, where the MPs stand with loaded automatic rifles and shotguns. The Military Police jeeps that move about the town carry fully armed soldiers, both side arms and rifles. Everyone is on alert at the moment for it is expected that some major incident will follow the bombing of the oil depots near Hanoi by American aircraft. Whole areas of the city serve no other purpose but to cater for the troops—bars, tailors, junk curio shops. And at any time the sky seems to have at least one helicopter clacking its way overhead. . . .

The city is dirtier than I have ever seen it before, with garbage obviously uncollected for days in many areas and lying on the footpaths. And also on the footpaths are the black market stalls stocked with liquor (Chivas Regal no less), torch batteries, shaving cream, even underpants still in their Department of Defense wrappers, all the product of the massive theft which takes place on the wharves, or the blackmarket that has grown up about the commissaries.

This was the city a tourist brochure I had picked up on arrival at the airport the day before described as, "A happy combination of old Oriental civilisation and blooming modernism."

Life in the provinces was different, as I observed later when travelling to the Mekong Delta, Tay Ninh, Hue and the Central Highlands. Away from Saigon there were concentrations of American troops in every location I visited, but there was less of the immediately obvious squalor that was so much part of the capital, with the stench of rotting garbage pervasive even along Tu Do Street running past the Continental Palace Hotel in the centre of the city up to the Catholic cathedral. Yet life in the provinces could still be very grim, as I found visiting an Australian surgical team working in a hospital in the capital of Long Xuyen province later in the month. We had flown from Saigon's Tan Son Nhat airport to Can Tho, where there was much debate as to whether it was safe to drive to Long Xuyen. Finally we did, driving the sixty kilometres to the hospital at helter-skelter speed and passing the occasional lonely, little forts along the way with their watch towers that were an instant reminder of the passage in Graham Greene's *Quiet American*, where Fowler and Pyle sheltered for a time in such a tower on their way back from visiting Tay Ninh. Once in Long Xuyen we met the medical team:

. . . the team members are leading Melbourne doctors who

come on three month stints, aided by Australian theatre sisters and radiographers. They live a pretty isolated life, sitting down in deepest insurgent territory. The town is quite safe but the war is not far away. A trip through the wards brought human tragedy very close to a privileged observer—occupancy of a bed by two or three persons, the few war victims with wretchedly incapacitating injuries such as double amputations, children with problems which hardly occur in a highly medicated society such as bone disease which in a western country would have been arrested by antibiotics but now will cripple the child for life . . .

History and the present

With great kindness Michael Curtin from the Australian embassy offered me a place to stay as a paying guest while I was in Saigon, and the use of a bicycle; and after a week I had slipped into a routine. Pedalling in and out of the centre of the city each day, my time was dominated by two widely different interests. There were the hours spent on research linked to the nineteenth century in the archives and the National Library, and there were opportunities to join in conversations that focussed on little else but the war. Reading about the nineteenth century French colonials as I pursued my research reinforced for me how much of a legacy they had left behind. There was the physical legacy of the streetscape of central Saigon, with buildings such as the central post office, the former Hôtel de Ville, and the Catholic cathedral. At a different level of impact, there was the continuing widespread presence of men and women who spoke French, not just to foreigners but also among themselves. And as a reminder of France's former commercial role in Vietnam, as well as adding to the city's terrible pollution, there was the host of tiny blue and white Renault taxis that scuttled about the streets like busy beetles, their ancient engines spewing forth exhaust smoke. But only a romantic would see these legacies as dominant even if there were still sections of the city that had not entirely shed their character as remnants of the time when the French had been in control. The terrace of the Continental Palace Hotel, was still the place to sit and watch the passing parade, but there were few French men or women sipping their *apéritifs*. Now the drinkers were almost all Americans and the drink of choice was beer rather than wine or a *sirop*. The venerable La Pagode, long Saigon's best-known *maison de thé*, continued to function, with a few French old hands drinking their coffee as if independence had never come, and with the aged waiters treating everyone with the superb disdain that had always been their hallmark.

As for the conversations with a range of expatriates, they seemed endlessly repetitive, marked by a constant resort to abbreviations and acronyms and almost always concluding without firm conclusions. RD (Revolutionary Development) was or was not succeeding, while the VCI (Vietcong Infrastructure) was either growing or diminishing. The "big war", a much used term at this time, was "going well", but most of those to whom I talked agreed that the "little war" was not. This seemed to be the view of the anthropologist Gerald Hickey of the Rand Corporation, whom now I met for the first time. Having read his valuable book, *Village in Vietnam*, and knowing that he had been working in Vietnam since 1956, when he first went there as a University of Chicago graduate student, I had hoped to see more of him than I did on two brief occasions. I determined that if and when I was next in Saigon I would make an effort to spend more time listening to him. He clearly was well informed and sensible in his estimations of what was happening.

Conversations with Vietnamese about politics and the war—a surprisingly large number of them—seemed just as inconclusive, though inevitably my contacts were with a possibly misleading, educated sample. At a time when ill-informed foreign commentators were still peddling the fiction that the north and the south of Vietnam were fundamentally different ethnically, I was struck by the force of a comment from a photographer I met, a Mr Diem, who observed in a conversation, "Vietnamese blood is Vietnamese blood whether it is shed in the north or the south." Then there was the prosperous businessman told me of his fear of communism only to end our conversation by remarking that it was the communists rather than the southern leadership who understood the true character of his compatriots. A newspaper owner, Dang Van Sung, who had been a member of the old right-wing Dai Viet party that had long since lost any popular support, lapsed into fantasy as he told me his party would return to a position of strength in the future. In a frank assessment of contemporary politics another newspaper man, Nguyen Van Tuoi of the *Guardian*, spoke of how the members of the National Liberation Front, and even those who formed the Hanoi government, were "above all nationalists", only to conclude there was no end to the war in sight, unless the government in Hanoi altered its character. And, welcoming as he had been in 1963 but still as mournful, there was Duong Sanh at the library.

"Les trouristes" are to blame for port congestion

If Duong Sanh still clung quietly to something of his French-educated past, there were others who proudly proclaimed their link to that earlier time. I found this to be so when, rather improbably as it seemed at the time, I was invited by Charles Truong Vinh Tong to attend a dinner meeting of the West Saigon Lions Club on 21 July. Charles was a grandson of an important nineteenth-century Vietnamese scholar, Pétrus Truong Vinh Ky, who had worked closely with the colonial administration and whose career I eventually wrote about in some detail in my Cornell dissertation. In particular, Pétrus Ky, a Vietnamese Catholic who had studied for the priesthood in Penang but never been ordained, had played a vital part in the spread of *quoc-ngu*, the Romanised script to render the Vietnamese language. Now his grandson Charles worked for Shell and I had met him through an introduction given to me by one of his colleagues in Phnom Penh. In every way the dinner was an interesting occasion, as I recorded:

> . . . in the evening I went to the Majestic Hotel, by the waterfront, for the dinner. The club meets on the top floor of the hotel, and the members were gathered in the bar before going into dinner when I arrived at 8 o'clock. There were only about twenty of them—with one exception, a Frenchman, they were all Vietnamese. And they spoke French among themselves. This should have given me, and in a sense did, a clue to the evening. I was seeing a reunion of Vietnamese Francophiles, the last ditch stand of the Cochinchinese bourgeoisie, this time gathered under the aegis of the Lions Club. The view from the Majestic is always striking, even at night. But it had an eerie quality as the river was

bathed in the blue shaft of a searchlight which kept sweeping the river as a precaution against insurgent attempts on the mass of shipping gathered there.

When we went in to dinner the French quality persisted in the speeches that were made handing over the presidency of the club from one member to another, and in the French kissing on both cheeks that accompanied the ceremony. Next came the evening's speech. . . It was given in French by an extremely articulate, and even witty, young Vietnamese on the subject of port congestion. Before long it turned into a sharp criticism of the Americans, presented in the form of satire only lightly disguising bitterness. The Americans, this Vietnamese described always as *les touristes*, and he blamed them for the port congestion, as for the troubles of the country. If I had been an American at the dinner I would have been very tempted to leave. God knows the Americans are open to criticism on a whole range of counts, and there is no one better placed to criticise them, and with more justification, than the Vietnamese. But it is these businessmen/ Cochinchinese bourgeoisie who share a deep responsibility for the troubles that afflict their country. Their families—and it was the families of many of the men, and types like them who were at the dinner—who were those who limped through the years after 1946, compromising with the French at every turn, just as long as the payment was sufficient. And it is the types who sat happily drinking their claret, this Thursday night, who would be the first to fall and suffer if the "tourists" suddenly did go. And whether the "tourists" are right or wrong, a great many of them are being killed while the Saigon businessmen are concerned with the cluttering of the port. One's mind goes back to the words of General de Lattre de Tassigny when he came to Vietnam as Commander-in-Chief of the French forces in Vietnam in 1950, and when at that critical stage of the French-Viet Minh War he addressed young Vietnamese and urged those who carped at French policy to go and join the Viet Minh or to remain silent, for at least the Viet Minh were brave men fighting for an ideal . . .

The carping tone continued later when I went to have a final drink with Tong beside the river—beside the My Canh restaurant, too, which was a bit disturbing as it had been bombed by a Viet Cong sapper squad the year before with resulting heavy casualties. Tong was silent but his acquaintance kept on in the same tone while illumination flares floated down just outside the city and the sound of small arms fire was distinctly audible from some engagement on the outskirts.

Hue was another world

After ten days in Saigon I set off to make a long hoped-for visit to Hue, the old capital of Vietnam under the Nguyen dynasty. I had wanted to see this city—the architecture of its imperial citadel its a scaled-down version of Beijing's Forbidden City—for years. And I had an added reason to make the visit since I had been told that some of Father Léopold Cadière's papers were held in a Benedictine monastery outside Hue (Cadière had been active in Vietnam around the end of the nineteenth century and had written widely on the country's traditional administration and culture). It was a visit that turned out quite differently to what I expected, leaving me with yet another reason to have the warmest of feelings about the Australian army.

Nowadays Hue caters generously to tourists, but in 1966 there were none and finding a hotel proved to be a difficult enterprise. I finally did find accommodation in an institution that labelled itself a hotel, *khach san*, but which clearly made its money through a more short-term clientele. Neither soap nor towels were provided and I immediately took note of the fact that the walls of the rooms ended before reaching the ceiling. I feared it was going to be a noisy night. Still, I was in Hue with its striking setting on the Perfume River with the hills rising close behind the massive walls of the "Forbidden City", and the next step was to find a way to reach the monastery.

The problem was solved by my finding two Vietnamese Jesuits who were about to travel to the monastery and who were happy to take me with them. Reaching there I found a peaceful scene with the buildings of the monastery sitting close to the hills and surrounded by pine trees. Surrounded, too, it became apparent when I talked to one of the fathers, by Viet Cong forces. "Oh yes," he said, "'they all know what goes on here, but they do not trouble us." Apart from this slightly unsettling fact I gained nothing from the visit. I was able to look at Cadière's papers, but quickly realised that they were manuscript versions of published articles I had already consulted in Paris.

I had much better luck later in the day. As I walked along a road near the river a jeep suddenly pulled to a stop and I was greeted in a familiar and comfortingly Australian fashion by "Mac" McArtney, who had noticed I was carrying a red Qantas travel bag that Michael Curtin had lent me. Through "Mac" I met his colleagues, "Lofty" Moran and "Chicka" Ison, all three Australian army warrant officers and members of the Australian Army Training Team Vietnam (AATV) based in Hue. Formed in 1962 and initially commanded by Colonel Ted Serong, the Team worked and fought throughout Vietnam in close association with both the South Vietnamese Army and regional and irregular forces, quite separately from the Australian Task Force in Phuoc Thuy province. No fewer than four members of the Team were awarded Victoria Crosses.

Not only did "Mac" and his colleagues instantly offer to provide me with an alternative to my "hotel" accommodation in the MACV (Military Assistance Command Vietnam) camp, they kindly and happily acted as tour guides to Hue, taking me to both the old Imperial City, the Tien Mu Pagoda and some of the emperors' tombs. In Saigon it was possible to forget just how strong the Chinese model was for the rulers of Vietnam in the nineteenth century, and before, but not in Hue. The throne room within the Forbidden City, the *Dai Noi* in Vietnamese, or "Great Within", was a testament to how much had been borrowed from China—a colour scheme of red and gold, red pillars with golden dragons encircling them, and an array of beautiful ceramics, including one great shallow vase of rich, royal purple with Chinese characters decorating it in gold.

The members of the Team offered a highly critical assessment of the efforts of the American marines based in Hue, not of their courage but of their tactics—this coming from men who had served in both Korea and the Malayan Emergency. As for the Vietnamese whom they trained, this was what I recorded "Mac" as saying:

Quite apart from the recent political difficulties in Hue—a reference to Buddhist protests against the Saigon government—virtually no progress has been made against the insurgents in the past twelve months. The enemy still holds the same amount of ground. As "Mac" noted very accurately, it is impossible to see any progress coming in a situation where the Vietnamese opposing the insurgents are so divided among themselves. He has high praise for many of the Vietnamese he trains—popular forces not regulars—but he noted they are asked to do tasks for which their training hardly prepares them. He noted with some disgust the treatment given prisoners by the Vietnamese. And in a very practical fashion asked, "How do they think they are going to get them to talk when the moment they are captured they beat the fuck out of them?"

The best I could do for these generous hosts was to pay for a Chinese meal, an inadequate expression of thanks for an unexpected and very welcome reconnection with Australian realities.

* * *

Not long after returning from Hue I made a visit to Tay Ninh on 15 July. This was a further reminder of the problems confronting the Americans in Vietnam, for it was accepted that Tay Ninh was one of the most solidly insurgent provinces in the country. Just to the west of the town is an area that had been under the control of insurgent forces for more than twenty years. I was making this visit with friends from the embassy and they were there to see what was happening with the American RD program. Our guide was Jim Morris and his problems, which he readily acknowledged, were immediately apparent when we came upon his Vietnamese RD team.

The revolutionary development team in the hamlet did not know we were coming. And so we found them sitting under a tree in the shade. This was the first in a series of instances showing the almost impossible task the Americans have set themselves. They [the Americans] want to control the scheme, but they have to work through the corrupt and inefficient province and district officials. The leader of the team we encountered was asked if there had been any probing by the insurgents into the hamlet where they we working, "No" was the answer. And are you living in the hamlet, "Oh Yes". But then we found that they had in fact moved away from the hamlet to the village office, because the insurgents had probed into the hamlet. A defensive mud wall which the team was supposed to be organising had not, despite assurances that it would be, been begun. And to cap it all seven men had gone on leave without permission. This last discovery was made in a tortuous series of interpreted exchanges which, because the sentences were short and the vocabulary simple, I could mostly understand. And it was abundantly clear that the interpreter was not particularly competent and accurate.

In a revealing contrast with the problems of Morris's RD team, a visit to a Catholic refugee hamlet in the afternoon showed what is achieved when action is joined to motivation. This was a hamlet composed of Vietnamese who had fled to the south after the partial communist victory in 1954, and led by their priest they were ready to defend themselves with an armoury that included rifles, a couple of heavy machine guns and mortars. As so often happens in Vietnam, there were evocations of Graham Greene. In this case of Fowler's visit to the Phat Diem—not, of course, with the results of the massacre that Fowler sees, but rather for the sense of Catholic outpost in an insurgent-dominated world.

* * *

My month in Saigon ended in a general sense of pessimism and without my realising, as I made my farewells, just how many times I would be returning to this sad country. Writing then, I recorded the following in my journal:

> Duong Sanh at the National Library was as depressed as ever. He has a brother in France and undoubtedly the contrast between the untroubled life that his brother lives and the difficulties of Saigon are just too real to be ignored.

> And Pétrus Ky's grandson is leaving for France, another Vietnamese with French nationality who is getting out. When I went to say goodbye to him he was making his final plans to leave by ship in September. So often in Saigon one feels one is witnessing human dramas—always tragedies never comedies— which are being repeated over and over again among the city's population. There are clearly other Vietnamese, just like Truong Vinh Tong, who are getting out while they can, but without any clear knowledge of what they are going to do once they get to France. There must be so many men like the little librarian who can see no path ahead but despair.

1967

A year and a half later I was briefly back in Saigon. By now, in December 1967, American troop numbers in Vietnam had reached almost 500,000 and the daily sound of bombing and artillery had become a constant of life in the city, shaking the walls of buildings. Through unofficial help from the Australian embassy I was able to fly from Saigon to spend a day in Tay Ninh, escorted around the city and through villages deemed to be "safe" by a young American army lieutenant. I quite failed to recognise the significance of an informal intelligence briefing he gave me. After a day spent speeding by jeep between villages, and shortly before I was due to fly back to Saigon, he showed me his unit's "war map". He drew attention to what he described as an unusually large number of communist forces located just a short distance northeast of Tay Ninh. "I think they are there for a reason," he said. "But my superiors don't agree." The communist troops were, as it later became clear, part of the build up of their forces for what became the Tet Offensive, an event that resulted in huge communist losses but had a devastatingly negative effect on American opinion about the war and President Lyndon Johnson's decision not to contest the 1968 United States presidential election.

6

Vietnam, 1969-1970

In 1968 I returned for a brief visit to Cambodia after attending a conference in Kuala Lumpur, but did not go to Saigon. But I more than made up for this "lapse" in late 1969 and early 1970, when I spent a month and a half based in the city. I was there in privileged circumstances through the assistance of a fascinating figure, now sadly long dead, Phung Nhat Minh. I had met Minh in Melbourne, when he visited the city as a member of the South Vietnamese foreign service. During the Franco-Viet Minh War he had fought on the side of the Viet Minh as a non-communist nationalist, but his experiences at that time, particularly the readiness on the part of the Viet Minh to resort to terrorist tactics, led him to conclude that his loyalties could not be with Ho Chi Minh and the government in Hanoi once the war ended. Very much an intellectual as well as having been a man of action, he cultivated an air of weary cynicism which belied his deeply held humane feelings.

To talk to Minh was to have an opportunity to absorb a deeper understanding of Vietnamese politics than was usually present in contemporary discussion in the late 1960s. For this was a period when most discussion of the war in Vietnam, in Australia and the United States, let alone as I had found in France, took place without any acknowledgement that there might be shades of grey in the ever-changing picture of contemporary developments. When in the latter part of 1969 I expressed an interest in the possibility of living with a Vietnamese family in Saigon to Minh, he quickly arranged this, and from 11 December 1969 to 26 January 1970 I was generously welcomed into the home of Senator Le Tan Buu. His home was, in fact, just inside the boundaries of Cholon, Saigon's twin city with its majority Chinese population, rather than in the capital itself. Le Tan Buu was a former engineer officer in South Vietnamese army who between 1963 and 1966 had held a senior position in the South Vietnamese National Police. (Only recently have I learnt that he remained in Saigon to the end of the war when he was taken into custody by the victorious communists in 1975 and held in "e-education" for twelve years. He was finally able to emigrate to the United States, where he died in Virginia, aged 90, in 2012.).

Charting Vietnam's revolutionary past

I had been uncertain just what such an arrangement would involve when Minh made them for me. As it turned out staying with Buu and his family gave me a very comfortable base from which to carry out research in the National Library and archives. My research concerns were chiefly with the activities of those Vietnamese who, in contrast to the revolutionaries, were ready to work with the French in the 1920s, and to a lesser extent in the 1930s. They were ultimately history's losers and a neglected, and frequently vilified, subject of discussion because of their lack of nationalist zeal. But they were an interesting group of individuals nevertheless, for the extent to which, during a brief period, they seemed to justify French claims there could be a truly shared interest between the colonial government and its Vietnamese subjects. That this expectation was never transformed into political or social reality reflected the fact that ultimately France was not ready to concede any real power to the Vietnamese, even those who most earnestly wanted to work with it.

I was also concerned to read contemporary documents and newspapers dealing with the major revolts against French rule that took place in 1930 and 1931—the other side of the coin for the period. These revolts which took place in the north-central provinces of Nghe An and Ha Tinh, and also in the Mekong delta, reflected both severe social disadvantage—the presence of famine in Nghe An and Ha Tinh—and deep resentment of colonial rule. Celebrated by communist writers, the revolts may not have been started by communist agitators but there is no doubt that the fledgling Vietnamese communist movement sought to take advantage of them. Not even the pro-administration character of the Saigon newspapers of the time disguised the horror of the period as they reported on starving peasants confronting the force of French-led troops even as, like skeletal figures, they fought each other for a handful of food. Later, working in the French archives in Paris in 1973, I found reference to an order that instructed the troops of the French Foreign Legion, which had been sent in to suppress the revolts, to execute nine out of ten prisoners taken in the course of their operations (Archives Nationales de France, Section Outre-Mer, Nouveaux Fonds 2634). I have never found conclusive evidence that would make clear the extent to which this order was followed, though the existence of indiscriminate killing by French troops was reported by French left-wing writers at the time—most notably by Andrée Viollis in her 1935 book, *Indochine S.O.S.*

But I certainly found considerable confirmation, both from documents in the archives and in the newspapers of the period that the loss of Vietnamese life as the result of French military action was very high, certainly well in excess of two thousand persons.

Sitting in the National Library or in the building housing the archives in Saigon as I did my research bordered on the surreal. I was there alone, turning over the musty pages of newspapers and documents while the almost constant sound of helicopters flying overhead intruded and, every now and then, there would be the sound of distant artillery. These hours spent reading material from the 1920s and 1930s gave me a picture of colonial life in Vietnam that was quite different from the standard view so often presented in French writing, both in public official documents and in the writings of a range of commentators. Once popular French travel writers such as Roland Dorgelès, Pierre Billotey and Guy de Pourtalès could wax lyrical about France's Indochinese possessions to their readers: a "world so beautiful and so strongly seductive", in Billotey's words. But the reality was very different. For all the conviction the French undoubtedly had of the worth of their role as colonisers, particularly as purveyors of a *mission civilisatrice*, much of what I read about the period left the distinct impression that many of the French men and women living in Vietnam were at least subliminally fearful of the future.

French officials were not in the 1930s contemplating the ultimate achievement of Vietnamese independence by the limited number of revolutionaries who were calling for this goal. But there was an underlying sense of fear that was part and parcel of colonial life, a fear that persisted despite France's overwhelming control of the forces of order. It was reflected in the detailed accounts given by newspapers of executions of both criminals and those Vietnamese who made a direct challenge to the state. This was the case with the punishment of the militia men who mutinied in the northern military post of Yen Bai in 1930, when fifty men were guillotined, one after another, while their condemned comrades were forced to look on. And it was apparent in the harsh prison conditions to which those suspected of communist revolutionaries tendencies were confined, notably on the prison island of Poulo Condore (modern Con Son), with its notorious "tiger cages". For those who presided over this repression, and above all for senior figures in the colonial *Sûreté général*, such as Louis Marty, the acting director of its political section, France was confronting not just the challenge of revolutionary communism but also the inherently savage nature of the "yellow race".

Travelling with General Tran Van Don

While staying with Le Tan Buu and his family meant I could pursue these historical issues, it also quite unexpectedly opened a door to frequent travel throughout South Vietnam as an unofficial, and as far as I could tell never fully explained, supernumerary in a group of senators and their aides led by General Tran Van Don. He had been one of the key plotters, in concert with Generals Duong Van Minh and Ton That Dinh, in the overthrow of President Diem six years before and by 1969, when I met him, Don was the leader of a political faction within the South Vietnamese parliament. Don's travel throughout South Vietnam was both a duty for him as the head of the senate's armed services committee to assess the state of security and an opportunity for him to try and rally support for his political grouping. It was travel marked by contrasts, and for reasons of security it was almost entirely in military helicopter and fixed wing aircraft. Repeated journeys in "Huey" helicopters means I have a sharp memory of that moment just after takeoff when the helicopter's nose dips disconcertingly towards the ground before the aircraft reassuringly and rapidly rises vertically. And journeys in an assortment of fixed aircraft made me aware of the distinctive character of Pilatus Porters, Caribous, C-130s and an assortment of others that I was not able to identify. Apart from landings at Saigon's Ton San Nhat airport, many of our descents were made in tight spirals as the aircraft, whether a helicopter or a fixed wing machine, manoeuvred to avoid possible ground fire. So far as I am aware it never came.

We were served meals on our travels that sometimes deserved to be described as banquets and at other times were simple offerings from army messes. Accommodation was usually basic in barrack rooms, often sleeping dormitory style. In a notable departure from the austerity of miliary camp accommodation, when the travelling party reached Da Lat, on 3 January 1970, we were lodged in the Dalat Palace Hotel, a leftover from the days when Da Lat was a hill station retreat from Saigon—renovated it continues to function today as part of the Sofitel chain. That particular visit concluded with General Dinh, who had accompanied Don on this occasion, insisting the day should end in a seedy Da Lat cabaret and with the consumption of multiple bottles of champagne. To add to the unreality of the scene, the cabaret's manager, dressed in a dinner suit that had seen better days, crooned French *chansons* and between times spoke of his hope to return to Paris where he had once lived. I could be pardoned for thinking this was a "twilight of the gods" occasion, or the other, more obvious comparison, Nero and his lyre in ancient Rome. But just as had been the case on when I had previously travelled with these South Vietnamese politicians, the following morning their first task at 6 o'clock was to make the effort to tune into the BBC World Service news on the powerful transistors they all carried. It was the one news source they trusted.

Security in the countryside

South Vietnam at the end of 1969 was a very different place from the year before, and even more notably than 1967. Despite the shock of the 1968 Tet Offensive, main force battles were now few and far between and almost entirely confined to the far northern provinces and, with tentative peace talks secretly taking place between Washington and Hanoi in Paris, the number of American soldiers in South Vietnam was steadily reducing. In this general atmosphere almost all major urban centres were fairly firmly in the hands of the Saigon government, or at least gave the impression of being so, whatever clandestine presence communist representatives might have had in them.

The extent to which security prevailed outside these urban settlements was a very different matter, for there was little conviction, even on the part of observers sympathetic to the Saigon government, that the regime's writ was really established in the countryside. As a result, the preoccupation for the South Vietnamese government and its allies, most particularly the United States, was with ways to gauge the extent to which it exercised control over the thousands of settlements in the countryside. In an effort to do so, a "Hamlet Evaluation System" (HES) had been devised and reporting of where a hamlet stood in this system —"A" good, "C" marginal but on balance under government control, "D" unsatisfactory and contested—was supposed to provide an answer to the state of security. To say the least, the highly subjective aspect of deciding just what degree of control the government exercised over a particular hamlet made the system of dubious value. And, over and over, the briefings I observed travelling with Tran Van Don's group involved claims that the majority of hamlets in a particular region were at least deserving of being classified as '"C" in character.

From the Delta to Tuy Hoa

During the six weeks I spent in South Vietnam on this visit, and as I have already noted with travel by road strictly limited because of security concerns, I made no fewer than 16 helicopter flights and 17 flights in fixed wing aircraft to twenty-three different locations away from Saigon. So I saw a great deal of Vietnam from the air as we travelled to towns that once were familiar names to anyone following the progress of the war and now are becoming better known as tourist destinations— Can Tho, Chau Doc, Da Lat, Nha Trang, Phu Quoc--and others that remain less well-known, Ca Mau, Tri Ton and Tuy Hoa. The Mekong delta, seen from the air, is a vast, flat expanse of bountiful agricultural land intersected by the broad arms of the river flowing to the sea. Just a important to its fruitfulness are the countless canals that have been dug over the centuries to drain the swamps and provide easy routes for travel in what would otherwise be a watery land. The flatness of the land makes the sudden presence of the Seven Mountains on the delta's western edge seem both dramatic and mysterious as they rise sharply like giant, misshapen beehives from the paddy fields, their sides a mixture of dense green foliage and bare rocks and screes. Given their stark contrasting presence with the surrounding dead flat landscape it's not surprising that both Vietnamese and Cambodians have regarded these mountains as both holy and sinister, and they have been a magnet for hermits and bandits alike for centuries. Flying above much of the highlands was to realise how challenging a topography Vietnam posed to any military force seeking to operate in these vast jungle forests. Yet other highland areas were quite different, as was the case with the area around Da Lat where the gently rolling hills were covered with native grasses.

Flying in to Tuy Hoa on 2 January 1970 left a notably vivid memory. We had started the day flying from Saigon to Kon Tum in South Vietnam's central highlands. Next we flew to Qui Nhon, which nowadays is gaining a reputation as a largely unspoiled coastal destination that has escaped the worst "modernising" excesses that have overtaken Hoi An and Nha Trang. At the time my journal records that Qui Nhon was "a grubby little town in an attractive setting located on a curved bay beneath the foothills of the mountains that, in Binh Dinh province come almost down to the sea". But for scenic impact, the best was yet to come.

The sun was close to setting as we flew out of Qui Nhon for Tuy Hoa, travelling the seventy or so kilometres south along the coast to the last stop for the day. There is virtually no agricultural littoral along this part of the coast so that the mountains rise sharply behind wide, sandy beaches. As the light faded over the craggy headlands but continued to

119

illuminate the small, rocky islands lying just offshore, the impression was of a Chinese painting, or should that be a Vietnamese one, with dark shadows on rock faces contrasting with remaining areas of light that gave a sense of glistening silk to the swirling, slate-coloured sea.

It was dark by the time the aircraft finally came to a halt and we went, first, to a briefing on security that was cast in the same broadly optimistic terms as those heard earlier in the day, except that afterwards the Deputy American Provincial Adviser, a colonel, told me that it was the "usual load of bullshit". Then, after dinner, I accompanied Tran Van Don to call on the chief *bonze* (the French term used by Don for a Buddhist monk) of the region:

> . . . It really was a rather mysterious scene at the monastery with the light of flickering candles and just a few people sitting while Don talked with the frail old man wrapped in his dark maroon coloured robes, and with the chief monk's assistant, an almost gross figure reminiscent of the fat, laughing Buddhas one finds carved from ivory. The conversation was inconclusive. Don repeated his policy. Strikingly, when Don spoke of "freedom", *tu do*, the monk immediately broke in to pose in opposition, *hoa binh*, "peace".

Tran Van Don and Ton That Dinh

What sort of a man was Tran Van Don, this elegantly handsome individual who during his active service had been a three star general and President Ngo Dinh Diem's Chief of Staff? And what might be said of these other former generals with whom I travelled? These were questions I repeatedly asked myself as I sat beside Don time after time and talked to him at length. I think the fact that as a result of earlier research I was able to tell him that I knew something his father's career as a doctor and, briefly in the 1920s as a politician in colonial Saigon, played a part in his readiness to talk to me. The American journalist, Stanley Karnow, describes him as "more French than Vietnamese", noting he was born in Bordeaux, educated in France, and served in the French army. The accusation that his true allegiance was to France was one Don was at pains to deny in conversations with me.

He was equally adamant in denying that he and Ton That Dinh had intended to assassinate Ngo Dinh Diem when they participated in the coup that overthrew the South Vietnamese president in 1963, a coup that ultimately had the support of the United States. In the aftermath of the coup Diem and his brother Nhu were killed while expecting to be given safe passage out of the country. While responsibility for the deaths has been endlessly debated, it seems most likely that it finally rested with Duong Van Minh, and the personal grievances of two of his subordinates. To the extent there is any consensus on this issue, Don's claim that he and Dinh did not seek Diem's and Nhu's death seems correct. They had wanted him out of office and a new approach to the developing war, but just what that "new approach" was to be, or could have been, was never really clear as the result of my conversations with Don or any of his colleagues. Certainly it did not seem to have developed into a coherent, workable plan when I was able to talk to Don in 1969 and 1970.

Don and his associates often spoke of the need for a "social revolution" that would respond to the interests of the seventy per cent of the population he argued was not committed either to the communists, who had the support of twenty per cent, or the existing government, which held the support of only ten per cent. Whether these figures were soundly based was difficult, indeed impossible to know. What did seem clear was the lack of reality in Don's belief that it would be possible to convince the government in Hanoi that it should accept the existence of a separate southern state. And the dubious nature of this view was underlined by his observation to me that if President Nixon's commitment to "Vietnamisation" continued the result would be "very grave". In short, he doubted the capability of the southern forces to withstand the north.

So was he just a dilettante, someone playing at politics with no expectation that he would ever have to put his ideas into practice despite his undoubtedly commanding presence? I really don't know, but it is worth noting that he stayed almost to the end of South Vietnam's independent existence, leaving without money and initially finding employment as a waiter in the United States. All this said, I have to record a considerable debt to Tran Van Don. He was always affable, generally ready to talk without restraint. He gave me an opportunity to see Vietnam in a time of war in a way that would not otherwise have been possible. Yet, at the end of this visit it was the assessments made by one of Don's fellow senators, former general Nguyen Van Chuan, which seemed the more likely guide to the future. Chuan had been a soldier in both the French army and later fought for a period with the Viet Minh. Talking to me during my travels with Don he said without qualification, "We are losing the war," and on another occasion, "If the government really controlled the numbers which it claims to do, the war would have been over some time ago."

In contrast to Don, his co-conspirator in 1963, Ton That Dinh, seemed too easy to analyse, and frequently not to his advantage. In my journal I ventured the assessment that he was, in Australian terms, something of a larrikin, but that way of describing him does not cover enough of his qualities, both good and bad. With distant connections to the Vietnamese royal family, he could be sensitive to perceived slights, which also meant that he was susceptible to flattery. He gave the impression of living for the moment and he always wore a pearl-handled revolver at his waist as well as another pistol in a shoulder holster. It was as if he was mimicking General George Patton, at least in the way he armed himself. He never seemed to be short of large amounts of money, which he spent with abandon. The general consensus of observers is that he was only persuaded to join in the overthrow of Diem because he saw some personal advantage in doing so, not because of the political implications. Yet if this pen portrait is critical in tone I have to record that he was an amiable travelling companion who often made astute and appropriately sceptical comments on the unconvincing nature of the briefings we received as part of Tran Van Don's entourage. Often he did even pretend to listen to the briefing, instead ostentatiously reading a newspaper as the presentation was made.

Australia in Vietnam

There was an Australian dimension to this visit, and given the fact that I was lecturing on Vietnam at Monash University it could not be otherwise. Members of the Australian embassy, from the ambassador down, were generous in the time they gave me. The personnel of the Army Task Force, based in Phuoc Thuy province were equally generous. And the unofficial assistance I again received from the Australian Army Training Team provided me with one of the most interesting experiences of all the visits I made to South Vietnam.

It did not take long for me to find that there was a considerable difference of opinion about the state of the war between the embassy and the military. With variations, the military view was that the communist forces were not in a position to "win" the war so long as the force levels opposing them remained as they were at the beginning of 1970. But the South Vietnamese and those forces allied to them, primarily the Americans but including the Australians, were not winning either. When I visited the Task Force at Nui Dat, in Phuc Thuy province, on 15 December, here is how the commander, Brigadier Stuart Weir, put the situation to me in a briefing that he said was not the usual "smarmy bullshit" and which he partly conducted as we travelled in his command helicopter to an outlying fire support base:

> . . . He had the gravest doubts about "Vietnamisation". In his view the province of Phuoc Thuy would return to a 'shambles' should the Australian troops be withdrawn over the next twelve months. He has little respect for the existing political apparatus in the province and even less, it would seem, for most of the RF (Regional Forces). As things stand at the moment, the Australian forces can keep the Viet Cong and the North Vietnamese forces off balance, but the moment an Australian operation ends he is

fully aware that the other side moves its troops back into the same areas again.

Weir's view was reinforced by the thoughtful comments of his deputy, Colonel Ken MacKenzie, who had clearly taken a lot of trouble to study the historical background to the war and the presence of communist forces in Phuoc Thuy before 1954. As he said:

. . . He is disgusted by the venality of the Viet officials and scathing in his criticism of the regional forces who are supposed to have primary responsibility for guarding villages. He notes that the major insurgent force in the province, Regiment 274, has been operating for 20 years and although it may have more difficulties now it continues to operate. Meanwhile smaller guerrilla groups are able to operate among the population. Examples he cited included: the resettlement village of Suoi Nghe has had three village chiefs assassinated and the present one does not dare live in the village (hamlet); Hoa Long, just outside the ATF's perimeter is still strongly pro-Viet Cong in sentiment and nothing can prevent it acting as a resupply centre for the insurgents; in Dat Do there is a Gilbertian situation in which bunkers which were built to defend the village are being blown up by guerrillas coming from the village.

. . . Among the great myths he sees perpetrated is that which suggests that the harmless villager is only coerced into cooperation by the vicious VC (Viet Cong). This makes no sense in a province where most of the villages have relatives in the VC and where there are few reasons to support the government. He and all the other officers with whom I spoke had considerable admiration for the dedication of their opponents.

I spent much of the next morning with the officer overseeing the Task Force's civil aid action, Lieutenant Colonel Peter Gration, the later Chief of the Australian Defence Force. Less outspoken than Colonel MacKenzie, he clearly held similar views and later, at lunch in the mess, he deplored the lack of awareness among both Australian politicians and other army officers who had not served there about the difficulties the Task Force faced in Vietnam.

* * *

A little over a week later, on 23 December, I spent an hour with the Australian ambassador, Ralph Harry, who gave me his strikingly upbeat views on the war. Armed with a set of viewgraphs that contrasted the situation a year ago with how he saw matters at the end of the year, he presented himself as an optimist on Vietnam, though not really ready to commit himself on whether the improvements he catalogued were permanent. For Harry, positive progress was apparent through the activities of the People's Self Defence forces, the growth in the number of Popular Forces platoons, the greater acreage of rice under cultivation and increased numbers of children attending school. As I recorded at the time, "he seems to feel that the North Vietnamese have been so badly mauled that this is their reason for limited activity at the moment . . ."

Then two weeks later I received another extended briefing, this time from Lieutenant Colonel Russell Lloyd, the commander of the Australian Army Training Team in Vietnam. Because of his position and the fact that he visited members of the Team throughout South Vietnam, his view of developments was particularly well informed. What he had to say contrasted sharply with the ambassador's assessment. As I noted when I wrote up my journal, on this occasion in the evening:

> He is convinced that the allied military situation is a great deal less satisfactory than is claimed. There has, he is sure, been some improvement. But first it should be remembered that the improvement has to be placed against the pitiful state in which things were two or three years ago. Secondly, and he made this point over and over again, one cannot place too much emphasis on the extent to which the present apparent improvement reflects the enemy's decision not to stir the pot too much. He regards this as capital. He is sure the Front (National Liberation Front) and NVA (North Vietnamese Army) forces have a greater capability than the Americans and the South Vietnamese allow them to have and that they are working with a great deal more political success than is generally admitted. He is scornful of the significance of pacification figures [based on Hamlet Evaluation statistics] as they are regurgitated from the computers each week.

One by one Lloyd went through the points that Ambassador Harry had posed as reflecting progress to question or demolish them and particularly discounting Regional and Popular Forces and the Revolutionary Development Teams. He was very critical of "Operation Phoenix", the CIA-backed program to seek out and kill or capture members of the Viet Cong "infrastructure". He believed it was a "bloody disaster" and that contrary to claims made for its success that the program has only eliminated very low-level cadres.

Not least, Lloyd was critical of the performance of the American military:

> He states that morale among the [American] troops is very bad and that there has been a dramatic decline in military efficiency since he was here in '67 and '68. The Marines in I Corps (the northern part of South Vietnam) are badly affected by drug taking and the discipline of the 9th Division, which recently left the delta, was deplorable—it is currently being investigated for alleged indiscriminate firing on civilians.

After two hours of Lloyd's pessimistic assessment he gave me one immediately encouraging piece of news. Having heard that I was planning to go to Hue he said he would be in touch with members of the Team there so that they could look after me. This was an entirely unofficial offer of help, and very welcome because of it. Just as had been the case in 1966, the Training Team were ready to help without going through the rigmarole of seeking and obtaining official approval for their actions.

Overnighting at Nam Hoa

And help they did when, after yet another trip with Tran Van Don— this time to the Phu Quoc, where the chief intent of the visit seemed to be to sample *nuoc mam*, the Vietnamese fish sauce, for which the island is famous—I flew to Hue on 12 January not having had not been to the city since 1966. So I had not seen the effects of the savage battles that took place in Hue during the 1968 Tet Offensive. Travelling in from the airport it was clear many of the houses that had been damaged were now repaired but there were at least as many gaunt skeletons of buildings, the roofs blown off and with great jagged shell holes in the walls. When I later saw the old Imperial City it too showed clear signs of damage; not as much as I feared would be the case, but substantial nonetheless. One immediately apparent aspect in the Imperial City was the disappearance of the multitude of blue and white ceramic planter pots that I had found so charming in 1966, and more importantly the absence from the throne room of a wonderful collection of fine ceramics, the famous "Bleu de Hue" manufactured in China for the Vietnamese emperors in the nineteenth century. No one seemed to be able to say what had happened to these items.

Members of the Australian Training Team were waiting for me when I reached the US MACV (Military Assistance Command Vietnam) compound, where they were housed, as was an engineer major, Gordon Brown, who was currently seconded to act as District Senior Adviser for a region west of Hue. He invited me to spend the afternoon and the night at his post in Nam Hoa district, about twelve miles by road outside Hue. This was the start of an interesting twenty-four hours:

> We drove out to Nam Hoa along a road that skirts near various royal sites . . . The road is secure in daytime, but Brown observed that he would not make the trip at night without some urgent necessity. It is an indication of how limited the coastal littoral is that we were, when we had reached Nam Hoa, very close to the hills that roll back from Hue. And there was the district post.

> One immediately thought of Beau Geste. The fortifications of the post were originally constructed by the French so that there is the inevitable small watchtower. This, a couple of concrete

bunkers, and a few untidy huts compose the post. Around these buildings spreads a mass of mud. After years of neglect Brown is endeavouring to develop some proper trenches and this has involved shifting earth with bulldozers. Then around the muddy earth is the barbed wire. Outside the wire is supposed to be a minefield, but the mines were laid so long ago that it seems doubtful if the minefield provides much protection any more.

Enemy activity is building up around Nam Hoa and an attack is expected in the next couple of weeks. Because of this, and shortly after I arrived, Brown and the grizzled and very tough Australian warrant officer, Tom McNee, who also serves at Nam Hoa, carefully took me around the "bug out routes". These are the planned escape routes to be used should the camp be overrun. Being shown the escape routes was a slightly unnerving affair, but not half as unnerving as the observation that we were examining them without Vietnamese present since it was assumed that an unknown number of the Vietnamese Regional Forces troops in the compound were, in fact, members of the enemy.

Another indication of the situation in the area around Nam Hoa was the fact that we slept with our clothes on, our boots ready to slip on beside the bed, and a fully loaded carbine plus a belt of ammunition clips within arms' reach. (I had been given a quick introduction to the use of a carbine and paid careful attention on the basis that the other side was unlikely to recognise my non-combatant status if they should break into the post!)

The post is suffused by an atmosphere of gallows humour. Exposed as it is and with the two Australians and five Americans, who man the radios and act as medical orderlies and messengers, uncertain of the quality and loyalty of the Vietnamese this tendency to grim humour is not surprising. McNee, a man of infinite profanity, was a master of the genre. He is also a walking compendium of the horror of the war. He has served in the Delta, in Phuoc Thuy and Nam Hoa before his present reposting there. He can speak of Catholic leaders that the Viet Cong "belly gutted" in Binh Gia before letting loose starved pigs to eat their entrails while their families were forced to look on; of the priest from Binh Gia that the Viet Cong crucified; of the fourteen year-old girl that the Vietnamese at Nam Hoa suspected of being a spy who was thrown over the perimeter fence on to the minefield to be blown to pieces; and of the routine torture which has been used by both sides to gain information from prisoners.

As Brown and I talked until late in the night, sipping on mugs of sweet Vietnamese rum, I was not surprised to hear of his doubts about the war. If the security situation had indeed improved in the district he did not think this reflected commitment to the government. As for the events of the Tet Offensive, when communist troops massacred hundreds, and probably thousands of people, he dismissed the suggestion that the large number of people killed while the communists held the Hue citadel were victims of government and Marine Corps artillery. Instead he had come to the conclusion that, in addition to having list of those to be assassinated, the communists also killed many of Hue's inhabitants because of their reluctance to align themselves with the communist cause. There was a large plastic bag under my bunk containing the bones of victims who had been killed during the Tet Offensive and buried in a mass grave not far from the Nam Hoa outpost that had only been discovered recently.

I slept remarkably soundly despite the sound of intermittent Harassment and Interdiction artillery fire, to wake to the sound of a helicopter gunship spraying bullets around the area outside the post's perimeter as a precaution against infiltrators having crept up to the outpost under cover of darkness. Then, and after a breakfast of sausages and bacon that was testimony to the supply capabilities of the American army, I took advantage of Nam Hoa's location west of Hue to visit the Emperor Minh Mang's nearby tomb. After some hesitation Gordon Brown agreed to my visiting the tomb, on two conditions. The first was that I should be accompanied by one of his Nung bodyguards. The second was that I should go equipped with an American issue Colt 45 pistol. I had never worn a weapon at any time while visiting Vietnam but I was determined to see the tomb and duly belted the weapon in its holster around my waist, to my later embarrassment.

Ming Mang had reigned from 1820 to 1841 and his tomb is an architectural testimony to his deeply Confucian cast of mind. I had not seen it when I visited Hue 1966. Now, in 1970, I was able to observe it in its fundamentals; sadly in disrepair but with the emperor's final burial site reached through a series of pavilions. Looking like something painted on a willow pattern plate, each one blocked the view of the next and led to a more impressive successor. Apart from my Nung mercenary escort the only other people present were three old people, one man and two women who still played some role in preserving the complex from falling into irretrievable ruin.

Returning to the post at Nam Hoa I made my embarrassing mistake.

. . . Before returning it [the pistol] to Gordon Brown I did, as one should, carry out the routine clearing operation, this at least was something I remembered from my time as a member of Sydney University's rifle team, detaching the magazine and firing the action. It was not, of course, a weapon I was used to and I had not realised that there was still a bullet in the chamber. Fortunately I was acting correctly on the one vital part of this whole operation. I pulled the trigger with pistol pointing firmly at the earth. It was more than a surprise when instead of a click as the action cleared I had the full-throated crack of a heavy calibre handgun . . .

* * *

As my departure from Saigon loomed, the Australian ambassador, Ralph Harry, kindly talked to me again over lunch. His account of the situation in Vietnam was much the same as before, though perhaps with a little more sense of uncertainty:

. . . Harry admitted the errors of the past—even with a bit of professional back-stabbing making it clear whom he thought, amongst his colleagues, had given too optimistic a view of developments in the 1954-1955 period—but retreated to the tried and true position of the serving bureaucrat, "Whatever happened in the past, the problem has to be solved in terms of current demands." He was honest enough to admit that one of the Australian government's chief preoccupations was to try and show that its participation in the war was not a mistake. When the Task Force troops are withdrawn from Phuoc Thuy the government does not want it to appear that little has changed there. (Here the government has a problem and Harry knows it. He could only grin rather wryly when I observed to him that it was no secret that his military advisers in Phuoc Thuy have a much more pessimistic view of developments there than he does.)

Harry seems to have followed the Americans in becoming a considerable spokesman for President Thieu. This I do not understand. It is a dangerous position to assume, as the Australian high commissioner in Pakistan, General Cawthorn, found in 1958 when he was identified totally with President Iskander Mirza who was overthrown by Ayub Khan.

Yet having made that last remark, I did, towards the end of our discussion, wonder whether Harry is not, to some small degree, beginning to realise that he has been over-optimistic, and that matters are not moving in the direction he has suggested with anything like the speed he has tended to see.

I was interested to find that he agreed with my view that the Americans really are working on the assumption that if the Vietnamese cannot handle their own problem in military terms, then it is almost impossible to conceive of a renewed American escalation.

* * *

I left Saigon for Phnom Penh on Australia Day, 26 January 1970, without regret. I had already summed up my feelings about the city a month earlier, on Boxing Day when I wrote:

I find from my latest copy of *Newsweek* that this "might be the worst city in the world". I find it hard to think why the word "might" was put in. The human tragedies of this city which one must encounter every day, even if one tries to become inured to them, are of staggering proportions. The poverty, the beggars— mostly maimed—the sleazy bars and the prostitutes, all these leave one tired in spirit at the end of the day. But there is another element. The dirtiness and the noise of Saigon have become much greater since even December 1967 and certainly since 1966. There is less obvious garbage in piles about the streets; that is until one finds oneself by chance in the back streets and remembers that is the back streets that really make up the greater part of the city. In these fetid and narrow lanes the piles of garbage are, if anything, larger than was the case in 1966 that was the height of the apparent garbage problem. For then, in 1966, the garbage was spread throughout the city. Now it has become concentrated into more restricted areas and the density of the population in the areas where it is dumped for days before some effort is made to take it elsewhere has grown.

I think, however, that if one had to isolate the worst of the [environmental] problems which this city faces it would be the noise and dirt which has followed the Honda revolution . . . There are probably 750,000 of them [motorcycles]. No one knows for sure but this estimate of three-quarters of a million seems generally accepted. . . . There have always been a considerable number of worn-out two stroke engines polluting this city, but now with the Hondas (and the many fewer Suzukis and Yamahas) belching out their blue smoke the haze hangs like a miasma throughout the day. It is so bad that the old trees along the streets are dying and it affects the plants in the gardens of houses, stunting them and withering their leaves. And the noise. The roar is there from six in the morning until near curfew time at one in the morning.

7

Cambodia, Uneasy calm before the storm, 1970

I had made two very short visits to Phnom Penh in 1967 and 1968, so that more than a year had passed since my last visit to Cambodia when I returned to Phnom Penh on 26 January 1970, just in time to attend the embassy's Australia Day reception: "certainly no worse than the others I have attended, but then that means it was no better—too many people in a temperature which even at this time of the year becomes overheated with all the people, too much noisy conversation and nowhere to sit down". (I think that jaded assessment, which I recorded, reflects a carry-over of my feelings after spending more than a month in Saigon.)

Among the Cambodian elite and in diplomatic circles two issues dominated discussion during the three weeks of this visit. There was, first, a very overt concern with the continuing problem of the rural insurgency that had broken out in 1967 and had continued to grow in intensity. This was despite the draconian measure being taken to combat it —just how draconian depended on whom I spoke to. Donald Lancaster, Sihanouk's English-language secretary, spoke of bounties being paid for severed heads being brought to the capital in army trucks to show that repression was indeed taking place. Cambodian friends, such as Khao Song Beng, referred to reports of the army hurling prisoners over the cliffs at Bokor, the mountain retreat above Kampot on Sihanouk's orders. And when I told these friends that I planned to travel out of Phnom Penh I was told that there was no question of my going to some parts of the country because the government had lost control over key regions to the insurgents: parts of Battambang province, western Pursat province, much of Svay Rieng, Mondolkiri and Ratankiri provinces were all said to be too dangerous to visit.

Secondly, and, in a way that I had never encountered before, Sihanouk's future was being discussed widely, both by Cambodians and foreigners. Whereas the expressions of discontent I heard expressed in 1966 were about politics generally, now the focus was on Sihanouk himself. This discussion was prompted by two main factors. The first was the manner in which the government elected in 1966 had increasingly shown it was ready to act with remarkably little deference to the prince. The ministers, led by General Lon Nol, Sihanouk's long- time army commander, and Prince Sirik Matak, Sihanouk's cousin and frequent critic, had not been opposing him in a direct fashion. Rather, they largely disregarded him and managed to get away with it. The second factor was Sihanouk's decision to go overseas at a time when he surely knew that his control over state affairs had slipped badly. In the past he had gone in to temporary "exile" in the expectation that his opponents would beg him to return. Now, when he departed in early January 1970 for his long-delayed weight-loss "cure" in Dr Pathé's clinic in Grasse, he was in a foul and resentful mood and people were seriously wondering if he intended to return. Certainly there was no emergence, sudden or otherwise, of calls for him to return.

Gossip dwelt on the claimed fact that he had left with a much larger amount of luggage than was normal when he had travelled to France previously. Not that his absence meant his "voice" was stilled, for the newspapers printed copies of his frequent telegrams which recommended, scolded and praised this and that. The official newspapers had also taken to printing selections of Sihanouk's words in a little box on the front page each day. It was difficult not to find them banal, downmarket versions of the "Thoughts of the Great Helmsman", as the prince observed, "When one considers the achievements of a people one must consider what factors enabled them to make progress". A lighter note was struck in the account of his doings that appeared in the newspapers just before he entered Dr Pathé's clinic. Sihanouk told readers that, on 6 February 1970 and in anticipation of his "cure" he had eaten "his last good meal" of trout and almonds cooked with Provençal herbs at the "modest but charming inn, Chez Danny".

Overall there was a mood of general disquiet, partly linked to the embarrassing character of yet another of Sihanouk's "feature films", *Joie de Vivre*, that had just been released and more obviously to the extraordinary scenes that were taking place in the Phnom Penh casino. While members of the elite could well afford to lose money at the casino, it was evident that many of those who flocked to gamble there were among the capital's poorest citizens—they were the customers for whom an enterprising Chinese businessman had set up a shoe rental booth in front of the casino, since patrons were not allowed to enter unless wearing shoes. Amid stories of fortunes lost and suicides of disappointed gamblers, and with appeals to Sihanouk from wives to stop their husbands losing all their money there, the government decided to close the casino. I went to see its operation on its final night, 31 January:

> . . . Money was being thrown away as if it was not merely out of date, but unlikely to have some antique value in the future. It was impossible to find a place at the cheaper stakes roulette tables, and there was a waiting queue to get into the roulette room where one plays for minimum stakes of US$3 a time. But the great majority of those present did not seem to be persons who were interested in playing *with*, as opposed to *for*, high stakes. In general the gamblers were very ordinary people intent on indulging their desire to gamble in a legal way until the very last moment, despite the heat, the crush and the noise.

Gauging opinion

Against this rather gloomy background, I made a fruitless visit to Battambang to see Father Tep Im, the scholarly Catholic priest whom I had first met in 1966, only to find that he was absent from the town; travelled to Angkor for a short visit to the temples; and ventured down to the seaside town of Kep on the shaky rail link that had been constructed from Phnom Penh to the country's deep water port at Sihanoukville. As I made my round of old friends and acquaintances, Prince Sisowath Entaravong, my good friend Prince Phandaravong's father, was as welcoming as ever. And true to form he was full of royal family gossip. Sihanouk, he maintained, had been seriously thinking of reclaiming the throne as a way of reasserting control over Cambodia's politics and had put this idea to his mother, Queen Kossamak. His proposal had been roundly rejected by his mother who, Entaravong recounted, had very firmly told Sihanouk that he would be a fool to do this after the many times he had vowed that he would never mount the Cambodian throne again. This maternal rejection of his suggestion was, Entaravong said, yet another reason for Sihanouk's air of discontent.

As I flew out of Phnom Penh on 13 February I kept thinking of what Bernard-Philippe Groslier, the *Conservateur* of the Angkor temples had said to me when I lunched with him in Siem Reap on 10 February. Of all the Frenchmen I had met in Cambodia over the years, Groslier had to have been one of the best informed about the country's politics. He was the fourth generation of his family to have had a career in what had been French Indochina, and his long residence in the country with the personal contacts he had established at the highest levels of society were, I think, unmatched among expatriates. It had been a good lunch, very much in the French style with a pleasant white wine accompanying the dishes. With the wine bottle wrapped in a white napkin, Groslier grinned as he asked me if I could identify the wine. I was flummoxed, as I unsuccessfully ventured every major French region that I could think of and Groslier looked on with his grin growing wider. As I admitted defeat he removed the napkin to show me that we had been drinking a wine from Western Australia, Houghton's White Burgundy, as it used to be called. I was suitably shamefaced. Then, as I was shaking his hand on departure after lunch, he remarked, "I am not sure they (he meant the government in Phnom Penh) are going to give Sihanouk a visa to return."

Next day I took a country bus back to Phnom Penh, seated in a position of honour as a white foreigner at the front and so in the most dangerous place in the vehicle, and beside another honoured traveller, a Buddhist monk, who chewed raw garlic during the whole five hours of our journey. Just over a month later, on 18 March and while he was still in Europe, Sihanouk was voted out of office by the Cambodia parliament. For the moment the Kingdom of Cambodia with its links back to the Angkorian Empire was at an end and the country was about to experience two decades of unrelieved tragedy.

8

Cambodia at war, 1970

I was back in Phnom Penh before the end of 1970, flying in from Singapore on 19 December to a city and country at war. As I wrote in my journal:

> Tourists do not fly to Phnom Penh any more. It was very apparent from the loading of only eight persons on the Air Cambodge flight that only those who have to go to Phnom Penh travel there nowadays. The rest of the passengers were French businessmen and two Indian women—Pondicherry Indians—with French passports.

> At the airport the representatives of the multiple travel agencies that had sprung up in palmier days battled to get my custom for a ride into town. Both at the airport and along the way there are a mass of banners which seem such an essential accompaniment to any regime—whatever its political coloration in Southeast Asia: "Long Live Cambodia Independent and Neutral", "Corruption is a disease for the Whole Nation", "In a Democracy property is the right of all people". There seems to be khaki everywhere; men and women in khaki, the military police in very superior khaki; others in drab, unironed fatigues. Sandbagged strong points surround key

government ministries with roads running past them cordoned off with barbed wire. It is all very reminiscent of Saigon.

Over the next two days I had discussions with a range of observers including Graham Feakes, the Australian ambassador and a friend, Phandaravong and Khau Song Beng, other Cambodian friends, the local Shell manager, and visiting journalists, including Kate Webb of UPI and Peter Sharrrock of Reuters. All of them spoke of the reality of war in Cambodia. Large areas of the country were out of the government's control while many other areas were contested, changing hands according to whether government forces, which practically included South Vietnamese troops fighting alongside Cambodians, or the insurgents, which included North Vietnamese troops, were present at any time. Many of the principal highways were cut, notably the roads to Siem Reap and to Battambang. In the case of the latter, there was now serious concern as to whether it was going to be possible to bring the rice crop down the road from Battambang when it was harvested early in the coming new year.

Everyone I spoke to referred to the tragically high cost of lives among the students who had rallied to the new government's cause and marched off to confront the enemy, poorly trained and poorly equipped, to die in their hundreds or even thousands. The enthusiasm the students had shown immediately after Sihanouk's overthrow had waned dramatically, but they remained an important element in the political equation, acting as something of a ginger group to push the government in one direction or another. Already the war in the countryside was pushing peasants into the city, as I saw when I breakfasted with Phandaravong at La Taverne on 21 December:

> As we drove to La Taverne for breakfast, I was amazed to
> see a great double line of *cyclopousses* waiting with their riders to
> be checked by the police. Ratsody (Phandaravong's nickname)
> explained this as the result of the massive influx of peasants into
> Phnom Penh following the spread of the war. The *cyclo* riders
> we saw were seeking some way of living and they turned to the
> classic job taken on by country boys in the city: pedalling a *cyclo*.
> Phandaravong put the figure of refugees who have come into the
> city at half a million. This may well be correct, but apparently no
> one has any exact figure.

> Other obvious signs of the changed situation which one
> encounters in moving about Phnom Penh include the number of
> small shops that have closed down. The "Jade" photo shop to
> which I have gone for years, for instance, no longer functions. It
> was owned by Vietnamese and they, along with so many others
> sharing their ethnic background, had fled from Phnom Penh at
> the time of the massacres of Vietnamese in April and May. Petrol
> remains in short supply with only Shell having sufficient stocks so
> that its bowsers are besieged by motorists and by motorbike and
> scooter riders. And through the day there is that familiar sound, so
> often heard in Saigon in the past, of heavy artillery and mortars
> firing in the background.

Much had changed, but some things did indeed remain the same, as
I recorded:

> . . . The [elite] Committee of Cambodian Women recently

held a big bazaar to raise funds for the troops. The focus of interest was the tombola that had as its major prize sets of tickets for return trips to Paris. These prizes were all won, to no one's great surprise, by members of the Committee

Visiting Battambang to see Tep Im

With both the road and the rail links to Battambang closed because of the war the only way to travel there to see Father Tep Im was by air, by a new airline called Khmer Akas which was, in fact, Continental Airlines operating with a subsidy provided by the United States. The flight to Battambang on 22 December, in a DC3, was without incident and with little choice I made my way to the Hotel Samakki, where I had stayed once previously. It was just as seedy as before:

. . . the manager looked as if he had been specially cast for his role of pimp and procurer in a tenth rate Hollywood quickie. Assured that my requirements did not include one of his women, he settled down to the less demanding task of adding about ten per cent to the price of the soda water I asked him to get for me and to leering wistfully whenever I passed the reception desk, hoping to imply that I did not know what I was missing.

I had come to Battambang to see *Father* Tep Im, and it was by that style I had referred to him when asking a couple of French priests in the town about his whereabouts, and they did not correct me. So it was to my considerable surprise that I found he was now Monsignor Tep Im, Apostolic Prefect for Battambang, a status close to that of a bishop but without the authority to ordain priests. (Writing about Tep Im previously I have incorrectly identified him as a bishop—a reflection of the ignorance of a lapsed Protestant! But I have also found Catholic sources referring to him as "Bishop" Tep Im, so my error might be excusable.) He was welcoming as ever as we talked for the better part of four hours in a conversation that traversed contemporary politics, the reasons for Sihanouk's overthrow, the unforgivable massacre by the police and soldiers of Vietnamese near Phnom Penh earlier in the year, and the problems, as he saw them, associated with the papal encyclical *Humanae Vitae*. He was deeply concerned for Cambodia's future and for that of his small Catholic flock of about two hundred ethnic Cambodians and three thousand ethnic Vietnamese for whom he had responsibility. As for Battambang town and province in this time of war, he spoke of both being calm, largely detached and separatist in inclination, a view that accorded well with the region's history. The Khmer Rouge in the region he numbered at around two thousand with their activities mostly directed at preventing rice being shipped down to Phnom Penh.

Looking back at the coup that had overthrown Sihanouk, Tep Im ventured a view that I had already heard offered in Phnom Penh by other elite Cambodians, for he was certainly among that number despite his religion. He simply could not understand why the Prince had not returned to Phnom Penh immediately he learnt of what was happening in the days before the actual coup took place. Here Tep Im was referring to the period from 11 March when mobs stormed the communist Vietnamese diplomatic missions—an action we now know took place with Sihanouk's approval—with the actual deposition, which took place on 18 March. If he had returned, Tep Im argued, the plotters for all their bravado would have caved in to Sihanouk's physical presence and the awesome consequences of their act in confronting the man who had dominated Cambodian politics for so long. This judgement could only be another of history's "might have beens", and it tended, I thought, to discount the years from at least 1966 onwards when the power of Sihanouk's authority had already been deteriorating. More convincingly, he spoke of the final months of 1969 as a period when there were already several plots against Sihanouk being contemplated but when the men who finally acted against him, Prince Sirik Matak and General Lon Nol were far from agreement on whether to act and if so to do so together.

The massacre of Phnom Penh's Vietnamese

Just as had been the case when I first met him in 1966, it was clear that Tep Im continued to have contacts with the governing elite. He did not participate in the formulation of policy but those who had that responsibility consulted him from time to time. He was a man who moved easily in the upper reaches of Cambodian society despite his religion setting him apart from his Buddhist compatriots. So I was not greatly surprised when he told me he had been consulted by Yem Sambaur, the foreign minister in the government that came to power after Sihanouk's overthrow, seeking advice after the massacre of Vietnamese in April and May.

Even today the reasons for this massacre are something of a mystery. Starting in late April and continuing through May 1970, Cambodian soldiers and police massacred upwards of a thousand Vietnamese inhabitants of the Chruoy Changvar region, just across the Tonle Sap River from central Phnom Penh. At one level it seems to have been a reflection of atavistic rage against an ethnic group seen as traditional enemies. Possibly, too, the soldiers and the police were venting their anger against the Vietnamese in response to the high casualties Phnom Penh's troops were suffering as they fought against Vietnamese communist forces within the country. For at this stage of Cambodia's civil war regular Vietnamese troops provided the main military muscle for communist force arraigned against the Phnom Penh regime.

For the new regime in Phnom Penh the massacre was a public relations disaster of the worst kind as it was widely reported by the international media that had flocked to Cambodia to cover the new war. Against this background Yem Sambaur had asked Tep Im for advice on how the Phnom Penh authorities should explain the massacre to the South Vietnamese government that was now its ally. In response Tep Im had counselled Yem Sambaur to make a frank admission of responsibility coupled with an explanation of the circumstances that led to the killings. Interestingly, Tep Im argued that the massacres were the result of local factors and decisions and were not of any decision by the new leaders. But, not to his surprise, his advice was not taken.

As I left he asked if I could arrange to send him a copy of the *New English Bible*. He had begun the task of translating the Bible from English into Cambodian, in order to replace an existing edition prepared by evangelical missionaries and which he felt was too literal in form. He had, he told me, copies of the Bible in French and Latin, but what he was looking for in the *New English Bible* was a contemporary rendering of the text. I was able to send him a copy from Phnom Penh and this led to my receiving the last communication I ever had from him. He wrote to thank me for sending the Bible and to tell of how he spent some time at the end of each day continuing with his task of translation, using all of the texts he now had available.

9

Vietnam 1970-71 – Misleading calm

Flying in to Vietnam from Cambodia at the very end of 1970, on 29 December, I was once again welcomed into Le Tan Buu's house and into a period in the Vietnam War that, in hindsight, was misleadingly calm. Even the chronically gloomy Duong Sanh, at the National Library, was ever so slightly optimistic. And Phung Nhat Minh, who had met me at the airport on arrival, seemed prepared to qualify some of his usual world-weary cynicism. He spoke of the security situation as "very considerably improved", though in his view this in part reflected the choice of the National Liberation Front and the North Vietnamese forces operating within South Vietnam not to initiate action. This said, he almost immediately referred of the problems in II Corps, the region running from the central highlands to the coast, where Saigon's forces were under continuing pressure in the provincial areas around the towns of Qui Nhon and Quang Ngai. This assessment, though Minh did not say so at the time, reflected the fact that while American casualties had fallen sharply in the last months of 1970 South Vietnamese losses continued to be quite high in the fighting taking place in II Corps.

In an indication of the atmosphere of the time, Buu was preoccupied with multiple business ventures rather than the war. He had plans to set up a rural bank; to establish a joint venture with Japanese capital for a new fishing fleet to operate in the Gulf of Thailand; to build an "international class" hotel in Saigon; and to promote a school of self-defence based on a Korean form of karate. In addition to all these plans he continued to have profitable farming interests in the Mekong delta and his lucrative massage parlour in Saigon itself. Just what additional services the parlour offered beyond massages was something I never felt impelled to ask.

Anti-American feeling

As had been the case in all my previous visits to Saigon, I was again conscious of an underlying feeling of anti-Americanism among the Vietnamese I met on this visit. It was a feeling stemming from a peculiar mixture of resentment that it had been necessary to rely on the United States and its allies for survival, combined, in some cases with a readiness to contrast the "brashness" of Americans with the supposed "subtlety" of the French, even if they had been colonisers. At least this was an attitude to be found among those who had lived through the final stages of French colonial control. I well remembered an occasion the previous year when two young Americans from their embassy had called at Buu's house to offer him "advice" on the positions he should take in relation to particular political issues. He was deeply offended and bluntly indicated that he thought the Vietnamese language they used in talking to him was deficient. He had insisted on their talking to me in English and having me translate the subsequent conversation backwards and forwards in French during this difficult meeting.

At the time of this visit in early 1971 the fact that the security situation appeared to have improved undoubtedly played a part in the readiness of this anti-American feeling to surface. It would be wrong to say that the feeling was universal, and who knew how the peasants in the countryside felt. But I heard sharply critical comments about America from Buu and his associates, from Duong Sanh and from Phung Nhat Minh. And there was no doubt about the feeling of the university students in Saigon, who periodically rioted to show their disapproval of both the Americans and the government. A particular and widely held gripe was the belief that the Americans were ready to intervene to ensure General Thieu was re-elected president when elections were held in 1972. Buu blamed the incumbent American ambassador, Elsworth Bunker for this readiness to interfere. In Buu's view Bunker was "too old, had been in Saigon far too long and was too rigid in his outlook".

Duong's Sanh's view of the world was very different to Buu's, reflecting the contrast between their two positions within South Vietnamese society. Although, as I have just noted, he was marginally more optimistic, he dwelt at length on the extent to which Saigon had become a lawless city and the problems faced by civil servants like him. They faced increasing tax demands from the government, but that same government was ready to let the corrupt and the powerful escape paying their share. Commenting on the diminished activity of the communist forces:

> . . . he argued that whatever optimism is generated by this
> state of military affairs is very quickly dissipated by the fact
> that the communists remain entrenched politically both in the

countryside and in the cities. He and his friends do not believe that the government has been successful in its campaign against the VCI (the Viet Cong Infrastructure, and a reference to the Phoenix campaign, the program which involved assassination of known and suspected communists). And he believes that continuing United States troop withdrawals from Vietnam can only work to the advantage of the communists.

Walking back the three or so miles from the centre of Saigon, where the library was located, to Buu's house in Cholon I wondered whether Saigon had not slipped a little further down the scale of cities where one does not want to be. I glimpsed a couple GIs scoring a drugs deal in a laneway; the black market stalls were more in number and seemed to have a larger range of goods for sale; there was surely more dirt and more fumes than when I was last here; and the footpaths along which I was walking had crumbled even further since my last visit. It was not, I reflected, Calcutta in terms of the overwhelming sense of poverty on the streets, but it was no less a sad and tortured city.

The Australian Task Force

In contrast to my previous extended visit to Saigon, I was only based in the city for just over a week. During this time I visited the Australian Task Force at Nui Dat for two days. In contrast to what I had found during my previous visit, there appeared to be a much greater concern that visitors, any visitors, might find something that might lead to critical reports appearing in Australia. This was despite the fact that the security level was, on the face of it, better than a year before. I could only presume that this overly cautious attitude at Nui Dat was a reflection of the extent to which Vietnam was now such a contested political issue within Australia. Once back in Saigon I went on yet another of Tran Van Don's flying visits around the delta, with our helicopters calling at Ca Mau and two fire bases in the U Minh Forest before a final call at Can Tho. The most memorable aspect of this trip with Don was the fact that on one of the legs of our trip the helicopters we used had neither doors nor seats, and so no seat belts. My Vietnamese companions were quicker off the mark that I was and managed to place themselves in the centre of the craft. I had no shame in using my trouser belt to fix myself firmly to a stanchion as we flew on to our next destination.

Meeting Son Ngoc Thanh's brother

Back in Saigon, on 7 January 1971, I managed with the help of Peter Timmins from the Australian embassy, to interview Son Thai Nguyen, a senator in the South Vietnamese parliament and the brother of Sihanouk's long-time enemy, Son Ngoc Thanh. The son of an ethnic Cambodian father and a Vietnamese mother Son Ngoc Thanh had been born in 1908 in Vietnam's Mekong delta—part of the southern region of Vietnam area known as Cochinchina in colonial times. In the 1930s, and like a number of other members of the ethnic Cambodian minority in Vietnam, he saw his future as linked to Cambodia rather than in French-administered Cochinchina. Thanh emerged into prominence in the period of the Second World War and had at one stage seemed likely to play a major role in Cambodian politics. Indeed, and to Sihanouk's deep annoyance, he could claim to have been one of the country's earliest modern nationalists.

But along with his undoubted nationalism there was an authoritarian streak to his personality that shaded rapidly into life-long enmity towards Sihanouk when the latter, with French help, bested him politically in the post-Second World War period. By the 1950s Thanh and Sihanouk regarded each other as bitter enemies and after 1954 Thanh was ready to cooperate with the South Vietnamese regime in the hope of bringing Sihanouk down. Whether he was personally involved in the plots against Sihanouk and his family in 1959 is not clear, but Sihanouk was convinced this was the case. And there is no doubt that Thanh was active in supporting right-wing Khmer Serei insurgents who carried out guerrilla attacks against Sihanouk's regime in the 1960s. When I visited the army camp at Kompong Chrey in southeastern Cambodia commanded by my friend Captain Kim Kosal in 1966, he told me of how Khmer Serei agents were active in sabotaging infrastructure, such as bridges, in provinces close to the Cambodian-South Vietnamese border. Son Ngoc Thanh's direct involvement in the overthrow of Sihanouk in 1970 was widely suspected. Now, with my meeting with his brother, I hoped to pin this issue down.

We met Son Thai Nguyen in a nondescript house near the Wat Chantavangsay, a Theravada Buddhist pagoda in Saigon patronised by members of the sizeable community of ethnic Cambodians who lived in the southern provinces of Vietnam, an area that several centuries previously had been under Cambodian sovereignty. This, as I wrote in an article in *The Age*, was a case of bringing to life a "ghost" who so often in 1960s had been rumoured to be either dead, through assassination, or mad. I was aware that Son Ngoc Thanh now held an official position in Phnom Penh, but he remained a man of mystery. Speaking of his brother in a mixture of awe and pride, Son Thai Nguyen gave me an extended account of the developments leading up to Sihanouk's overthrow on 18 March 1970 that placed great importance on his brother's role. Some of what he told me was probably true and I included parts of his account in my biography of the former Cambodian leader. But even if Son Ngoc Thanh's role in bringing Sihanouk down was not as pivotal as his brother suggested, the fact that Thanh was still alive seemed remarkable enough given his dangerously murky past. Ultimately, his involvement in Sihanouk's overthrow availed him very little. Falling out with Lon Nol regime in 1972, Son Ngoc Thanh exiled himself to Saigon and he was still there when the Vietnamese communists marched into the city at the end of April 1975. They took him into custody and he died in prison in August 1977.

Gerry Hickey's pessimism

At the end of this hurried and busy day I managed to find time to call on Gerald Hickey, the American anthropologist who had worked for the Rand Corporation for many years and whom I had first met in 1966. His continuing link to an American government-funded think tank had led to opponents of the war in the United States denigrating Hickey personally and discounting his research. On the basis of my previous meetings with him and his publications, I had the highest respect for his integrity and his scholarship, which were based on some ten years spent in Vietnam and a fluent capability in the Vietnamese language. Against the optimism that I had encountered elsewhere on this visit, Hickey had a very different view. As I recorded at the time his summary of the situation in South Vietnam, for the government and its foreign backers, was that it was "bad".

In an extended review of the state of the war, he started by making a frontal assault on the views of Ted Serong, the former senior and controversial army officer who had at one stage headed the Australian Army Training Team in Vietnam and had retired with the rank of brigadier. By the time I was talking to Hickey in 1971 Serong was occupying a range of advisory roles for the South Vietnamese government and for the United States, including the Rand Corporation for which Hickey worked. Hickey argued that Serong, who had become a leading advocate of the view that the war was going well, relied too much on the statistics compiled by the Americans and far too little on personal observation and contacts with knowledgeable Vietnamese. The suggestion from Serong that the war was over, Hickey stated, was "sheer nonsense". Rather, the war had changed character:

> . . . but this change is as much a reflection of the enemy's conscious estimation of the need to return for a period to guerrilla war as it is a reflection of the losses which they have suffered. Hickey is emphatic in his stress on the manner in which the Viet Cong Infrastructure is intact. He says that even John Paul Vann [the subject of Neil Sheehan's book, *A Bright Shining Lie*], who has been touting progress to the skies, will admit in private, and when pressed, that the VCI remains intact and effective in the delta. The efforts to root out the VCI, particularly through the Phoenix Campaign, have failed—and worse than failed they have alienated substantial numbers of Vietnamese through the torture and counter-terror methods that have been used. While he expects that military activity will remain at a relatively low level in IV Corps (the

southern region of South Vietnam covering the Mekong Delta), he sees a resurgence of activity in I and II Corps (roughly the top half of the territory of South Vietnam) with, possibly, a return to the old enemy strategy of making it appear that they intend to cut, or have the capacity to cut, the country in two. Still on the military side, Hickey claimed that the desertion rates amongst the ARVN (Armed Forces of the Republic of Vietnam) have reached staggering levels, greatly above those admitted by the government. He also spoke of the lack of discipline of Vietnamese government troops . . .

In Hickey's judgment there was a solid core of support for the National Libration Front of around twenty per cent among the population—an interesting agreement with the judgment given me by Tran Van Don a year before. What this meant for the future was that there could be no end to the war without a place for the Front. His final summation to me was deeply pessimistic:

> The whole thing saddens Hickey. He finds himself criticised by those in America who condemn anyone who has anything to do with the government of Vietnam. He is saddened by the way in which the American army is behaving in Vietnam. He is saddened by the apparent fact that the massive American effort here is more than ever likely to leave resentment as its chief legacy. It (America) has not, all official statements to the contrary, won the war. And, he maintained quite unemotionally as his most careful judgement, the bulk of the population has now come to the point where they now have a single, demanding desire for peace. He contrasts this with a period of even two years ago. But now, he maintains with great emphasis, this has become the general, central hope.

* * *

I did not know at the time that this would be my last time in Vietnam for just over ten years. My visit ended in a dinner party that I would look back on for years as symbolising the contrasts and the absurdities, not to mention the unrealities that abounded in Saigon and the country as a whole in 1971. With both Tran Van Don and Le Tan Buu among the guests, and an annoyingly bumptious Jean-Claude Pomonti from *Le Monde*, whom I now met for the first time, we dined at Rumanchos, the restaurant of choice at that time. My record of the evening was deeply pessimistic:

> . . . Much was said of the unreality of optimistic comments on the war. In fact, as on so many previous occasions, there was a "Twilight of the Gods" air to the whole thing. Here we were in the expensive ambience of Rumanchos, shielded briefly from the noise of Saigon by the air conditioners, all agreeing that the place was shot to pieces; that the VC strength in the delta remained great and that the situation in II Corps is deteriorating. But what did this all mean for the Vietnamese? Did they really see an end to it all? Or does the knowledge of bank accounts overseas remain as a guarantee of their future security? I do not know the answer but on this as so many occasions I felt like the outsider standing by watching the grief of others, yet the grief was being sublimated with good food and wine so that there was almost the air of a relaxed wake.

10

No Good News From Cambodia

After I left Cambodia at the very end of 1970 and having seen Tep Im in Battambang for what proved to be the last time, it was another ten years before I visited the country again. As the war raged there seemed to be no good news from Cambodia. By 1973 it had become abundantly clear that the United Front forces fighting against the Phnom Penh regime and the Royal Government that Sihanouk nominally headed from his exile in Beijing were dominated by men on the extreme left of Cambodian politics. Sihanouk knew this, though in his ingrained self-referential fashion he seemed to think there would be a place of importance for him once the United Front toppled the regime in Phnom Penh. But only those in the West who were ready to let romantic hopes triumph over reason could believe that an eventual victory by the forces of the Front would mean a return to anything like the "normality" of Sihanouk's pre-1970 Cambodia. Indeed, many on the left of politics in Australia, Europe and the United States fervently hoped that a victory by the Front would radically transform Cambodian society—into quite what was never very clear, other than it would be a symbol of the defeat of "American imperialism", since the United States was backing the regime in Phnom Penh.

Such a hope was not one I shared, but I did want to find out more about the Kampuchean United National Front and the opportunity came in the course of a visit Paris in the summer of 1973. I learnt from French acquaintances that the Front had offices in Paris and was ready to receive visitors. And so one afternoon in early July I knocked on the door of an apartment in a building in the Place de Barcelone which, given its location in the smart Sixteenth Arrondissement, was strangely nondescript in character. After a long pause the door was opened and I was received by Ok Sakun, the representative for the United Front in Paris He stood in a room crowded with desks piled high with papers and propaganda material. I had never before met Ok Sakum, though I did have a vague memory of a reference to his name having been on a list of "subversives" submitted to Sihanouk in 1963. A slim, dour figure Ok Sakun did not smile once in the thirty minutes I spent talking to him, and he was frank in stating his political orientation and in providing a brief account of his personal background.

Like Pol Pot, though this was a name unknown to me as I was talking to him, Ok Sakun told me be had been a student in France. When he had returned to Cambodia in the late 1950s he had been the editor of a left-wing newspaper in Phnom Penh before the authorities closed it down, at which point he again left for France. Later research has confirmed this outline of Ok Sakun's background, but added much more information about him. He was, indeed, a student in France, but one of rather more academic talent than Pol Pot. Arriving in 1949, he completed a baccalaureate in France but then failed to be accepted into the Ecole Centrale to study engineering. Like other Cambodian students who were to rise to prominence in the Cambodian communist movement, Ok Sakun had lived in an apartment in the rue Saint-André-des-Arts in Paris'

Latin Quarter. And he, too, had been a member of the *Cercle Marxiste* that met to discuss communist theory and to plan for a revolution in their homeland.

Returning to Phnom Penh after his failure to enter the Ecole Centrale, Ok Sakun took up an appointment with the Cambodian railways. Later, and with his French wife, Ok Sakun returned to France for further study in the 1960s, finally gaining an engineering diploma and studying political science for a period. He returned to Cambodia again and joined men like Khieu Samphan in the maquis in 1967 before once more moving back to France to become the United Front's representative until the Khmer Rouge victory in 1975. So he was, in every way, at the heart of the Cambodian communist movement.

As he talked to me, Ok Sakun handed me various propaganda brochures, many containing photographs of his colleagues who were fighting in Cambodia. I was not surprised to see photographs of the so-called missing deputies—Khieu Samphan, Hou Youn and Hu Nim —men who were supposed to have been killed on Sihanouk's orders in 1967; for by this time the fact they were alive was widely known. What was a surprise was the sight of one of my Cambodian acquaintances I knew had gone into the maquis in the late 1960s, but about whom I knew nothing more. But here he was, Poc Deuskoma, scion of one of the great Cambodian official families, occupying some form of leadership position with the insurgents. He was shown smiling and dressed in black peasant clothing. And he was no longer the tubby figure I had known both in Canberra, when he served in the Cambodian embassy, and in Phnom Penh in 1966, where he revealed his radical left-wing sympathies to me over dinner. Only many years later did I learn he was probably already dead at the time I was looking at his photo in 1973, whether in battle or, as some have suggested, as the result of malaria I have never found out.

As I leafed through at the brochures Ok Sakun had given me, I was listening to him talk and suddenly realised that he was describing events of great importance in Cambodia about which I had absolutely no knowledge. Yet he was describing a major event that had occurred in 1960, the time when I was working in the Australian embassy. I had some small sense of the clandestine politics that had existed while Sihanouk was firmly in charge of the state, but now Ok Sakun was telling me of the foundation of the Cambodian Communist Party as an organisation separate from the Vietnamese Worker's Party, the official name for the Vietnamese Communist Party. It took me a while to recognise just how important this information was, as Ok Sakun spoke in some detail and with obvious pride of this event. In late September 1960, Ok Sakum stated, he and a small number of communist colleagues—we now know the actual number was twenty-one, including Pol Pot, or Saloth Sar as he was known then—met in the house Ok Sakun occupied behind Phnom Penh's railway station. It was from this point, he told me, that he and his colleagues had begun their march towards the victory he had no doubt they would achieve.

Ok Sakun was to return to Cambodia after that victory was indeed achieved in 1975 and to survive despite his loyalty to the cause apparently being called into question. When the American journalists Elizabeth Becker and Richard Dudman, and the Scots radical academic Malcolm

Caldwell from the School of Oriental and African Studies in London made their visit to Cambodia in December 1978 Ok Sakun helped to escort the small group. As Becker reported in her important book, *When The War Was Over*, Ok Sakun was poorly nourished and hesitant to engage in conversation, leaving the impression that he had just been released from hard manual labour in the countryside. Whether this was actually the case, he was a survivor, and in the 1980s he resurfaced as Democratic Kampuchea's representative to UNESCO in Paris.

Separate from the information Becker provided on Ok Sakun, her book recounts the dramatic events associated with the assassination of Malcolm Caldwell when, on what was the last night of the trios' visit to Cambodia, he was killed in a government guesthouse. It seems most probable that Caldwell was killed by agents of the Khmer Rouge regime he had idolised in his writings, But it is unlikely there will ever be a definitive conclusion and some other suggestions—such as that by Pol Pot's biographer, Philip Short, that the killing was done by Vietnamese commandos—as to who was behind the assassination cannot be discounted. The "confessions" to his murder by two Cambodians at the Tuol Sleng extermination centre, or S-21, can scarcely be relied on and seems far too like window dressing by the regime in the days just before Pol Pot's regime was overthrown. But even if it was agents of the regime who carried out the killing the question of motive remains unresolved. Everything points to Caldwell having found his visit to Cambodia and his lone conversation with Pol Pot—he was accorded this privilege separate from Becker and Dudman—had provided confirmation of his beliefs in the virtues of the regime.

Perhaps the best known of the Western propagandists for the Pol Pot regime before its defeat by the invading Vietnamese at the beginning of 1979, Caldwell had taught at London University's School of Oriental and African studies and was a cult figure among a small group of radical students as well as gaining support from other critics of the Vietnam War. I had met him at SOAS on one or two occasions in 1972 in the course of a visiting appointment at that institution. But he had a larger place in my mind after he and a Cambodian-born radical, Lek Hor Tan, published their book, *Cambodia in the Southeast Asian War*, in 1973 that plagiarised material from a book I had published the year before. Their plagiarism was "even handed", reproducing unacknowledged material from other authors including Wilfred Burchett.

11

Cambodia on the Rack

"But why didn't you tell us what was happening, comrade?"

I am still angered by the way in which some academics welcomed the victory of the Khmer Rouge in Cambodia in April 1975 and then wrote and spoke warmly of the subsequent rule of the Democratic Kampuchean regime almost to the very end of its existence. It was not just that the apologists for the Khmer Rouge regime were "useful idiots," in the phrase famously, but probably incorrectly, attributed to Lenin. They were something worse, individuals who sheltered under the cloak of scholarship but abandoned any pretence of adhering to scholarship's standards in their skewed and ideologically based celebrations of the Khmer Rouge's triumph. And this behaviour was in relation to a regime that cost the lives of nearly a quarter of Cambodia's population.

Getting it wrong

Today these academic commentators are totally discredited, and in any event not remembered outside of specialist circles, but in their departure from reasonable standards of evidence they should not be forgotten. The names of Gareth Porter and George Hildebrand immediately come to mind and the fact that they had a Cornell association is a matter still, for me, of regret. Based entirely on their imaginings and ideological prejudices, they wrote a justification for the Khmer Rouge regime's forced evacuation of Phnom Penh in April 1975 in their book, *Cambodia: Starvation and Revolution*, published in 1976. Even more dispiriting for me personally was the readiness of George Kahin, one of my inspiring teachers at Cornell, to write an approving introduction to their book.

Among others who were unconvinced about the character of the Khmer Rouge regime was Noam Chomsky. With his colleague Edward Herman, Chomsky wrote about what happened in Cambodia informed not by knowledge but by ideological bias that included a determination to condemn the United States. I am at one with William Shawcross who commented on Chomsky in June 1981: "Chomsky's position [on Cambodia] has been disastrous ever since the Khmer Rouge victory in 1975. By continually concentrating on mistakes which journalists and writers have made and on the way in which western governments have exploited the stories out of Kampuchea, he has deflected attention from the far more important issue—whether or not gross abuses of human rights were being committed there."

Well before the end of 1975 there was consistent evidence available that something terrible was happening in Cambodia following the victory of the forces led by Pol Pot. I certainly had no mortgage on the truth of developments immediately after the Khmer Rouge marched in to Phnom Penh on 17 April 1975 and my initial expectation, grim though it was, anticipated a limited and targeted period of killing to take place. After all, the Khmer Rouge had repeatedly stated that they would kill the leaders of the regime in Phnom Penh once they were victorious. Then, when the new regime pushed almost all of the city's population into the countryside in a mass forced exodus immediately after their victory, it became clear that previous expectations of what was going to happen following the defeat of the Khmer Republic were no longer valid.

Getting it right

What was taking place did become apparent in a long article written by Henry Kamm of *The New York Times,* and published on 15 July 1975 on the front page of that newspaper—it was the first of a series of outstanding articles on Cambodia by a man I did not know at that time but who has become a good friend, and for which he was awarded a Pulitzer Prize in 1978. Reporting from Bangkok and on the basis of extended interviews with refugees who had fled into Thailand, Kamm described how the new government was pursuing brutal policies of forced relocation following the initial emptying of Phnom Penh. He wrote of the new regime's sanctioning the execution of any persons who failed to accept a new life of controlled and exhausting servitude in what were effectively agricultural forced labour camps.

The accounts that Kamm gathered from Cambodians who had managed to escape into Thailand were both remarkably consistent and full of detail that was later proved to be correct. His reports led a limited number of other journalists, including Denis Gray of Associated Press, to pursue the issue, but there was still a remarkable degree of scepticism in the academic world. Alert to the significance of this reporting, I read all I could while based in England and in Singapore during 1975. Then, in early 1976, I was able to talk to people in Bangkok who also had knowledge of the refugees' claims. As a result, I believed it was increasingly clear that an ongoing and deeply troubling Cambodian tragedy was occurring. And amid this grim picture of developments I found that I could gain no firm news of the fate of my Cambodian friends; nothing about Colonel Kim Kosal and his wife, nothing about Prince and Princess Sisowath Entaravong, and nothing about Monsignor Paul Tep Im Sotha, or any others.

In 1977 two important books were published that drew together the overwhelming evidence of the tragedy occurring in Cambodia: François Ponchaud's *Cambodge: Année zéro* (published in English as *Cambodia: Year Zero*) and John Barron and Anthony Paul's *Murder of a Gentle Land*. It remains shameful that both were attacked from the left as nothing more than propaganda, and in the case of Barron and Paul's book as a reflection of supposed subservience to the wishes of the CIA. But before these books appeared, and in the light of what I had been able to learn, I responded to an invitation in early 1976 to write about Cambodia for *Pacific Community*, a journal then published in Japan. My article was completed in May but not published until the journal's October issue. Addressing the issue of developments within Cambodia and the problem of not having full knowledge what was taking place there I wrote:

> No foreigner yet knows the full truth about developments in
> Cambodia; nor probably do many Cambodians. But the full truth is
> an elusive concept at the best of times even under ideal conditions,
> which are clearly not the circumstances in Cambodia in the second

year following the defeat of Lon Nol's forces. What has happened since then may never be clearly documented. Segments only of the overall picture are revealed with any clarity. Viewed discretely or taken as an incomplete assemblage these segments suggest a revolution of staggering proportions imposed harshly upon an already war-ravaged country. They suggest a resort to brutal methods that can only be explained by some deep and perhaps desperate fear that the revolution might be halted or even turned around. And they suggest that policy measures that might, in the abstract, be regarded as rational and desirable have been pursued in that terrible vacuum of unreality where the end justifies the means. It is difficult to use other descriptions for a situation in which there have been widespread killings of both former enemies and of those who had no clear links to the defeated regime, massive forced relocation of population, and a determination to attain food sufficiency at a human cost that can scarcely be comprehensible to those who are privileged to live in freer circumstances. There must be doubt about magnitudes. If, however, only ten per cent of the stories told by refugees fleeing Cambodia are correct the situation is of an awfulness that beggars description.

Concluding the article I wrote:

Throughout this article the need to recognise the inadequacies of our available information has been underlined. Few comments on developments can be made in an unqualified fashion, and there is a faint possibility that in some areas of the country, at least, the general picture of conditions accepted by foreign observers is less dark than is widely taken to be the case. There is even a less likely possibility that our general picture is wrong and that we have allowed ourselves to be swayed by over-publicised and deliberately distorted accounts of developments. If either of these possibilities should be borne out in fact the new rulers of Cambodia could justly claim to be the victims of an international smear campaign as calculated in falsehood as the concoction of the "Protocols of the Elders of Zion" and as wilfully deliberate in its intent to mislead as any past exercise in black propaganda. But if this is not the case, then to remain silent in the face of developments in Cambodia is, for those who in the past have claimed to be knowledgeable about that country, a contemporary treason of the clerks.

The shameful fact was that the "treason" continued into 1978, and even beyond that date. It is one thing for Wilfred Burchett to be described by Ben Kiernan of Yale University as "by November 1978, if not before" having become "convinced that the Vietnamese allegations of genocide against Pol Pot were largely true". But the author of that comment only reached the same conclusions earlier that year after having been a vigorous public supporter of the Pol Pot regime for nearly three years before he finally admitted his error. Other names of academic and journalistic commentators on Cambodia could be added to this list, including Laura Summers, David McKnight and Gavan McCormack.

When admissions of error were finally made by these doubters that something truly awful had occurred in Cambodia under Khmer Rouge rule, it was done grudgingly. Here, as an example, is Gavan McCormack, then based at the Australian National University, writing in the *Journal of Contemporary Asia* in 1980:

> [The] truth about the Kampuchean revolution is extraordinarily difficult to discover . . . Till some time in 1978 the case against Kampuchea was of such a dubious nature that many socialists and progressive people refused to give it any credence. It is likely some fabrication/distortion of evidence is still going on, but in my view the balance of probability has now shifted heavily towards the

view that the Kampuchean revolution between 1975 and the end of 1978 was a terrible travesty . . .

Since I am not a psychologist I cannot explain this apparently wilful ignorance, except as a case of ideological conviction overriding the facts that were there for all to see, at the latest by 1976, and indeed before then for the readers of *The New York Times*. It was wilful ignorance that was maintained after both Ponchaud and Barron and Paul had published their books. The whole issue was summed up for me in the question put to me by a left-wing Australian academic, Bruce McFarlane, at the Australian National University in 1979, by which time the Pol Pot regime had been overthrown. Posing a question in the familiar Labor Party-speak of the Whitlam period he asked, "But why didn't you tell us what was happening, comrade?" But, of course I had, and others had done so in greater detail and more cogently. It was simply the fact that men like my questioner had not wanted to listen, for to have done so would have been to upset their carefully constructed, but utterly unrealistic, view of the world.

* * *

So there was no smear campaign or exercise in black propaganda. Indeed, even after the Vietnamese overthrow of the Pol Pot regime and the installation of their Cambodian protégés, in early January 1979, it still took time for the full horrors of Democratic Kampuchea to be revealed to the world—in part this was so because of the initial refusal of the Vietnamese to allow all but a handful of international observers into the country. But as an example of a startling revelation that emerged *after* the Vietnamese marched into Phnom Penh in January 1979, it was only then that S-21, the Pol Pot regime's extermination centre at Tuol Sleng, was discovered. And, as the continuing discovery of mass graves in Cambodia confirms, there is still more to be learnt of the country's national tragedy even now after more than forty years.

12

A World Of Refugees

Beginning in 1980, and quite without any plan to do so, I became closely involved with efforts to find a solution to the presence of more than one hundred and seventy thousand unwanted Cambodian refugees in Thailand. The fact that these Cambodians were in Thailand was part of a much wider refugee problem in Southeast Asia. There were, for instance, other refugees in Thailand who attracted much less attention in the world press—groups of hill people, Hmong and Yao, held in camps in the far north of the country, many of whom had been there for a decade after they had fled fighting in Laos. When I visited one of these northern camps at Chiang Khong close to the Mekong River in December 1979 I found only one aid worker present, a German doctor who spoke bitterly of how the refugees he looked after were forgotten by a world more preoccupied with the activities of the Soviets in Afghanistan. Then there was the growing number of refuges from Vietnam who continued to leave that country following the communist victory in 1975. Some of these refugees were in camps in Hong Kong and Macau; they were mostly ethnic Chinese. Thousands of other Vietnamese refugees were in a holding centre on the Indonesia island of Galang, in the Riau Archipelago.

Perhaps most remarkable of all were the Vietnamese refugees on the tiny island of Pulau Bidong off the coast of Malaysia. There, as I saw when I travelled the four hours by small boat out to Bidong from Kuala Trengannu, in 1980, some 40,000 refugees were clustered in a land area just over one square kilometre in size. They lived in primitive structures of up to three storeys in height, jumbled one against the other and built from material donated by aid groups and flotsam and jetsam that had washed on to this tiny island. The refugees had formed all manner of committees providing an "administration" for the island, an impromptu "police force" and a jail—an even smaller island to which wrongdoers were exiled. The whole place worked in a remarkably efficient fashion, not least as the refugees waged a constant war against rats. In every way the community on the island reflected the determination and resilience of the Vietnamese who had reached there after they fled from southern Vietnam following the communist victory of April 1975.

That there were refugees in all of these places, and in others, was a reflection of the enormous upheaval that had occurred following the end of the Vietnam War. More than forty years after that climatic moment it is difficult for those who did not live through the events of the time to realise how dramatic a period it was. To think only of some of the highlights in what occurred makes the point. The regimes in Cambodia and South Vietnam, both backed by the United States, has been defeated by their communist opponents in April-May 1975. The situation in Laos was more nuanced, but the accession to power of a communist regime in Laos at the end of 1975 meant that the whole of the region that had once been French Indochina was now under the control of regimes that embraced their own visions of communism. Then the Pol Pot regime that fought its way to power in 1975 was conquered in turn by the Vietnamese invasion of Cambodia that declared victory in January 1979. In response to this defeat of the Pol Pot regime, which had enjoyed the firm backing of Beijing, the Chinese then invaded northern Vietnam, beginning in February 1979, to punish the Vietnamese for their actions. All of these events generated waves of refugees. Viewed at the end of 1979 the overall situation offered little promise of an end to instability, only the promise of more refugees leaving their homes.

The "Cambodian Refugee Problem"

Although the overthrow of the Pol Pot regime in January 1979 was seen by most observers as a development to be welcomed, the manner in which this occurred, through the invasion of Cambodia by neighbouring Vietnam, posed geopolitical problems for the future that would not be resolved for more than a decade; that it also raised problems of international morality was another matter. More immediately, the end of the Khmer Rouge government was soon followed by a new and urgent challenge to the international community as Cambodia descended into a new and near-deadly period of chaos. One aspect of these developments was a major exodus of part of Cambodia's population into Thailand. It became common usage to speak of the events of this period as "the Cambodian Refugee Problem". (Technically, the Cambodians seeking refuge in Thailand were not refugees. In the eyes of the Thai government, which is not a signatory of the United Nations Refugee Convention, they were illegal immigrants.)

By the end of April 1979 the Vietnamese invaders had established control over Cambodia's previously depopulated towns and the main road system, but some tens of thousands of Cambodians remained under the control of the retreating Khmer Rouge forces in the west of the country. For the remainder of the population at this time their life was at first immeasurably better than it had been. Food was available and they were free to move about the country as they sought to return to their home villages. Then disillusionment began to set in. It became clear that the Vietnamese were in charge and intended to remain so. Next came rumours that the Vietnamese might embark on a forced resettlement program of their own within Cambodia. And international politics began to intrude in a dramatic fashion: the American government rejected the recommendation of its Bangkok embassy that urgent aid should be given to Cambodia and the Soviet Union appears to have urged its Vietnamese ally not to accept international assistance. The tragedy of this period of deliberate and shameful decisions, massive muddle and a general failure to appreciate just how complete the societal collapse of Cambodia was after the fall of the Pol Pot regime, meant that by mid-1979 the country was poised before a potential disaster of enormous proportions.

Fear of famine sparks an exodus

And now the fear of famine began to stalk the land. With the population that had been moved from their homes by the Khmer Rouge seeking to return to their villages, the normal pattern of the agricultural year was ignored so that there was little planting of rice at the beginning of the wet season in June. Stocks of grain were consumed without considerations for the future and draught animals were slaughtered for food. Whether true famine ever faced Cambodia's population in 1979 has been debated, with some observers doubting that this was the case. Perhaps the best judgment would be that the level of food deprivation varied greatly throughout the country and was acute in some areas. That there was genuine fear of famine is surely beyond dispute. Among those who suffered the worst within Cambodia were the many thousands who remained under the control of the rump Khmer Rouge forces. They had been held in desperately grim circumstances in remote regions in the west of the country, starved of food and still controlled by unrepentant cadres. It was Cambodians from this group who, in the closing months of 1979, were to be seen stumbling across the border into Thailand, skeletal in appearance and almost literally dying on their feet. By the end of 1979 more than 170,000 Cambodians had taken refuge in eastern Thailand, most in the region around the scruffy border town of Aranyaprathet, where they were accommodated into two hastily prepared camps at Khao I Dang and Sa Kaeo. At least 250,000 others—some estimates were of 400,000—had moved into what were termed "border agglomerations" along the Thai-Cambodian border. The disturbing, indeed in many ways shameful, details of this period are brilliantly captured in William Shawcross's *The Quality of Mercy: Cambodia, Holocaust and the Modern Conscience.*

This situation was an enormous challenge to the international community, to Thailand in particular, and to the United Nations High Commission for Refugees (UNHCR), which was the organization that by late 1979 faced finding some solution to an unprecedented problem. At one level a temporary solution had been found through the establishment of the official camps within Thailand's borders just mentioned—though even this "solution" was beset by a range of difficulties. The camp at Khao I Dang had no natural water on site, so as well as supplies of food water had to be trucked in. At Sa Kaeo, the camp site had previously been used for rice cultivation and digging latrines in the ground proved to be extremely difficult. But at least these were sites that were developed by an international agency. Much more problematic was the question of what the international community was going to do about the "unofficial" camps that straddled the Thai-Cambodian border. When I spent December 1979 and January 1980 in Thailand I saw something of the scale of the problem associated with the unofficial camps, first at Non Mak Moon (usually simply called Mak Moon) and later at Sok Sann.

Mak Moon and Sok Sann

At the time of my visits the sprawling and chaotic settlement at Mak Moon was a dominated by a self-proclaimed "marshal" Vong Atchivong and his associate "Prince" Norodom Soryavong. The former was in fact a notorious teak smuggler whose real name was Vann Saren. Incongruously, he received visitors wearing a pork pie hat and had a cross hanging from the string of pearls he had draped around his neck. The self-proclaimed "prince", who had no connection whatsoever with the Cambodian royal family, was in fact a French citizen named André Ukthal. Together in an atmosphere of desperate uncertainty, and with the help of a few hundred armed bully boys, these two men dominated the camp, bought and sold gems and gold at great profit for themselves, and claimed to be preparing to liberate Cambodia from the Vietnamese. This claim was a nonsense, but the fact these two rogues could exercise power as they did was a reflection of the general sense of disorientation, bordering on millenarianism, that prevailed among the hapless people they controlled for a period.

Vann Saren even showed he had some sense of the world away from the squalor of Mak Moon. Making my first visit to the camp in December 1979 I found the bizarre sight of a German film-maker at work filming a mass being celebrated by a Sino-Thai priest in a white soutane and a baseball cap, assisted by a grey-clad nun. The priest was ministering to a pathetic half dozen members of his faith who scarcely seemed much moved as they stood in the searing sun. The real satisfaction seemed to be associated with the filmmaker who told me, his eyes glinting in anticipation of the fee he could command, that the film would have a marvellous impact shown in wintery Germany at Christmas-time. And what's more, he told me, Vann Saren had only charged him a nominal sum to do his filming.

So I wondered, as I went to speak to Vann Saren, if I too was going to be asked to pay for an interview, but this was not the case. Instead, when the "marshal" found I was an Australian, he told me he was looking for support from the United States and Australia, indeed of "all the Western nations", and for an immediate monetary donation of $800 million. "Tell your prime minister, Mr Andrew," he went on, of our need for aid." He must have seen the doubt on my face for he asked, "Mr Andrew does hold power, doesn't he?" Told that, in fact, the prime minister was Mr Fraser, while Mr Peacock was the foreign minister, he was not abashed, saying, "Then tell Mr Fraser *and* Mr Andrew of our needs." He paused, as if Australia's constitutional arrangements remained a puzzle for him. Then he asked, "Who is the president of Australia?" When I started to speak of a governor general it was clearly all too much and Vann Saren firmly brought our conversation to an end by repeating that I should "tell Mr Andrew and Mr Fraser".

Quite a different atmosphere existed in the other border camp that I visited with a group of foreign observers, mostly journalists, in December 1979. This was the camp established at Sok Sann (Peace Village), located in a wooded valley on the Cambodian side of the Thai-Cambodian border in the Phnom Malai mountains, which are close to the boundary between the two countries. After reaching the border in the evening we first travelled in a trailer pulled by a tractor along a rough logging track, with an escort precariously perched on the front of the tractor with their Armalites and AK-47s. Then, when the track ended, it was necessary to make the rest of our journey on foot, along steep mountain paths. It was still dark when we reached our goal, but in the morning we found that we were in a long valley surrounded by hills covered with thick jungle, and crucially outside the control of the Vietnamese troops occupying Cambodia.

This was a base for the *Khmer Sereika*, or Free Cambodians, led by Son Sann, the man who had been Sihanouk's most trusted economic adviser in the 1960s. He had returned from exile in France, hoping to play a role in efforts to return Cambodia to independence from the occupying Vietnamese. With perhaps 3,000 men ready to follow his lead, and that of others, such as former general Dien Del, who were aligned with him,

Son Sann was establishing a politico-military force called the Khmer People's National Liberation Front (KPNLF). He was still the gracious men I had known two decades before, remembering me from that time and wryly contrasting the period when I had called on him as a minister in Phnom Penh with his situation in a remote jungle camp.

Spending two days at Sok Sann was a salutary introduction to what was to become a long period of moral ambiguity so far as finding a way to end Vietnam's occupation of Cambodia was concerned. With the Thai government determined to see an end to Vietnam's presence in Cambodia it was already making clear it would follow policies of self-interest no matter what the human costs of such policies might be. So, at Sok Sann, there had already been a heavy loss of life over the preceding months as there was a determination in Bangkok that medical supplies should be withheld from the camp until its leaders were ready to cooperate in the policies the Thais dictated. I was told that no fewer than 1,000 persons were said to have died because of this embargo on the arrival of medicines, most from tropical diseases. Those who were currently ill could be seen in the camp's "hospital", where they were attended by a young man who once had received two years of medical training in Phnom Penh—no one else in the camp had any medical training. Malaria and malnutrition were taking their toll, with some of the children in the hospital little more than skin and bone. Their heads were more like the skulls of the dead than those of healthy humans, while their arms and legs looked as if they could be snapped like twigs. They could have been figures in a Second World War photograph of prisoners in a liberated concentration camp. To look again at the photos I took then is to bring back a sense of the time that remains shocking.

Above all, I was struck by the terrible air of lassitude of the children in the makeshift hospital as they looked, uncomprehendingly, at us visitors.

Yet depressing as this camp was, when I spent time in the large, unofficial border camps close to Aranyaprathet only two months later, I found that it was possible to see much worse, not so much of malnutrition but of human squalor. But that experience was still to come, and for the moment my final memory of the visit is of the physically demanding trip out along the same mountain paths. This time I was carrying much of Neil Davis's camera equipment, for the famous Australian combat photographer who was part of the visiting group was struck down by malaria in the final stages of our visit.

13

Consulting for UNHCR

Shortly before I was due to travel back from Thailand to Australia in January 1980 I accepted an invitation from Zia Rizvi, then the senior UNHCR representative with responsibility for Thailand, to return and undertake a survey that might explain why so many Cambodians had either fled their country into Thailand or moved to the border camps, such as Mak Moon. What were their plans for the future? Were they seeking resettlement in third countries, and if not under what conditions would they return to Cambodia? What had been their experiences under the Pol Pot regime and to what extent did those experiences determine their current expectations? So after a brief time in Australia I returned to Thailand and began my work in February 1980 and handed in my report at the end of April. In retrospect many of the answers to the questions I set out to try and answer may now seem obvious, but that was not the case at the beginning of 1980.

Composing and conduction the survey

My problem was to find a way to reach some judgments that had general validity, given the large number of refugees involved. There were the two major camps, Khao I Dang and Sa Kaeo, and six additional small camps under UNHCR control in Thailand. In total the refugees in these official camps numbered in excess of 150,000 people. Separately there were three border camps, or agglomerations, at Nong Samet, Mak Moon and Nong Chan that had to be visited, since some of those living in these camps were believed to be planning to move into Thailand. While the total numbers involved could only be roughly estimated, particularly in relation to the border camps, there was general agreement that at least 250,000 Cambodians, and possibly as many as 400,000 had fled into or near to the Cambodian-Thai border.

I concluded that my principal aim should be to find out why Cambodians had fled their country, for unless this was clear there was no way of determining the circumstances under which they would return; the need to establish these circumstances rested on the well-founded assumption that there was little prospect that the majority of the refugees would be accepted for resettlement in third countries away from Thailand. And directly associated with this first question I further decided that it was vital to know the extent to which the refugees had direct experience of the Khmer Rouge's notorious readiness to execute its presumed enemies. This was not simply an academic issue since I surmised that such awful personal experiences had played their part in motivating the exodus. The killings and deaths of tens of thousands of people had to have had a terrible negative impact. And there was another point that I felt had to be addressed. Although few now questioned the fact of the Pol Pot regime's awfulness, there was a new line of left-wing commentary that needed to be assessed: the suggestion was being put about some on the political left in Western countries that "only" members of the Cambodian bourgeoisie had suffered seriously under the Khmer Rouge. Even without the evidence that I subsequently gathered this seemed at best a dubious and more likely a disgraceful proposition.

With Khao I Dang as my main base to test my assumptions, but planning to visit all of the seven other camps controlled by UNHCR, I developed a questionnaire to put to a sample of one hundred refugees that at least approximated Cambodia's pre-civil war demographic profile; I knew there was little possibility of establishing an exact replica of the actual profile of that period, when approximately ninety per cent of the population were peasants. Moreover, it was clear from a very preliminary survey carried out by UNHCR before the end of 1979 that Khao I Dang's population was not reflective of Cambodia's broad demographic profile, containing as it did a much higher proportion of educated people —this was less the case in Sa Kaeo, and in Mak Moon among the border agglomerations. So, consciously weighting my sample to minimise the number of educated and socially elevated respondents, I began a program of extended interviews with the able assistance of my interpreter, Ouch Samsan, with some interviews taking place entirely in Cambodian, some in a mixture of either French or English and Cambodian, and in a few cases in either English or French alone. The key questions in the interviews established the home bases of the refugees; why the refugees had taken the decision to leave Cambodia; whether close members of their families had been executed; whether they had ever seen executions taking place; and whether, or under what conditions, refugees were prepared to contemplate returning to Cambodia.

Each day I would drive from my base in Aranyaprathet to start work around seven in the morning, seldom concluding until late in the afternoon. It was a hot and tiring business, since before conducting each interview I had to be sure that I was developing a sample along the lines that seemed appropriate. So Ouch Samsan and I would move from hut to hut, checking about backgrounds in detail before actually embarking on the interview process. And beyond the tragedies that were so often revealed in the interviews, some were conducted in trying circumstances. This was particularly the case in the Sa Kaeo camp where many of the refugees were former Khmer Rouge soldiers whose officers maintained a strict control over them and sought to terrorise the remaining non-Khmer Rouge people in the camp. On occasion I would be conducting an interview only to have a former Khmer Rouge soldier forcibly seek to prevent my informant talking to me. Overall, the process took place in circumstances that were different from any previous experience I had ever had. I did not have any preconceptions about how a massive refugee operation of this kind would unfold, but I soon came to realise that international assistance to cope with such a massive human problem came in many forms. And no matter how hard I tried to remain emotionally detached, the raw facts retailed to me by the refugees were seldom less than disturbing and at times heartbreaking.

I had not been in Thailand in the early months of the international response to the Cambodian refugee influx in the latter part of 1979, but as William Shawcross makes clear in his book, *The Quality of Mercy*, almost all involved at this time—governments and NGOs—were found wanting in the face of the challenges the refugees represented. By time of the two and a half months I worked to complete my survey, starting in February 1980, UNHCR was acting vigorously at the forefront of the assistance program, with Zia Rizvi as a man of great energy pressing the effort forward. And that energy was matched and supplemented by the UNHCR representatives in the field, most notably Mark Malloch-Brown who had responsibility for the administration of Khao I Dang camp. As Lord Malloch-Brown today, he has written of this period in his book, *The Unfinished Global Revolution*, in which, very practically, he points to the importance, indeed necessity, of digging latrines as one of the earliest tasks in setting up a refugee camp.

In addition to UNHCR the International Committee of the Red Cross and the International Rescue Committee were prominent among major aid and assistance groups, with the former making up for serious missteps in the early stages of the crisis. But I was struck by the additional presence of what could only be described as a motley group of other aid organisations. These ranged from Christian evangelical missionaries to those whom the more experienced in international aid management called, derisively, "crisis groupies". All bustled about the camps, some making a genuine improvement in the lives of the refugees, others pursuing goals I found distasteful. To hear hymns being sung in Khao I Dang on any day of the week was a signal that the American evangelists were at work, seeking to convince their sadly gullible audiences that conversion to Christianity would ensure they would be selected for resettlement in the United States. Other developments were more sinister. Such was the readiness of a few "aid practitioners" to offer the promise of resettlement in return for sexual favours, while there were dubious programs to arrange adoption of unaccompanied children in both Switzerland and France—not always with certainty that their parents had vanished. Backbiting among the various aid groups that worked in the

UNHCR camps was common, as was a disturbing reluctance for many not to cooperate in their endeavours.

Good, bad or indifferent in their efforts, many of the expatriates of the aid groups could be seen at the end of each day in the limited eating opportunities in Aranyaprathet, notably at the less than stellar establishment that was ironically given the nickname "Maxim's". It was here from six in the evening that there was a passing parade of aid workers, including a French surgical team that turned up regularly still wearing their surgical scrubs, more often than not flecked with blood. The fact that the hospital in which they had been working was thirty kilometres distant from the restaurant and they had had plenty of time to change their clothes was not lost on the rest of the clientele. As in so many situations, the unreality of Aranyaprathet eventually came to assume a degree of "normality", so that after an indifferent meal and a couple of glasses of Singha beer it was not too difficult to accept the dormitory accommodation that I was initially afforded. Graduating to a room of my own was a very acceptable advance in privacy, though I was still far away from the "grandeur" of my second spell consulting for UNHCR the following year when I had the occupancy of a haunted house all to myself.

Ping Ling's Nightmare

The most remarkable surprise in the course of my work for UNHCR was encountering Ping Ling, an acquaintance from the time I spent in Phnom Penh in 1966, in Khao I Dang in March 1980. To find someone I knew, as I was walked through the rows of basic, tiny huts, with the pervasive camp smells of sweat, shit and marijuana in a camp of over 90,000 persons was an extraordinary event. But more extraordinary was Ping Ling's own account of his time in Cambodia during the Pol Pot regime. Always thin when I had known him in Phnom Penh all those years before, he had lost yet more weight during the Khmer Rouge years, so that I could count his ribs through his skin. But he was in surprisingly good health, and in good heart, too, as arrangements were already in train for him to go to Australia where he had relatives.

He had been forced out of Phnom Penh in the April 1975 exodus and put to work as an agricultural labourer in a region northeast of the capital, close to a town called Skoun. Then, after labouring for about two months, he was identified as an engineer and brought back to the capital to service the machinery that even the Khmer Rouge needed to run their odious government. Just how he was found and identified at this time while he worked in the rice paddies he never knew. His summary of the period he spent in Phnom Penh was that it was a "nightmare that lasted a thousand days" as he never knew whether he would survive. He did, but others who shared his barrack-like accommodation in the city were taken away to "seminars" never to return. There was never any doubt in his mind that they had joined the ever-growing list of men and women who were being executed.

What was striking about Ping Ling's experience was the fact that the bulk of his time under Khmer Rouge rule was spent in Phnom Penh. In this his account contrasts with the now substantial number of memoirs written by survivors of the period while Pol Pot and his associates were in power. For the most part these memoirs tell of survival in the forced work camps in the countryside. The very few exceptions to this pattern include Ong Thong Hoeung's, *J'ai cru aux Khmers rouges*, and Laurence Picq's, *Beyond the Horizon*, both of which focus on their authors' life in Phnom Penh.

As we sat and talked about the past, with the reassuring knowledge that he was shortly to travel to Australia, his account of those years had a terrible fascination. His sense was that the policies pursued under Pol Pot were the reflection of a fundamental determination to erase Cambodia's past, a judgment that seems to be verified by all of the evidence that has accumulated since the Khmer Rouge's overthrow at the beginning of 1979. Surprisingly, to me, he doubted whether the Khmer Rouge leaders had a clear picture of what was going on in the country as a whole, and he thought that when they travelled away from Phnom Penh they were taken to see what he called "model provinces". With the benefit of hindsight I doubt this was correct. But his judgment that, while the killing of former Lon Nol soldiers, "capitalists" and "intellectuals" was central policy, much of the other killing that took place was done by indoctrinated peasants, particularly young men seems at least partially justified by later evidence. These were people who had rallied to the Khmer Rouge before the victory over the Phnom Penh government in 1975 and then had become privileged to order life or death. As for his own experiences, he had only seen two people killed, and that was during the exodus from the capital; he had lost count of the number of people he knew were taken away to "seminars". To this account he added a macabre footnote. After the Vietnamese invasion took place and before he was able to escape into Thailand, he saw corpses exhumed from beneath the trees that the Khmer Rouge had planted around the grand market in Phnom Penh, the *Psar Thmei*—two corpses per tree. And in the course of a brief spell of manual labour near Kompong Speu he had seen a mass grave of recently killed victims.

In his role as a designated engineering "fixit man" for the regime living in Phnom Penh, he said that he ate reasonably well as he moved about in hospitals and ministries. But if he was assigned to carry out work in factories, where there was a predominance of people who had not been under Khmer Rouge control before 1975, then the food offered was poor. As for the leadership of the Khmer Rouge, he judged they lived well in Phnom Penh, and all later evidence supports his view. Interestingly, he was convinced of the important role played by the wives of Pol Pot and Ieng Sary, the two sisters Khieu Ponnary and Khieu Thirith, in a leadership that he believed to have been heavily factionalised.

Ping Ling had not waited long to escape from Cambodia after the Vietnamese had captured Phnom Penh on 7 January 1979, and he seized an opportunity to do so on 16 January. He then took seven days to reach the Thai border. He had been lucky, he said, managing to hitch rides on a range of vehicles and evading efforts made by the new rulers in Phnom Penh to bring him back for his technical capabilities.

Refugees drawing water from a primitive well at Mak Moon, January 1980.

Mak Moon camp in March 1980 with inhabitants reacting to a mortar shell falling on the edge of the camp as they bring in a man wounded in a previous shelling.

14

The Border Camps—Mak Moon, Nong Samet and Nong Chan

I did not conduct formal interviews in the border camps or agglomerations of Mak Moon, Nong Samet and Nong Chan, but I made several visits to each of them in an effort to gauge the attitudes held by the Cambodians living in them in the course of informal conversations. With a total of at the very least of 250,000 Cambodians sheltering in these camps, it was important to reach some conclusion about their intentions, just as I was seeking to do in relation to the populations in the camps run by UNHCR. There were also two other border camps that I did not have permission to visit. These were the camps at Phnom Chat and Ta Prik which housed Khmer Rouge soldiers and their followers The soldiers in these camps were already receiving support from the Thai military and they were later to become the chief Cambodian weapon of the forces opposed to the Vietnamese occupation. As for Sok Sann, which I had visited in December 1979, this camp was too far away for easy access as well as being seen by the Thais as part of their future plans to confront the Vietnamese occupation of Cambodia.

Visiting the border camps proved to be surprisingly easy, armed as I was with a Thai laissez-passer. I would drive to the last Thai military post close to the border, show my document, and then take my car closer to each camp before leaving it to walk the distances of between a few hundred metres to a kilometre to each camp's location. My presence seemed to cause little reaction among most of the camp dwellers and, with the exception of the events I describe in an account of my visiting Mak Moon, I seldom felt any concern for my safety—at least not in 1980, though there were a few unsettling moments such as the occasion when a clearly drugged soldier in Nong Samet pointed his rifle a me before dropping it down and allowing me to take a photo of him as he looked at me stone-faced. Walking on my own through the camps and stopping to talk to individuals, when it was clear they were ready to talk, gave the whole experience a rather unreal character. And it was this unreality that was most striking for the camps were both literally and figuratively in no man's land and beyond anyone's authority.

Mak Moon

When I had visited Mak Moon in December 1979 it had at least a vague sense of its being an organised grouping of people, even if it was under the dubious control of Vann Saren, the former teak smuggler and his supporters. By March that partial sense of order was deteriorating for the 25,000 persons I estimated were in the camp. The area around the grouping of huts at the centre of Mak Moon was littered with deep holes dug for water and all-too-apparent patches of ground used as open latrines. Piles of discarded plastic bags lay everywhere, as did heaps of rotting food being picked over by scraggy dogs. I quickly noted down some rough notes about the camp immediately after my visit, on 15 March 1980:

> A visitor arrives to find a scene from "The Inferno"—thousands, perhaps 4,000, of persons milling about in the heat and dust of a "free market" on the Thai side of the border, with very considerable evidence of cross-border trade as well as "immediate" trade in cloth, drinks, cigarettes, food, Thai whiskey, and much, much more. I observed a dozen heavily laden ox carts heading back to Cambodia as well as bicycles in their scores—heavily laden also . . . some with food in "Distributed by USA" bags.

> I was "received" by Vann Saren—purple silk shirt, cross now on a plain chain rather than hanging from a string of pearls . . . New headquarters now built and hung about with banners, "We heatly [sic] thank the Pope who pray for us every day." "Go down the Vietnamese." "We fear genocide."

> An event brought near panic. A rocket, claimed to be Vietnamese, fell about two kilometres from the camp, and was said to have killed four people, two were being brought in, one seriously hurt in a litter. Then mortars in the camp opened fire and a single M-16 shot into the camp brought people racing everywhere and motorbikes manned by two or three "soldiers" roared off to the camp's outskirts.

> The whole place is a particular vision of hell. A world gone quite mad. Filth, death and degradation. Millenarianism rife. Buddhist charms. "Soldiers" in bizarre dress.

> The final image of Mak Moon on this day was of a young boy carrying a huge cassette player through the filth of abandoned fields with their pervasive smell of shit, and with the cassette machine playing "My Blue Heaven".

When I attempted to visit Mak Moon four days later, on 19 March, I saw the results of an attack on the camp by factional opponents of Vann Saren. Frightened occupants of the camp were streaming away from fighting that had been taking place and I could hear the sounds of rapid gun fire as I stopped my car about 100 metres from the outskirts of the camp. When I asked what was happening I was told that as many as forty people had been killed in artillery fire directed on the camp. I had no way of knowing if this was true but the gunfire I could hear was that of small arms and not of any larger weapons. With no chance of being accepted into Thailand, the unhappy fugitives I saw fleeing had no choice but to return to Mak Moon once the fighting ended or to look for acceptance in one of the other border camps.

By the time I visited the camp again, on 6 April, its progressive deterioration had continued. The so-called soldiers seemed fewer in number, and most of those that were still there were grouped together drunk, and getting drunker in their "military" lines. On a previous visit I had notice that some of the "soldiers" were dressed as women, and now I noticed that among the drunken group there were some who had their faces daubed with rouge and their fingernails painted with nail polish. Overall numbers in the camp had fallen dramatically, probably to a quarter of the size I had observed three weeks before. If Mak Moon had any meaning now it was as a transit point for cross-border trade, and standing at the extreme eastern end of the camp I watched as an endless line of bicycle smugglers passed by without a break over fifteen minutes. That noted, Vann Saren and his associates were still running an exploitative foreign exchange operation

By the middle of April Mak Moon had been abandoned as the result of a final burst of factional fighting, first on 10 April and then two days later; Van Saren and his offsiders, like "Prince" Norodom Soryavong, had disappeared, probably having been killed; and the remaining 25,000 people who had been grouped there had dispersed, some returning to Cambodia, some going to the other unofficial camps at Nong Chan and Nong Samet.

Nong Samet (Camp 007)

The impression I gained when I visited Nong Samet, on 16 March 1980, was very different to that provided by Mak Moon. The camp had been affected by factional fighting in January, but by the time of my March visit it had an air of "normality," if it is possible to use that word about a settlement of perhaps 75,000 people living in temporary huts on the edge of a country occupied by the Vietnamese. This air of normality was the result, I concluded, because of the presence within Nong Samet of a significant number of members of Cambodia's pre-1975 educated class—not nearly as many as in Khao I Dang, but a sufficient number to make a difference. Although the nominal leader of the camp, In Sakhan, was a former captain in the Lon Nol forces, he appeared to have ceded much of the organization of the camp to a range of "committees"— these included gathering places for "Intellectuals," the existence of a folk dance troupe and another group forming a *théatre populaire*.

I was shown around the camp by Ton Vann Pchang, a former student at the Faculty of Fine Arts in Phnom Penh and who was introduced to me as the "Chef du Bureau de l'Information." An intelligent man, he recognised the fragility of the camp, and the fact that many in it would be ready to go to Khao I Dang, if the Thais would permit them. Others, he said, would prefer to be somewhere other than Nong Samet but were reluctant to think about the possibility of going to Khao I Dang, even if the were allowed to do so because it would mean they "had lost their freedom". Overall, Ton Vann Pchang said, there was a general lack of unity among the Cambodians currently living in the camp, except in wanting the Vietnamese to leave their country. There was not much to raise a smile about what I was seeing in Nong Samet, but I couldn't fail to do so when I was introduced to a former Phnom Penh cinema star from pre-war days. Smoking a pipe and with a bandana carefully knotted around his neck he managed to give the impression that he was "only resting", and introduced me to a number of young men whom he described, in the fashion of an impresario, as his *protégés*.

Nong Chan

The smallest of the border camps near Aranyaprathet was Nong Chan. Originally established by General Dien Del, who had later moved on to be with Son Sann at Sok Sann, the small base of the Khmer People's Liberation Front. Nong Chan then briefly became a base for another would-be warlord, Kong Sileah, an associate of Mak Moon's Vann Saren. By the time I first visited it on 15 March 1980, it had an estimated population of around 5,000, and owed its existence to its character as a distribution point for food, both for it and the other border camps and most importantly for the population inside Cambodia. On those days when food distribution took place the number in Nong

Chan increased sharply, to as many as 20,000 by my estimation. To the extent that anyone exercised authority over the camp it was international agencies, most importantly the ICRC. Indeed, it was widely known that a missionary turned ICRC representative, Robert Ashe, regarded Nong Chan as his personal fief.

In the eyes of some observers, and particularly in the view of the ICRC representatives, Nong Chan's role as a distribution point for food represented a breaking of the barriers the Vietnamese-backed regime in Phnom Penh has placed in the way of international aid to Cambodia. And there was an important measure of truth to this judgment. But there was another way of looking at Nong Chan's role, and my inclination was to adopt this alternative point of view. This other judgment was that a system of food distribution that depended on thousands of Cambodians travelling to the border, often for five or six days, in order to receive donations of food, could only be regarded as a palliative solution to a continuing problem. It also carried with it very obvious and desirable political overtones, from the point of view of he Thai authorities. For by distributing food through Nong Samet this became a way of reflecting the incompetence of the authorities in Phnom Penh. In short, opting for a system of food distribution through Nong Chan rather than finding a permanent solution to the existence of hunger was another instance of the compelling need to find a political solution to Cambodia's problems. And at this time the need for such a solution looked nowhere like being addressed.

Food distribution

Whatever the rights and wrongs of Nong Chan's existence, I was a fascinated observer of what took place on 16 March, one of the days when food distribution took place at the camp. I arrived around 10.30 in the morning by which stage I estimated that there were at least 20,000 people waiting in disciplined lines for the distribution to take place—this was dramatic increase from the 5,000 I had seen the day before. Packed tightly together, they were standing in the harsh sunlight of a cloudless day, strangely quiet apart for an occasional hoarse cough. It was if to talk could put at risk the food supplies they waited for. And as the crowd waited in their lines Robert Ashe drove up and down the assembly, standing in a Land Rover, very much the general reviewing his troops. I could readily see why his critics argued that much of this procedure was an ego trip for him. Around eleven o'clock a convoy of twenty rice trucks arrived in a vast cloud of dust and carrying their cargo of rice bags, each bag containing one hundred kilograms of rice. With surprising speed the bags were unloaded, but still the lines of waiting Cambodians remained in place. Then, at a signal from Ashe, and with an extraordinary show of discipline, groups of six Cambodians at a time came forward to take their bags. It was a remarkable sight, the whole scene shrouded in dust, as once they had their bags the majority set off immediately back into Cambodia with loaded ox carts and bicycles.

15

The Survey Results

By the second week of April 1980 I concluded that I had done as much as was possible in terms of my interviewing program and the more informal assessments I had been making in terms of the border camps. I had conducted the bulk of my survey in Khao I Dang, but had also conducted interviews in Sa Kaeo, and six other locations north and south of Aranyaprathet. Now was the time to write up my report to UNHCR and I left the dust and heat of the area around Aranyaprathet for the seaside location of Songkhla in southern Thailand. There, over a period of four days I wrote a report running to 80 pages. In it I noted that the results of my program of interviews could be quickly summarised. Overall, the refugees in UNHCR's camps and those in the border camps had left Cambodia because they feared for their lives or freedom, or both, under the Vietnamese occupation. This fear was heightened by what they had experienced while the Khmer Rouge regime had still been in power. Among the one hundred individuals whom I interviewed, 40 reported instances of the execution of close family members to a total of 88 persons; there were 33 reports of the execution of other family members; while there were 20 reported instances of the death of close family members through hunger or disease. No fewer than 42 persons reported having personally seen executions taking place—this figure included an admission of having taken part in killings from a self-admitted Khmer Rouge soldier. Against this background, only one person whom I interviewed indicated a readiness to return to Cambodia without any qualification. Among the remainder of the sample 63 individuals expressed an interest in returning subject to various qualifications; 34 said they had no interest in returning while two interviewees expressed no opinion.

Such a summary of my findings gives little sense of the human drama of each interview. Take the case of the second-last refugee I interviewed, in Buriram camp in northeastern Thailand, well away from Aranyaprathet. It was difficult to believe that she was only thirty-five years-old. She had the face of a haggard old woman who, when she spoke to me in impeccable French, showed the gummy, broken-toothed look that I had become accustomed to seeing among the refugees. She wept as she told me that her husband had been executed, as had her brother and sister. Her sister's two children had died of hunger, and by her count no fewer than twenty of her brother-in-law's family had been killed by the Khmer Rouge. I had no doubt about the accuracy of her account, but I asked if she had seen the executions she had just recounted. And to my lack of surprise the answer was no, for it had become clear that part of the terror that the Khmer Rouge visited upon the population was frequently to kill their victims away from observation.

But this was not always the case, as I found with several of the refugees I interviewed, and none more strikingly so than the account given to me a man who had one day been tapping juice high up under the fronds at the top of a sugar palm. Hearing cries in the distance, but within his line of sight, he looked down to see Khmer Rouge cadres executing about a hundred people before throwing their bodies into a bomb crater. And there was the man who told me of how he had seen a primary school teacher put to death by having his throat cut slowly with a crude saw made from a palm frond. As this took place, the man told me, the victim "cried out like an animal". Then there was the old woman who had no hesitation in telling me that she came from a prosperous peasant family, who emphasised her account of an execution she had witnessed with sharp gestures of her hand as she described victims being bludgeoned to death with hoes and staves.

In compiling my report for UNHCR I did not try to extrapolate a figure for the total cost in lives of the Khmer Rouge regime on the basis of the deaths reported to me. My concern was to document why the refugees were in Thailand and whether they might return to Cambodia at some future date, and under what conditions. The most important conclusion I offered was that there could be no settlement of the refugee situation without a political settlement of what had become known as "the Cambodia Refugee Problem". As I wrote in my report, "The refugees exist because of political developments in the past. The solution to their plight cannot be separated from a political settlement in the future." Today that may seem a very obvious conclusion, but it was far from clear at the time I offered it when it was thought there could be a quick end to the refugee problem.

I had another recommendation in my report to UNHCR about which I felt deeply. At a time when the Thai authorities were steadily developing their efforts to establish a Cambodian military force able to confront the Vietnamese occupiers of Cambodia it was clear that they would both support the rump of the Khmer Rouge still within Cambodia and were looking for means to reinforce that group. Against this fact, I was aware that the Thais were considering facilitating the return to Cambodia of the population of Sa Kaeo, Khmer Rouge and non-Khmer Rouge refugees alike. So I wrote, "I make no apology for recording in this report my strong personal judgment that the implementation of any policy that leads to the non-Khmer Rouge population of Sa Kaeo being returned to Kampuchea under the control of the camp's Khmer Rouge leadership and its associates would be an act of the most profound immorality."

* * *

Having already noted that I did not try to reach a conclusion on the total number of deaths that occurred during the Pol Pot regime in my report to UNHCR, it's still worth considering the extent to which the statistics derived from my interviewing sample reflected the human costs of those years—it says something about the world of scholarship that for some time there was sharp disagreement about the true costs involved. Now, there is general agreement that something of the order of 1.75 million Cambodians died who would have lived if the Khmer rouge had not been in power. Some thoughtful analysts would suggest that a figure of 2 million is more likely. Of those who died, perhaps as many as half a million died through executions. Going back to my interviews in 1980, an extrapolation of the figures resulting from my questionnaire would have placed the death toll under the Khmer Rouge regime at a million and a half persons. With figures of this size there is a temptation, which surely should be resisted, to suggest that the cost in human lives was so great that it is scarcely important to know the exact numbers involved. For it remains important to remember that a loss of 1.75 million lives in the Pol Pot years between 1975 and 1979 means that in those years nearly a quarter of the Cambodian population died who otherwise would have lived.

My consulting for UNHCR led me to reflect on many things, not least my own good fortune, so very different from the life led by the refugees. Perhaps most importantly of all it brought to me the realisation that the loss of life that occurred while Pol Pot and his associates ruled Cambodia had as deep a meaning for outsiders, such as I was, as it undoubtedly did for the Cambodians. It was not a realisation that resulted from comparing what happened in Cambodia with other tragedies, though this could certainly be done. What set the loss of life in Cambodia apart was the fact that ethnic Cambodians visited this awfulness upon their own compatriots. That this could happen revealed the depth of evil—that much over-used word—that could occur when a theoretical idea could be transformed into an unrestrained reality that deformed both attitudes and actions. It was an idea that gave those in power the right to take life for the "good" of the state, not in tens or hundreds of their compatriots, but in hundreds of thousands.

> Note: My report to UNHCR was never released publicly but I subsequently published an academic paper covering its findings and providing detailed statistical analysis of my interview program. The reference for this paper is as follows: Milton Osborne, "The Indo-Chinese Refugee Situation: A Kampuchean Case Study," in Charles A. Price, ed., *Refugees: The Challenge of the Future*, Academy of the Social Sciences in Australia, Fourth Academy Symposium, 3-4 November 1980, Canberra, pp. 31-68

Border smuggler, Nong Samet. March 1980.

(below) Cambodian refugees waiting for rice distribution, Nong Chan border camp March 1980.

16

UNHCR, Again - 1981

When I made a short research visit to Thailand at the beginning of 1981, it was clear that the "Cambodian Refugee Problem" that had been at the heart of my work for UNHCR in 1980 was far from resolved. Increasingly it was caught up in the geopolitical rivalries, and moral ambiguities that had followed the Vietnamese invasion of Cambodia. Vietnam's invasion had rid Cambodia of the tyrannical Pol Pot regime, but it had done so through a cross-border conquest that raised deep problems for the international community. A range of governments of quite different political systems looked askance at a foreign-engineered overthrow of an established government, no matter how awful that government had been. And nowhere were the issues flowing from Vietnam's invasion of Cambodia more a matter for concern than in Thailand.

In 1981, the controlling Vietnamese regime was still struggling to shape a protégé Cambodian administration. When Henry Kamm of *The New York Times* had spoken to Hanoi's proconsul in Cambodia, Ambassador Ngo Dien, the year before, the ambassador had said that the members of the Heng Samrin regime the Vietnamese had installed in Phnom Penh after defeating the Khmer Rouge were "below the standard required by their task". And despite efforts by the Vietnamese to promote the idea that the Cambodian regime in Phnom Penh was an independent government, it was clear to all but the most biased observers that this was not the case. The last thing the Vietnamese and their Cambodian associates wanted was the return of hundreds of thousands refugees, many of whom could be expected to be hostile to the regime now based in Phnom Penh. So if there was to be any return of refugees it had to be on Phnom Penh's terms. And those terms involved the recognition of the Vietnamese-supported Heng Samrin government of the People's Republic of Kampuchea (PRK).

Mirror images ?

It's tempting to describe the Thai attitude towards the continuing presence of some 150,000 Cambodian refugees on its territory, plus at very least 250,000 located in border camps who were sustained by supplies coming to them from Thailand, as a mirror image of the views held in Phnom Penh. For like the Vietnamese-backed Phnom Penh regime the Thai government saw political advantage in continuing to have Cambodian refugees on its territory. But the metaphor only works if it is noted that the image in the mirror was distinctly distorted. On the one hand the Thais were ready to see the voluntary return of Cambodians back to their country, but only if the refugees in question ended up in areas out of the control of Phnom Penh: this meant their returning to areas still under the rump of the Khmer Rouge or under the very limited territory under the control of Son Sann's Khmer People's National Liberation Front. On the other hand, while the Thais claimed they were ready to talk about a broader program of repatriation of Cambodian refugees, they were only prepared to countenance such a program if it did not involve recognition of the regime the Vietnamese had installed in Phnom Penh. In short, public statements from Thai officials apart, keeping a substantial population of Cambodian refugees under their control in Thailand suited their broader interests. And in holding to this position the government in Bangkok had the support of its fellow ASEAN members in refusing to recognise the regime in Phnom Penh. Additionally, and most importantly, it also had the backing of Beijing and, with some embarrassment, of Washington and Canberra.

This "heads I win tails you lose" attitude on the part of the Thais reflected the blunt fact that that they regarded the Cambodian refugees as pawns to be moved about the Thai-Cambodian chessboard solely in Thailand's interest. And while some Western commentators ridiculed the Thai concerns with the presence of Vietnamese in overall control of Cambodia, I had no doubt that these concerns were genuine, if frequently exaggerated. After all, Thai determination that Cambodia should not be under the sole control of a potentially hostile Vietnam was an attitude that had been present in Bangkok's thinking for at least two hundred years. In the nineteenth century it was an attitude that had almost seen the disappearance of Cambodia in the long-running wars between Thailand and Vietnam before the two countries agreed that Cambodia should be a buffer state between them, paying tribute to both Bangkok and to Hue. The colonial control France extended over Cambodia from the 1860s had put traditional rivalries into a deep freeze only for these to emerge again once when Cambodia became independent in 1953. And tensions were heightened after a single government in Vietnam gained control of the whole of that country's territory in 1975.

UNHCR's attitude to this complicated set of circumstances was essentially straightforward, but no more likely to succeed because of this fact. Its senior officials hoped to find a way that would see the bulk of the Cambodian refugees in Thailand, or in the border camps, returned to Cambodia as soon as possible. While they welcomed the programs that accepted resettlement of Cambodians that were operated by countries such the United States and France, and to a lesser extent Australia and Canada, the leadership of UNHCR recognised that the majority of the refugees would not be accepted for resettlement in a third country. And they were conscious of the fact that the international community had a limit to the amount of money it was prepared to spend to maintain the status quo. But how might the return of the refugees be achieved, given the attitudes held in Bangkok and Phnom Penh, or perhaps more correctly in Hanoi? Once again, and at the invitation of Zia Rizvi, I returned to Thailand at the end of February 1981 carry out a survey among the Cambodian refugees with the aim of finding out who among them would consider returning to Cambodia and under what conditions.

This time the survey was to be both larger and less in-depth in character by comparison with my 1980 efforts. It was to be carried out among Cambodians identified as peasants and low-level urban workers who had not been part of the previous regime's military forces, and it was to be completed in little more than two weeks. The exclusion of formerly more prosperous refugees from the survey endorsed my presumption, which UNHCR accepted on the basis of my previous report, that if there were refugees who ready to consider returning they would not be from the more educated or previously more prosperous refugees. Nor was it likely that former members of the military who had fought for the Phnom Penh regime before 1975 would be interested in opting to return. It was apparent that they saw their previous military service as making them likely to be regarded as potential opponents of the new regime the Vietnamese were mentoring. In any event, it was scarcely likely that these were persons who would be accepted by the Phnom Penh authorities.

So the rationale behind Zia Rizvi's invitation was clear. It would only be by showing that there was a body of refugees who were ready to return to Cambodia, with or without conditions, that matters could be moved off the top dead centre position in which they were stuck. My task was to see if such a group of refugees did exist. It was a task I believed was morally justifiable, though I was aware there were likely to be opponents of this view in the Thai political and military establishments. The suggestion that there was any real alternative to eventual repatriation of these former farmers and low-level workers to their homeland was either romantic or political. It certainly was not practical. Ultimately there was no other choice but for them to return or remain indefinitely in camps in Thailand. But if return was to be on a voluntary basis it was vital to find out on what basis they were ready to do this, and what matters were of concern to them.

The survey

My base once again was in Aranyaprathet, though this time accommodated much more grandly, by comparison with the year before, on my own in a large wooden house that, because it was allegedly "haunted", UNHCR was able to rent cheaply. I never encountered any ghosts and concluded that the supposed haunting stemmed from the fact that as the wooden structure of the house cooled in the evening the creaking noises this involved were unusually loud. But those noises were not as loud as the rock band that played until after midnight each night as the population of Aranyaprathet celebrated their hot season festival in the grounds of the Buddhist *wat* immediately behind the house. Their favourite numbers were from Boney M, particularly "Rivers of Babylon" and "Daddy Cool". I checked and found that none of the band members spoke English, but they had learnt the words to the songs perfectly and sang them without missing a beat. I can still hum the tunes of both numbers.

Over two weeks I interviewed a total of 205 Cambodian refugees who fell into the peasant, or farmer, and low-level urban worker category. The largest number, 155, were in Khao I Dang, still the biggest concentration of refugees in Thailand, with smaller numbers interviewed at camps in Ban Kaeng (Sa Kaeo), 30, and Kamput, 20. (I also visited and interviewed 24 people at the two camps located at Mairut.) The fact these camps were essentially transit bases for individuals who had been accepted for resettlement in the United States meant that there was no interest in discussing returning to Cambodia.) In addition, I carried out informal interviews in the unofficial border camps at Nong Samet and Nong Chan, since there were still upwards of two hundred thousand refugees resident in these camps and it was important to know whether their existence had any bearing on the attitudes of refugees in camps within Thailand's territory under UNHCR auspices.

This was a hurried process, with an average of more than twenty refugees interviewed each day, and I could not have carried the survey out if it had not been for the extremely able help I received from my interpreters. It was vital at the beginning of each interview to make clear that I was not in a position to decide what would happen to an interviewee in the future. It was difficult to know whether this was fully accepted and understood by those interviewed, but the fact that there was real variance from individual to individual in the way in which they responded to my questions suggested that, overall, it was. Once again, and as had been the case the previous year, my days were long and I was more than ready to return to my "haunted" house after a quick meal washed down by a beer at "Maxim's" to fall asleep, even with the Boney M wannabees playing in the *wat* compound behind me.

It was clear from this new survey that, as had been the case the year before, contemporary developments in Cambodia dominated refugee thinking about their country. The horrors of the Pol Pot period were fixed in their mind, but it was apparent that there was a widely present fear of what it would mean to return to a Cambodia controlled by Vietnam. There were varying degrees of understanding about the extent to Vietnamese control but an almost universal conviction that any form of Vietnamese domination of their country was bad. This attitude was not surprising to me. For while some left-wing inclined commentators have tried to discount the existence of ingrained ethnic antipathy towards Vietnamese among Cambodians of all social classes, my judgment was and is that the evidence is overwhelming for the existence of this feeling. It is a feeling fuelled by folk memories from the nineteenth century period of Vietnamese domination of their country that involved attacks on the Cambodian monarchy and harsh exploitation of the peasantry. And it was exacerbated by the role played by Vietnamese who worked for the French in Cambodia during the colonial period. They were seen as surrogates for the French and resented for their tendency to lord it over the Cambodians with whom they dealt. But while it was apparent that thinking about their homeland was a dominant theme in the minds of refugees, the extent of detailed and accurate knowledge about developments there was limited. Indeed, I reached the conclusion that it was almost universally inaccurate and notably out-of-date.

The survey's conclusions

In contrast to the attitudes that I had encountered in 1980, when there was a widespread feeling among refugees that living in a camp was tolerable for an indefinite time to come, it was now apparent that the limitations of camp living were affecting attitudes. Interestingly, this changed attitude was now present among refugees who were visibly better fed and less obviously troubled by the past than had been the case with those I interviewed the year before. This change in feeling was now combined with the growing realisation, particularly for the occupational groups I was interviewing this time, that they had little chance of resettlement in a third country. They knew the kinds of refugees who were succeeding in their aim of gaining such resettlement—educated, formerly prosperous and often Sino-Khmer—and they recognised they did not fall into that category. So a key question became, under what circumstances would these formerly less prosperous members of Cambodia's population consider returning to their homeland? The answer for 46 per cent of the refugees was that they were ready to return if UNHCR assured them it was safe to do so. Another 24 per cent indicted a readiness to return with an assurance of safety from UNHCR, but added to that a series of qualifications of various kinds. These percentages left some 18 per cent of those interviewed who stated that they would continue to seek resettlement in a third country, while the remainder indicated they were prepared to stay in Thailand indefinitely.

Having presented these figures to UNHCR, I went on to make a number of recommendations while recognising that some of these might not be politically acceptable to the Thai government or practical from UNHCR's point of view. Central to my recommendations was the proposal that UNHCR should indeed be ready to provide the assurance that the refugees sought: that it would be safe to return. In order to be able to provide this assurance UNHCR would have to establish what areas of Cambodia were safe and subsequently find some way to monitor what happened to the returnees. For UNHCR to be able to act in this way would require the agreement of the authorities in Phnom Penh, and I recognised the difficulty this involved. And I concluded, "The recommendations are also made in the light of the judgment I offered at the end of my previous, April 1980, report: "time is not on the side of those seeking a solution to the Kampuchean refugee problem." As events were to show, this conclusion was all too correct.

The border camps, again

Returning to Nong Chan and Nong Samet—Mak Moon had now ceased to exist as a settlement of any significance—I found events over the nearly twelve months since my last visits had brought about substantial change to these camps. Nong Samet was much smaller in size and Nong Chan remained much the same, but now both camps had become much more clearly political in character with activity linked to Son Sann's Khmer People's National Liberation Front present in both. This said, in conversations I had in these camps I found there was considerable scepticism about the extent to which the KPNLF could ever play much a role in efforts to dislodge the Vietnamese from Cambodia. As before, Nong Samet was marked by efforts to recreate something of a "normal" society, again with a camp "administration", schools and traditional dance groups. There was nothing equivalent in Nong Chan where the sense of fragility was very much present.

In Nong Chan, as I found on one notable occasion, the fact that the population within this camp was anti-Vietnamese in orientation did not mean there was no rivalry among the various armed groups that used it as a base. And so it was when, in moving through this unofficial camp, I was suddenly on the edge of a firefight taking place on its southeastern perimeter. Time spent lying in a convenient ditch solved the problem as the shooting ceased after about ten minutes. It was the only time in my association with the refugee camps that I actually felt truly afraid rather than, as I had on a few other occasions, somewhat anxious about personal safety.

As before, there were other border camps that I did not visit: most strikingly those of the Khmer Rouge. By this stage it was apparent that ASEAN, with Thailand and Singapore in the vanguard, were ready to rely on the remaining forces of the Khmer Rouge to head their military efforts to oust the Vietnamese from Cambodia. This was a policy that had open support from China and more clandestinely from the United States and, eventually, the United Kingdom. I have already referred to the ambiguities of this period and none was more glaring than the recourse made to the Khmer Rouge as a foreign policy instrument.

Thai Reactions

After considering my report, UNHCR chose to make it the basis for an approach to the Thai authorities seeking their permission to arrange the repatriation of a trial group of between 20,000 and 30,000 Cambodian refugees back to Cambodia. (I had not, in fact, recommended a specific number of refugees for repatriation in my report to UNHCR but as Mark Malloch-Brown, who was continuing to play a major role for UNHCR in Thailand, wrote to me later the figures of between 20,000 and 30,000 became known subsequently known as "the Osborne figures".) At the same time, copies of my report were leaked to the domestic and international press. The net result, which involved some direct questioning of both UNHCR's and my own integrity by authorities in Bangkok, was a Thai refusal to accept the validity of the survey and a decision to leave the refugees where they were.

So far as the Thais were concerned, the refugees' future had to be considered in terms of Bangkok's refusal to recognise the PRK government the Vietnamese had installed in Phnom Penh. This meant, for the Thai authorities, that the suggestions contained in my report and put forward by UNHCR were unwelcome at best and possibly malign in their intent. So, the secretary-general of the Thai National Security

Council, Squadron Leader Prasong, was quoted in the *Bangkok Post*, on 15 April 1981, as saying that the proposal to repatriate Cambodian refugees was "political". It was "meant to provide manpower for the Heng Samrin regime in Phnom Penh. The UNHCR, I [Prasong] believe, intends to please the Vietnamese who have set up the regime with armed forces and are now trying to conduct elections to try and legitimise the regime." And the same theme was taken up in a *Nation Review* editorial on 16 April, with the observation that "It is possible that the UNHCR representatives, when they acted as Gallup or Harris pollsters, loaded the question [as to whether refugees wanted to return to Cambodia]. They might have prefaced their question by saying that all is calm in Kampuchea except for minor skirmishes along the border . . . And if such a loaded question is asked, the refugees will naturally say they want to go back."

This was far from the end of Cambodian refugee story, but it was the end of my involvement in it. Attitudes within the Thai "establishment" became more complex with the passing years, as some officials, even within the military, reached the conclusion that repatriation of Cambodians would, after all, be in their country's interest. But as conflict continued in Cambodia throughout the 1980s, with anti-Vietnamese forces ranged against the Phnom Penh regime with its Vietnamese backers, the bulk of the refugees in Thai camps remained there. It was not until the Paris Peace Accords relating to Cambodia, of October 1991, that a program of repatriation was finally drawn up and implemented. Arable land was offered to the largely peasant refugees who had remained in the camps or, alternatively, provisions of money, food and household utensils. Most of the refugees opted for the latter choice.

The operation of returning so many refugees was massive in its scale, with the average number of refugees returning each week exceeding 30,000. Buses and trucks to a total of more than 450 were used in the operation that continued for several months. And once again UNHCR was at the forefront in overseeing the refugees' return, working close with the United Nations Development Program as new schools were built, water points constructed and health centres established. Like the broader Cambodian settlement itself, it was a remarkable achievement.

Khmer People's National Liberation Front soldier, Nong Samet camp, February 1981. High on drugs, he had pointed his rifle at me just before I took this photograph.

Vietnamese border slogan reading in translation 'The two peoples of Vietnam and China are friends forever.' It had clearly been recently repainted after the Vietnam-China border war of early 1979. Photograph taken in August 1981.

NHÂN DÂN HAI NƯỚC
VIỆT NAM - TRUNG QUỐC
MÃI MÃI LÀ BẠN BÈ.

17

Finding a way back to Vietnam and Cambodia

Shortly after I took up an appointment at the Australian National University in Canberra, in 1979, I called at the Vietnamese embassy to ask whether I could be issued a visa to visit Vietnam. I had never been to the northern section of the country, or indeed to any part of it since I had made my last visit in 1971. Now, as an external observer I was aware of the difficulties the government in Hanoi faced in making the transition from waging a war to managing peace and I very much wanted to make my own judgments on what was happening.

The difficulties the Hanoi government faced were abundantly apparent to the outside world in the growing outflow of refugees that had followed the communist victory in 1975 and which had accelerated after 1978. But concentration on this issue, important as it was, risked diverting attention from the other problems confronting the Vietnamese leadership. At the most fundamental level there was the cost in lives exacted by the Vietnam War. In southern Vietnam alone it was estimated that 16 per cent of the population had been killed or wounded, while 57 per cent of the population had been made homeless in the years between 1965 and 1974. Then there were the staggering costs in lives and damaged infrastructure in the north. With its plans to establish a "socialist economy" throughout the whole of Vietnam, the government was encountering a growing range of difficulties, not least as the result of natural disasters—first drought and then floods. And in the face of these ever-growing difficulties the government found it simply did not have the trained personnel to deal with post-war reconstruction. Plans for "New Economic Zones" were hampered not just by these managerial problems but additionally by the reluctance of former urban residents to exchange life in the cities for the rigours of working in pioneer agricultural settlements. Hoped-for international aid turned out to be much smaller in quantity than anticipated, and donors found that what they did provide was held up by bureaucratic delays. And misguided expectations that the United States would feel some obligation to assist Vietnam were quickly dashed.

Then, to add to all of these problems there had been the fundamentally irrational policies of the Pol Pot regime in Cambodia, which had led to the Phnom Penh government embarking on cross-border raids into Vietnam during 1977. These raids were a reflection of deep-seated ethnic antipathy, blended with irredentist longings to regain territory that had passed out of Cambodian control centuries before. And they involved grossly unrealistic estimations of the capacity of the small Cambodian armed forces to match the larger, better-equipped and battle-hardened Vietnamese army. In the official view of the Khmer Rouge leadership, as it set out in the regime's *Livre Noir* (Black Book) shortly before its overthrow, for Phnom Penh the nature of the Vietnamese was "that of an aggressor, an annexationist and a swallower of the territory of other countries". So in the minds of the Khmer Rouge leaders attacking such a country was entirely justified, if in the view of almost all other observers such a step was wildly irrational given he imbalance in power between Vietnam and Cambodia. When the Phnom Penh government disregarded the warning given to them by a short-term Vietnamese military incursion into Cambodia in December 1977, the stage was set for a full-scale Vietnamese invasion to overthrow the Khmer Rouge regime.

It came year later, with Vietnamese tanks entering Phnom Penh on 7 January 1979, just two weeks after their offensive had begun on Christmas Eve. The Vietnamese gloss on these developments was given by Premier Pham Van Dong just before Phnom Penh fell. It was a reference to the Vietnamese view of what might have been, couched in the language of socialist amity that had long since vanished: "Having at heart the militant solidarity and fraternal friendship between the two peoples, we have shown extreme patience . . . In the face of this serious situation our armed forces have been compelled to take action."

Defeating the main Khmer Rouge forces had not proved difficult, but it brought the almost immediate response of China's incursion into northern Vietnam as a "punishment" for Hanoi's gross temerity in acting against a Chinese client. For, as *The People's Daily* pronounced, "in dealing with the Vietnamese authorities restraint and forbearance were an invitation to more bullying". The Vietnamese took understandable pride in fighting the Chinese invaders to a standstill, with the Chinese forces withdrawn after a month but only after they had inflicted considerable damage on the infrastructure of Vietnam's most northerly provinces. So by the end of 1979 Vietnam's problems were considerable. It had an occupation force of 50,000 troops in Cambodia who had to be maintained at heavy cost and were beginning to sustain casualties, not least from malaria; an economy in great difficulties; and little external support beyond that afforded by the Soviet Union. Yet while few external observers thought that it would collapse, debate turned on how the government in Hanoi might find some way to reverse or eliminate the negative factors that seemed likely to be holding sway for some time to come. There was obviously much to learn if my hopes to visit Vietnam were ever realised.

Breakthrough

Throughout 1979 and 1980 the Vietnamese in their Canberra embassy were polite but firm in their negative responses to my requests for a visa. They were also, it was clear, well informed about my activities in promoting discussion of and writing about refugee issues—I had been closely involved in a major conference on Indochinese refugees at the Australian National University in 1979 and had been publishing articles on this issue in a number of journals and newspapers including *The Far Eastern Economic Review*, *The Bulletin* and *The Age*. And after 1980 they knew of my work as a consultant for UNHCR. My wish to obtain a visa, I was told, would be given favourable consideration if I were to become a member of the Australian–Vietnam Friendship Society. My reply, equally polite and firm, was that I was not, in the terms that the embassy and that society embraced, "a friend of Vietnam". I was anxious to visit

Vietnam as an independent scholar and writer, not as an acknowledged supporter of the regime. I was never quite sure how well my position was understood. And so for two years I made no progress in my hopes to visit Vietnam, nor indeed Cambodia, though in relation to this latter country I had let out some nightlines through various international organisations and NGOs in the hope that my interest in making a visit might be brought to the attention of the regime in Phnom Penh.

The first sign that attitudes towards my visa requests might be changing came in early July 1981, when I received an envelope posted from Bangkok, on 24 June, and bearing the address and logo of the International Committee of the Red Cross. The envelope had no message from the ICRC, but it contained a carbon copy of a "TELEGRAMME", dated 17 June, from Hor Nam Hong, the Vice-Minister for Foreign Affairs in the People's Republic of Kampuchea (Cambodia) government, with a single sentence of text: "May come Phnompenh third week of June." This unexpected and slightly mysterious document was not at any stage matched by my receiving an actual telegram. A few days later as I weighed up how it might be possible to accept this invitation in a situation in which there were no diplomatic relations between Australia and Cambodia, I received a telephone call from the Vietnamese embassy. The embassy, I was told would be happy to issue me with a visa and could I please come to discuss arrangements for visiting Vietnam with the ambassador.

What had happened? I think it was clear that somewhere in the Hanoi government there was a recognition that closing Vietnam's doors to those who were not its supporters was a mistaken policy, one that did little to bring a Vietnamese story to the outside world from observers who were not closely identified with the regime. So, buoyed by this apparent change of heart I duly made an appointment to see the Vietnamese ambassador. In talking to him I decided that polite audacity might be rewarded and after indicating my gratitude for his government's readiness to grant me a visa, I asked whether I might specify particular issues I would like to explore and people I would like to meet during my visit. The ambassador assured me that he would do his best to see that my requests were treated positively. In the light of this assurance I said that I would be grateful if it would be possible to interview the Vietnamese foreign minister, Nguyen Co Thach. And, so far as travel was concerned, in addition to visiting both Hanoi and Saigon, or Ho Chi Minh City, I was particularly interested in visiting the northern border region that had sustained damage during the 1979 Chinese invasion. The ambassador assured me that he would recommend that these requests should be met —as indeed they eventually were. And then he said, "While we are not the government of Cambodia, I believe we could assist you in arranging a visit to that country."

Shortly before I left to fly to Bangkok, and then on to Hanoi, the ambassador invited me to a one-on-one dinner to assure me that my program was all in hand, including arrangements to meet my particular requests. We talked quite late into the night and towards the end of the dinner he told me of how he had been at the battle of Dien Bien Phu as a political commissar. We both reflected on the heavy losses suffered by both the Vietnamese and the French in that epic siege with the ambassador, suddenly transported back to the moment of the Vietnamese victory, saying, "Yes, so many brave men died, but oh how we danced and sang when we won!"

18

Hanoi and Saigon
(Ho Chi Minh City)

Hanoi

On 14 August I left Bangkok and flew into Hanoi for the first time to be met at Noi Bai airport by the Australian ambassador, John McCarthy, who as a friend had kindly offered to put me up in his flat, the "residence" which was over the chancery "shop". After coping with modified confusion as I and the rest of the passengers—almost all Scandinavian aid workers—scrambled for our luggage, we set off on the 40-kilometre drive into Hanoi, crossing the iconic Long Bien Bridge —the Paul Doumer Bridge in colonial times—that the Vietnamese had defended against American bombing so tenaciously during the Vietnam War. Driving into Hanoi I found myself in a big city that nevertheless had immediate visual echoes of Phnom Penh and Saigon—creamy yellow paint on the old buildings, the same style of architecture, the same tree-lined boulevards. I had a strange sense, not of coming home, but of being in a city linked to what I had known in the rest of the former French Indochina.

The next morning I found I was in the hands of the Institute for

International Relations, a branch of the Foreign Ministry, with Tran Le Duc in charge of my arrangements and assisting a more senior officer, Le Thanh Tam. I was also the sole audience for a two and a half hour survey of Vietnam's relations with China, presented by Tam, a Dien Bien Phu veteran and former ambassador. I made notes as I listened to his presentation made mostly in English but occasionally, for emphasis, in French:

> It is all to do with China, and China has had it in for Vietnam since the pre-Christian era. . . . China has only sided with Vietnam when it did so in its own interest. Zhou Enlai and Deng Xiaoping are or were just as much committed to controlling Vietnam as was Mao. And China's aim is to control the whole of Southeast Asia after it controls Vietnam. There have been changes in some aspects of China's policies over the years. Thus in the fifties China was anti-US, in the 60s anti-US and anti-Soviet, and in the 70s anti-Soviet and pro US. But all the time it has plotted against Vietnam.

> China's intentions are clearly revealed in efforts it made to use Cambodia as a base. It now continues that policy by supporting the ousted Pol Pot regime.

With my program assured, including plans for a trip to Lang Son on the border with China the next day and a meeting with Foreign Minister Nguyen Co Thach in four days' time, I was caught up in a busy program, including visiting the Historical Museum and later attending a dinner at the Institute of International Relations: good Vietnamese food with an eccentric offering of drinks, ranging from a Grand Marnier-like liqueur as an apéritif to vodka with the crème caramel dessert. Then, later, attendance at a Dutch embassy party awakened so many memories of Phnom Penh in the sixties—a gathering of expatriates forced back on their own resources because of having little connection to the local community, a paucity of nocturnal alternatives, much heavy Dutch humour, and a refrigerator that could not keep the Heineken cold.

The next morning I set off at five o'clock with Le Thanh Tam to visit Lang Son, travelling north for over three hours on a bumpy road in a Volga sedan that had long ago lost its shock absorbers. At first we travelled through flat country with rice fields stretching back to the horizon. Then, about half way into the trip we began to enter what Tam called a *couloir*, a narrow valley between hills that had begun to rise on either side of the road, limestone *calcaires* to the west and more gently rounded hills to the east. And as we did so he grabbed my arm and said, "And now we are entering the killing ground." It took me a moment to realise what he was referring to—this was a time when the term "killing fields" had become all-too-widely known in relation to Cambodia, but he had said killing "*ground*". Then after a moment's thought I realised what he meant; he was referring to the great defeat the Vietnamese inflicted on the Ming Chinese occupiers in this area in 1428. It was a defeat that restored Vietnam's independence after a period of Chinese occupation and was celebrated in a famous poem by the warrior-scholar, Nguyen Trai. Fortunately, I was able to remember some of the lines of the poem and to quote them to Le Thanh Tam:

> We have our own mountains and our own rivers, our
> own customs and traditions.
> And these are quite different from a foreign country
> to the north.
> We have sometimes been weak and sometimes strong.
> But we have never lacked for heroes.

It wasn't quite Patrick Leigh Fermor being able to match General

Kriepe's quoting of Horace's ode, after the German had been abducted in Crete during the Second World War, but it was well received and, as I noted in my journal, attempts to force their way through the *couloir*, or passage, would have been a nightmare for any invading army.

As we drove into Lang Son it was clear the town, as I recorded, "had taken one hell of a beating physically during the Chinese invasion. All major buildings of consequence in the town were destroyed, as were 60 bridges in the province and much of the railway track running from the town to the border." But when we reached our destination and I was given a briefing on the Chinese attack there was no mistaking the pride of the Vietnamese as they recounted how their regional forces had forced the Chinese to fight for sixteen days before they could finally reach Lang Son, a distance of barely 20 kilometres from the border. There was even a nice touch of almost "British" self-deprecation in the briefing. Of course, the briefing officer noted, the Chinese were badly led, by officers who had gained their appointments through ideological conformity during the Cultural Revolution rather than through military skill. One of the briefers even showed me how the Chinese officers marched, in a performance of strutting arrogance that could have found a place in John Cleese's "Ministry of Silly Walks".

Vietnamese and Chinese Friends Forever

With the briefing over we travelled further north, to within three kilometres of the border line itself, close to the famous Porte de Chine, the border crossing between China and Vietnam that is so frequently mentioned in French accounts of the colonial period. My companions were visibly nervous as I took photographs looking towards China, where we could readily see the structure of Chinese radar equipment. Their apprehension reflected the fact that despite the truce that now prevailed there were still occasions when the Chinese fired artillery onto this no-man's land region. I understood their nervousness, but was more struck by a large concrete block on which there was a freshly painted slogan, which read in in Vietnamese capital letters, "NHAN DAN HAI NUOC VIET NAM TRUONG QUOC MAI MAI LA BAN BE", and which, I was immediately able to translate, not least because it is such a simple sentence, as, "The two peoples of Vietnam and China are friends forever." Now not only did this seem a curious statement given the Chinese invasion, but the fresh paint on the concrete did not disguise the way in which it had been chipped by bullets that had struck it. I couldn't resist taxing Tam with the irony of the slogan, given all things that had happened so recently, and for a moment he was at a loss how to respond. But he recovered cleverly, saying, "Yes, but you see, it is the two peoples who are friends forever, not the governments."

The following two days were spent in almost continuous meetings. I spent two hours with the Committee for Social Sciences, where there was an interesting argument put to me that French scholarship about Vietnam had given too much emphasis to China's influence on the development of Vietnamese culture and not enough to the underlying importance of influences from Southeast Asia, though quite what these were was not made clear. A meeting with Hoang Nguyen, the editor of *Vietnam Courier*, the official weekly newspaper published in English, which was disappointing as in initial conversation it seemed that he might depart from the party line. Instead, he was just a little more subtle than many of his associates, and I recorded my judgment that he had "a manner calculated to appeal to a Left Bank Marxist or a starry eyed do-gooder". And the next day, after an interesting visit to the Military Museum with its well-presented diorama showing the way in which the Battle of Dien Bien Phu took place, there was the inevitable visit to the Ho Chi Minh's mausoleum:

> What does one say? There is a thing that could be Ho or could be a waxwork in a glass case. Perhaps the only comment of validity is that the Vietnamese shuffling through seemed moved. I found the whole thing faintly distasteful. It would have more attraction for a Spaniard or an Italian Catholic with their love of relics.

These almost continuous visits organised for me meant that I had little time to move about the city on my own. It was easy enough to record my feeling that the officials I was dealing with were tough, ready to engage in discussion and unfailingly to put the position of their government, and more than just polite. But it was impossible to say much about "ordinary" Vietnamese whom I was essentially only seeing in passing as I moved from one appointment to another. And all of this was in a city that left an impression of grand colonial buildings and pervasive austerity. It was a sombre mood that was matched by the grey skies and the frequently present drizzle of very light rain, what the colonial French called the *crachin*, the "spit". Only briefly at the end of the day was it possible to cycle through the city with John McCarthy and to see the markets, including what nowadays might be called the pop up markets, where antiques were being sold off in these harsh economic times and the old quarter with its narrow streets and even more narrow shophouses.

Meeting Nguyen Co Thach

And then, on 19 August, I had my much-awaited meeting with Foreign Minister Nguyen Co Thach. At this time, and with good reason, he was regarded by the countries of ASEAN as the man calling the shots in relation to Cambodia for the Vietnamese government and doing so in a hard-nosed fashion. He was his country's foreign minister now, but he had once been a regimental commander in the Vietnamese army and that background was clearly as much part of his persona as any nod towards diplomatic niceties.

We met in what had been an important colonial building, the former residence of the French Résident Supérieur of Tonkin (northern Vietnam), located close to the well-known Métropole Hotel, and which was now being used as a government guest house. When I entered Thach greeted me warmly, with a friendly punch on my arm as he told his interpreter that his services were not needed—he and I would speak in English or French—and all that he said was "on the record". It was an impressive start to an interview that lasted for nearly an hour, with Vietnam's occupation of Cambodia as the central issue. And on this issue what Thach had to say was a restatement of the Vietnamese position, in a forceful fashion, as I recorded:

> The situation in Cambodia is "irreversible", Thach emphasised, in the sense that there can be no return of the Khmer Rouge. The key to the present situation is China's support for the ousted Pol Pot regime and its troops and so long as that support continues with Thai connivance there will be no withdrawal of Vietnamese troops. If the threat of Pol Pot was removed then the Vietnamese government would withdraw some of its forces.

This was all a fairly expected statement of Vietnam's policies so that it was when Thach offered less scripted observations that he was most interesting. When I asked if Vietnam felt isolated he was very firm in his response, saying, "We are much less isolated than when were fighting the French and then the Americans." As for United Nations resolutions calling for Vietnam to leave Cambodia, these did not worry the Vietnamese, after all "The West would not let us be a member for thirty years." I realised as I was listening to Thach that he was something of a showman, as he continued by saying, "I told the Secretary General, "Now you have to look after Pol Pot. I am glad I do not have to put up with the smell." He was making the point that at this stage Cambodia was still represented in the United Nations by representatives of the now-deposed Khmer Rouge regime. And when I asked if it might be possible for the regime in Phnom Penh to accept Sihanouk or Son Sann into its ranks, and so to broaden its appeal, his response was blunt. To give these two a place in Phnom Penh, both of them having been associated with the Chinese, would be "like inviting a thief into your house".

He had perceptive observations to make about ASEAN, correctly noting that there was much less unity within that organisation than public statements suggested—in his words the Philippines "did not matter", and there was sympathy for Vietnam on the part of Indonesia and Malaysia. Thailand was determining ASEAN policy and Singapore was very vocal. But despite Singapore's public stance that country continued to trade actively with Vietnam. "They are clever people in Singapore," Thach went on, "more clever than you Australians when it comes to mixing trade and politics." And then there was China. Even if ASEAN changed its public position of opposing Vietnam's presence in Cambodia, he was not sure that China would follow this lead. The Chinese are not pragmatists despite the fact that many people judge them to be so. The Great Leap Forward was not a practical or a pragmatic policy. The Great Proletarian Cultural Revolution was not pragmatic or practical.

It was only when, in the closing part of the interview, that I felt Nguyen Co Thach was less than fully convinced himself of the arguments he advanced as we talked about the refugee outflow from Vietnam—an outflow which he and I both knew involved a measure of official corruption and in some cases direct encouragement from the government, particularly where ethnic Chinese fleeing southern Vietnam was concerned. Here is what I recorded:

> The departure of ethnic Vietnamese is "bleeding us". The people who are leaving are persons of talent and training, doctors and technicians, or they are young men. But why are they leaving? In part it's because of the inevitable difficulties that persons associated with the former regime have in living under changed conditions. In part because hostile policies towards Vietnam created circumstances that lead people to want to leave. In part it is because various countries are seeking to encourage refugee departures.

> In response to my query as to why so few ethnic Chinese were now leaving from the south Thach said that the reasons is that "they are doing too well". He went on to say, however, that "we will break the Chinese commercial network in the south. The Saigon regime could never do it, but we will."

Overall, the interview provided a fascinating insight into the Vietnamese conviction that they held the whip hand, with the presentation of this view from Ngueyn Co Thach nothing less than a bravura performance. Unlike some of the other officials I met later in the south, and with the exception in part of his comments on refugees, he made no pretence that I was listening to him as a "friend of Vietnam". And even in relation to the issue of refugees, about which he admitted the existence of corruption, I could sense that the Thai foreign minister, Air Marshal Siddhi Savitsila, would have found Thach almost unforgivably abrasive, and very un-Southeast Asian. I did not say to him, but I thought to myself, his comments on "breaking" the Chinese commercial network sounded very much like a pious hope rather than a certain conviction.

Neither Thach himself, nor I, could have predicted when this interview took place that a new set of circumstances at the end of the 1980s would alter the balance of forces in relation to Cambodia and so undermine Vietnam's position in Cambodia. With the collapse of the Soviet Union China's role in relation to Cambodia became immeasurably stronger than Vietnam's. Whether it could be argued that Vietnam won the long game by eventually seeing its protégés confirmed in power in the final wash-up that was the result of the Cambodian settlement negotiated in 1991 may be a matter for argument. But there is no argument that, ultimately, Thach was a loser in what transpired. For he was forced out of office at China's insistence as part of the conditions laid down by China at a September 1991 secret meeting it held with Vietnam in Chengdu that was central to the final settlement of the "Cambodian problem".

Ho Chi Minh City, but still Saigon

With a 4 am start I left Hanoi for the former Saigon on 20 August. Stepping out of the plane on arrival at Tan Son Nhat airport, there was a brief moment when I was transported back to the last time I had been here as a group of helicopters clattered over head, for this was one of the sounds I most associated with the city's aiport. But in the same moment change was sharply evident. Instead of an airport that rivalled Chicago's O'Hare for the title of the busiest in the world, there was barely any sign of activity. No longer were the crowds lining the viewing platform overlooking the tarmac, and then once outside the terminal and driving into the centre of the city there was scarcely any traffic. The old Saigon was there in bricks and mortar, and in the readiness of its inhabitants to continue using that name. But the new Ho Chi Minh City was marked by a lack of traffic and of the animation that was once so much part of its character. It was immediately marked by another absence, the absence of women wearing the traditional *ao dai* tunics that were so much a part of Saigon during the war years. On this Thursday a drab, utilitarian clothing seemed the almost universal choice of the women I saw on the streets. And surely I was not imposing my reaction to the dourness of this new Saigon when I recorded that the women I saw in the street seemed to have the corners of their mouths turned down.

Meeting Madame Dai and her nephew

In the evening, and left to make my own choice of where to find a place to eat, I followed what had become a well-worn track by those visitors granted entry to Vietnam the early 1980s and called on Madame Nguyen Phuoc Dai. A lawyer and former senator in the South Vietnamese parliament, she had become famous after 1975 for her courageous readiness to speak critically of the new communist administration. But by now she was at least as well known for her efforts to defy austerity by running a small restaurant in her house, The Bibliothèque, named for its location in her private library. In every way she was a relic, not of the South Vietnamese regime but rather of colonial times.

Charming and sophisticated she most certainly was, for after all she had spent much of her life in France and her husband had been a French citizen. In essence she was a remaining member of the Cochinchinese bourgeoisie, and her genuine disdain for the new regime was a reflection of both her personal politics and what used to be called by the French *le snobisme Saigonnais*—the Saigon snobbery felt by inhabitants of this city for their compatriots elsewhere in Vietnam who had not absorbed French culture in the same measure. She was also had an expert eye for *Bleu de Hue* ceramics, and a good sense of their value. I readily admit to having been one of her willing, and very satisfied customers.

Her nephew, Pham Dinh Phuong, whom I met on another evening, provided a qualification to his aunt's views, one that I found more revealing. Perhaps because of our shared background at Monash University he was ready to speak frankly to me:

> Phuong stated that there are severe tensions between southerners and northerners. The former staff the local HCM City Committee government while the latter are the overwhelming bulk of the staff in the central government offices . . . In the Public Security Services and in the upper echelons of the police northerners are dominant. They tend to arrogance and to distrust the revolutionary zeal of their southern compatriots. It's not surprising, he observed with a wry smile, since there are reasons for their doubt. This said, he continued, it would be grossly wrong to think that there was counter-revolution lurking around the corner. There is much

dissatisfaction generally, and the north-south tensions will take a long time to dissipate, if ever . . .

Yet for all of his acceptance that there were serious feelings of resentment on the part of southerners, Phuong could not avoid observing that his compatriots in Saigon "loved to grumble". And having returned to Saigon from Australia in 1968 he could contrast the regime in place then with what existed now. For all his doubts he felt it was important that the whole of Vietnam was governed by a Vietnamese regime

Transforming the "corrupted past"

The next day, and after a guided tour of the city and its outskirts, I was received by, Le Quong Chanh the Vice President of the Ho Chi Minh City's People's Committee in what had once been the colonial Hôtel de Ville. The contrast with my briefings in Hanoi was striking. It was not the fact that Le detailed all the problems the city faced as it sought to transform society from its "corrupted past"; this I had more or less expected. But after the litany of Saigon's previous sins Chanh went on to tell me that all was now going well because of the revolutionary zeal of the population. Having spoken with Madame Dai the night before and seen the gloomy faces of so many of the people in the street, this was all too much, and I told Le Quong Chanh, once again, that I was not "a friend of Vietnam" and was well aware there was much that was not going well. Briefly the presentation became more frank, until Le Quong Chanh started citing figures for the number of ethnic Chinese who had left Saigon since *Giai Phong* (Liberation). The figures he gave were badly wrong, a suggestion that only 40,000 ethnic Chinese had left over six years. It was a nonsense as he and I both knew and, politely, I told him so. In the end I was left wondering whether the tone of the presentation was as much for the benefit of my escort officer as for me.

We have been colonised by the north

If meeting Madame Dai and her nephew at The Bibliothèque took place in an ambience of what might be called shabby chic, this was certainly not true of the dinner I attended in the home of Dr Duong Quyen Hoa. Dr Hoa was a hero of the Vietnam War, a Paris trained paediatrician who in 1968 left her practice in Saigon to go into the maquis and become the Deputy Minister for Health in the Provisional Revolutionary Government. Now, as she ran one of Saigon's hospitals, her home reflected her family's prosperous background, filled as it was with antique furniture and blue and white porcelain. This in itself was not as surprising as the views Dr Hoa bluntly expressed in flawless French as she spoke of how "we have been colonised by the north". The members of the Provisional Revolutionary Government had been discarded by the northern-dominated regime that had little understanding of the south. As for Vietnam's Soviet friends, she tolerated them for the moment for the aid they could provide, but they too would ultimately be transients on the Vietnamese scene.

. . .

My last full day in Saigon, 23 August, was a Sunday, and the mood had changed as the population was out promenading the streets, with some women in their *ao dai* and others in trim slacks and t-shirts. The black market stalls crowded sections of the footpaths in the centre of the city, selling everything from Swan Lager to expensive hi-fi equipment. The botanic gardens were crowded, but not the adjacent museum. And everywhere families were taking photographs of each other. I had one unpleasant moment, which, perhaps, said something about the mood of some of the people. In this city I had become used to children calling out *Lien Xo*, the Vietnamese for Soviets, for there was an assumption that white foreigners were from the Soviet Union, Vietnam's most important friend, and I had always replied by shouting back that I was *Nguoi Uc*, an Australian. But this time, as I took a shortcut through a back street the shouts of *Lien Xo* were accompanied by a hail of stones from a group of children. A sign of real antipathy or a chance occurrence, I didn't know. Certainly antipathy was not present in another scene I witnessed on this Sunday. In front of Saigon's cathedral a group of Soviet sailors were posed around a Vietnamese woman in an *ao dai* waiting to be photographed as a souvenir of their time in a foreign country. As I recorded my thoughts early the next morning I offered a tentative judgment on what I had seen and heard:

> I feel that Vietnam is, in relation to Ho Chi Minh City, rather like a boa constrictor. It has swallowed the former Saigon and is digesting it, but it is taking time. In this respect it would be wrong simply to dwell on the remnants of the past. For all the lissom ladies who still want to be part of the western present, for all of the fact that I found western pop and disco music for sale to local musicians (not to mention tapes—the taste is for Boney M, it seems), there are other developments that will, I judge, slowly put an end to the lingering links with the past.

That judgment seemed right at the time. Thirty plus years on it seems far from correct as the old Saigon has reappeared in a new guise that has indeed left the Party in control of government. But the people and the city that most of them still call "Saigon" are as linked, in so many ways, to the hi-tech, popular culture of modernity as the people and the cities in the rest of Southeast Asia. Saigon today, in a way very different from Hanoi, is a city where business, fashion, and for many a search for "the good life", are the dominant themes.

19

Return to Cambodia

Flying in to Phnom Penh on 24 August I was returning to Cambodia for the first time in ten years, and I had no real sense of what I would find. This was despite the long hours I had spent interviewing refugees and talking to a limited number of the aid workers who had been admitted to the country since the Vietnamese toppled the Khmer Rouge regime in January 1979. Above Phnom Penh the view out of the window of the Russian aircraft was comfortably reassuring —the Mekong and the Tonle Sap Rivers, the easily identified Royal Palace compound and the *Phnom*. But this feeling of reassurance was briefly overcome by the realisation that we seemed to be landing faster than normal and certainly were too low in our approach to Pochentong airport. The truth of the latter concern was obvious as we clipped the top of a sugar palm just before reaching the tarmac. But we landed safely with palm fronds stuck in the landing gear. The airport building looked much as before but it was as I was driven into the city that the new reality became apparent:

> Déjà vu at the airport, but after that it becomes hard to describe.
> One is prepared for something awful, but not really for the
> decrepitude that is there. Apart from a limited number of buildings
> such as the former National Bank, where a section of that building
> was blown up in the first days of the Pol Pot regime's control of

Cambodia, there is not all that much evidence of destruction. In some streets the wrecks of abandoned cars and trucks are piled up on top of each other. In other places there are simply open spaces where buildings used to be. So far as I can tell all of the Christian churches in the inner city—including the Catholic Cathedral have simply been razed. (This includes the large church opposite my first apartment in Kralahom Kong Street). On these open spaces are coconut trees as a reflection of the Khmer Rouge's intent to bring the country to the city. There is a sinister possibility that under each tree are the bodies of two executed persons.

Phnom Penh is full of people, living in conditions ranging from the acceptable to notably squalid. The garbage system—if one can use such a term—has broken down and there are great piles reminiscent of the July 1966 garbage strike in Saigon. In some areas people swarm. In other parts whole blocks are sealed off. Without any particular reason one seems to pass from heavily populated areas to ghost town conditions. There is a lot of traffic in the streets, with much more motor traffic than either Hanoi or HCM City. And there is a new element in the pony traps that were simply not a part of Phnom Penh before.

Accommodation is in the Monorom Hotel. Hot, noisy and grotty. But with a quite acceptable restaurant on the roof.

Petty trading is taking place at full blast, with goods from Thailand to be seen everywhere. At the minor consumer level money will buy almost anything.

The received wisdom is that the population now numbers 300,000 in the city, but how one could be sure is hard to know.

"Touring" Phnom Penh

On this first day I was taken on a mandatory visit to Choeung Ek, the infamous killing fields not far outside Phnom Penh and nowadays a much-transformed "tourist attraction". But at the time of my visit it was very different as the exhumation of remains was still taking place. At this stage more than 3,000 bodies had already been disinterred. Their bones and skulls were laid in rows, with some of the latter still with cloth blindfolds around them and almost all with the backs of the skulls split like walnuts—the Khmer Rouge executioners did not waste bullets on the condemned but bludgeoned their victims to death with ox cart axles. The smell of human corruption and decay hung over the site, and I later asked in my journal, "What does one say after looking at the two hundredth skull?"

The next two days were a jumble of visits and meetings travelling along streets with changed names, so that the Boulevard Norodom had become Tou Samouth Boulevard, named after a communist who was killed by Sihanouk's security forces in 1962, and Sothearos Boulevard, named after a member of the Cambodian royal family, had become Lenin Street. My first visit was to Tuol Sleng or S-21, the extermination centre, which left me with the deeply shocked feeling so frequently described by other visitors to this example of human depravity; to the Royal Palace, which as I recorded had a "forlorn" air, the buildings badly in need of painting and the formal gardens neglected; and to the old Australian chancery, which was accommodating squatters and had a pig tethered in the driveway where I once parked my car.

A visit to the 17 April Hospital left a grim impression, though this was qualified by the enthusiasm the Cuban doctors and technicians were showing for their duties amid the crowded and dirty wards. They spoke of malaria as a growing threat. Later in my visit the doctors at the World Vision-supported Paediatric Hospital indicated their chief concerns were malnutrition and TB. Children living in Phnom Penh, the doctors pointed out to me, were subsisting on a notably inadequate diet and the results of this were apparent in the cases of children suffering Kwashiorkor with their swollen bellies and reddish hair.

At a very different level it was a relief when visiting the National Museum to find so little evidence of damage or theft. I felt firm in this judgment since, free as it had been in 1966 and one of the few intellectual and aesthetic diversions available in Phnom Penh, I had been a frequent visitor. And I could not let this visit pass without a visit to the Hôtel le Royal, now named the Samaki, or "Solidarity" hotel, which had been taken over by permanent residents linked to those NGOs that were allowed to function in Phnom Penh. There was a brief but emotional moment when a waiter from ten years before recognised me and rushed to give me warm embrace.

Conversations with my escort officers swung between being surprisingly revealing and suddenly and firmly non-communicative. Just every now and then there was an oblique reference to the Vietnamese presence in the country and either by a grimace or a hesitation in our conversations a clear indication of resentments that this engendered. Sambath, the deputy head of the Ministry of Foreign Affairs Press Office, was unexpectedly ready to comment on the Cambodian political leadership, referring to Heng Samrin, then President of the Council of Ministers (or prime minister), of the People's Republic of Kampuchea as a "simple person". When I asked if he meant "simple" in the sense of "unassuming," he indicated this was so—Heng Samrin goes about like an ordinary citizen, rides a bike and drops in on families. But, Sambath said, he also meant "simple" in the other sense, that he is not very bright. Real power, he emphasised is in the hands of three key members of the politburo, Pen Sovann, supported by Hun Sen and Chea Sim. The passage of time has indicated how prescient this comment was. For although Pen Sovann was to fall out of favour not long after, thirty years later Hun Sen is still prime minister and Chea Sim was until his death in 2015 the chairman of the governing Cambodian People's Party and president of the senate. Heng Samrin holds the position of president of the National Assembly but does not appear to be a powerful voice in the councils of the government.

Journey to Battambang

Finally, on 27 August and after my near-continuous series of visits in and around the capital, I started my journey to Battambang, then Phnom Penh's second city and reputed to be a considerable contrast to the capital. It was a city, or town, I had visited many times before and which had once boasted a restaurant named "Australia". When, on one of my visits in the 1960s, I asked the owner why he had chosen this name, thinking there had to be a personal connection, he looked quite surprised that I should ask. It is a "nice name"', he told me. And "no" he had never been there nor had any connection with the country.

I had been told the journey would be slow, but the experience was more tiring, and tiresome, than I had expected. To cover the roughly 270 kilometres from Phnom Penh to Battambang took more than nine hours over roads that had been both neglected and deliberately damaged during the fighting of the past decade, in many cases by the "piano key" method—slit trenches dug in parallel on either side of the road, not necessarily across the whole of the road surface, but sufficient to prevent easy transit. There was scarcely a bridge along the route that had not been damaged so that most had been replaced by Bailey bridges. All of the bridges were protected, sometimes by Cambodian militia forces, occasionally by Vietnamese troops. The presence of the latter was both pervasive and unobtrusive, except for a company of recruits that I saw being drilled in Kompong Chhnang. And every now and then we passed the debris of war, burnt out trucks, a few Chinese tanks whose tracks had been shot off, the skeletons of buildings with their roofs and walls damaged by artillery.

* * *

Assessing Battambang the next day I recorded:

> Battambang now has a population of about 60,000. Although there are sections of the city that give one the impression of a ghost town, my overall reaction was that here is an urban unit that was functioning in a much more "real" fashion than Phnom Penh. There was none of the feeling of an anarchic population influx that is so striking in the capital. Certainly much of the town's return to life is associated with the border smuggling from Thailand, but there seems to be a solid base on the revival of rice farming and agriculture generally.

It was on this first day in Battambang, too, that I had further news of Monsignor Tep Im's death, for among the Cambodians I met was a man who had been on his staff and whom I had encountered in my last visit in 1970. I have incorporated what he told me in the "Epilogue" at the end this work, but for the moment it is sufficient to note that he told me no one knew where Tep Im was buried, or indeed if he was buried. And he mentioned the subsequently discredited suggestion that a skeleton had been found with the presence of Tep Im's pectoral cross.

Far and away the most interesting of my experiences in Battambang was the extended time I spent with Dr Ly Po, head of the health service for the province. His own experience during the Pol Pot period was all too typical, when he was initially held in prison but expected to train other health workers. Of the 480 who were in prison with him only 50 survived and he has seen photographs of some of those who did not do so in the confronting photographic display of victims mounted on the walls of the Tuol Sleng extermination centre in Phnom Penh. Apart from training health workers he had, during the reign of the Khmer Rouge been required to be a woodsman, a rice farmer and a cowhand. As he said with a rueful smile, with his family's peasant background he had been able to cope with all these tasks.

He was surprisingly optimistic about public health in Battambang, both in the city and the province generally. Hunger was not a problem now that rice farming was functioning adequately, though there was evidence of malnutrition in the western hills. The main problem was malaria and the need to contend with a new, virulent strain of the disease. Inadequate equipment was a concern, too, so that they had an X-Ray machine but lacked film. There are now only four or five lepers in the whole province: "Pol Pot's government solved the leprosy problem," Ly Po told me. "They killed all the lepers."

> All this information was given to me as I was taken through the city's main hospital, which contrasted sharply with what I had seen in Phnom Penh. The building and equipment were clean and the spirit of the staff was quite obviously buoyant. Ly Po pointed out instances where the staff had overcome the lack of equipment by, for instance, building their own unit to produce distilled water. I was even taken into a spotless operating theatre where an appendicectomy was taking place to observe the procedure.

As would be expected I was taken to see a mass grave site outside the city, at Phnom Sampeou. Whether for effect, or for other reasons, bones and skulls here had been left lying around near a former pagoda and surrounding caves and grottoes rather than grouped together as I had seen at Choeung Ek. But this visit was followed by a totally different call at the local soft drink factory, an occasion that made me wonder how successful the Phnom Penh government and its Vietnamese mentors will be in trying to establish a socialist economy. It also was a testimony to how much havoc the Khmer Rouge regime had wreaked with its efforts to destroy the technically qualified members of Cambodia's population. As I recorded:

> A very different visit came next with a trip to the local soft drink factory. This is located in the former Pepsi factory and has been brought back into production by a remarkably energetic man named Tes Heang, who is the province's Chief of Industry. He is a former tractor technician, but obviously a man of real organisational talent. He pointed out that not only does the soft

drink factory make money for the province, but it also means that there is no longer an incentive to smuggle soft drinks from Thailand. In reverse, ice from the factory is actually smuggled into Thailand and has been sold in Khao I Dang! He has plans to bring more rice mills back into production and to start a cigarette factory in Battambang. An index of his problems, and his energy, is the fact that in the whole province there are only seven electricians, two skilled technicians and one trained engineer.

Memories of better days

After a tedious return journey to Phnom Penh on 29 August, the following day, a Sunday, was clear of appointments and I was given the opportunity to travel outside Phnom Penh to Takeo, a small provincial town, about 60 kilometres south of Phnom Penh. I had known the town in better days, not least for a treasured memory of eating a breakfast of savoury Chinese soup in the Takeo market with Kim Kosal after I had spent the weekend with him at the army base he commanded in 1966. As noted earlier, the Khmer Rouge executed Kim Kosal almost immediately after their April 1975 victory. Now:

> . . . There was nothing of notable interest in the trip, but it was rewarding nevertheless, and rather saddening since it was a trip through a part of Cambodia that I knew so well and visited so often when I first came here. But so much has changed: the little hill with the pagoda on top, about 50 kilometres south of Phnom Penh, Phnom Kirivong, was used as a punishment prison during the Pol Pot years and is now abandoned. Kampong Kanthuot, which was one of the prettiest little towns near the capital, is a series of abandoned shells of buildings. As too, for the most part, is Takeo.

I had to use my imagination very hard to summon up a memory of that provincial town amidst the rubble and the destroyed houses, and the local Vietnamese detachment. Everywhere pagodas are damaged, abandoned, or simply completely razed. My total number of monks seen in all my travels is 30.

Meeting Mat Ly

On 1 September, my last day in Phnom Penh, I was given the opportunity in the morning to meet and interview Mat Ly, the vice-president of the National Assembly and deputy minister of agriculture. Before meeting him I had been told that he had been born in 1928 and was a member of the Cham community, the ethnic minority who are followers of Islam and suffered grievously under Pol Pot. As my meeting with Mat Ly revealed, he certainly qualified for the description of being a survivor, and I have later found out that he lived on into the present century as an apparently revered member of the Cham community, while holding a largely ceremonial office as vice-president of the national assembly. But then, as now, his career, which he detailed to me, raises some disturbing and unresolved questions. For, as he was to tell me, he remained working within the Pol Pot regime until 1978: that is for more than two and a half years after the Khmer Rouge came to power in 1975.

We met in the building beside the Tonle Sap River that I had known as the foreign ministry in the 1960s, in a bare room with the only decoration being four photographs hung on the walls: two of Cambodians, Heng Samrin and Pen Sovann, and two communist icons, Marx and Lenin. Most of what Mat Ly had to say I had heard already during my visit, though in fairness I should note that he offered considerable detail in talking about internal security, living conditions in Phnom Penh and the countryside, and "the development of socialism". In relation to all of these issues he showed the readiness, familiar in other leftist regimes, of being able to quote statistics almost down to the last decimal point. So, he told me there were 95,778 solidarity units (*krom samaki*) for agricultural production in the country, made up of 1,352,999 families. But he showed little inclination to respond to my questions that attempted to probe more deeply into the answers he had given. So after he had spoken of Vietnam and Cambodia having "a history of common struggle", and of Vietnamese "technical advisers" only being present until Cambodians were trained to take their place, I asked him about the resentment I had heard expressed about the presence of the Vietnamese in his country. He simply dodged the question, saying their presence was needed. As for the Vietnamese troops in Cambodia, he gave an answer that required a considerable amount of thought before I could makes sense of it. "This is the third time Vietnamese troops have come to help Cambodia," Mat Ly said, "In the past they have always withdrawn when there was no longer any need for their help."

Quite obviously the third instance to which Mat Ly was referring was the Vietnamese invasion that had overthrown the Khmer Rouge regime in January 1979, but what were the other two occasions? As I listened to him I realised he had to be referring to the relatively small part played by Vietnamese forces in Cambodia in the First Indochina War, the war against the French, as the first instance of Vietnamese help. And the second instance had to be the role of the Vietnamese communist forces that had aided the Khmer Rouge in their fight against the Phnom Penh regime in the early 1970s. This was aid that was vitally important for the ultimate Khmer Rouge victory, but by 1973 it had almost entirely ceased as relations between the Khmer Rouge and their former allies grew more and more antagonistic and ultimately poisonous. Although he did not make any reflection on his comment about the Vietnamese, it encapsulated the tortuous nature of relations between the communist parties of the two countries and bore directly on Mat Ly's own revolutionary background.

He spoke of having been born into a revolutionary family of leftists in Kompong Cham province and of having joined the Issaraks, or Free Cambodians, in 1948, and fought with them against the French during 1950-1953. In the latter year he was captured by the French, jailed and tortured, leaving him with a permanently damaged leg. By this stage he was firmly linked to the communist cause and he continued to work for that cause after his release in 1954. While his father had gone to North Vietnam for training in Hanoi in 1954, Mat Ly remained in Cambodia and in 1958 he was captured and tortured again, this time by Sihanouk's security services. He was released in 1959. He continued to live openly until 1970 although members of a "group" with which he had been associated had retreated into the jungle in 1966. By 1970 he had become the head of a communist district committee and he held this position until the Khmer Rouge victory in 1975. Later that year, Mat Ly stated, representatives from the central government in Phnom Penh— "members of the Pol Pot faction" -- came to see his father in Kompong Cham province, offered him medicine, which was in fact poison, and he died the same day. He offered no explanation for this action on the part of the "Pol Pot faction".

It was at this point in his relation of his personal history that Mat Ly's account began to raise questions in my mind, and they were questions that applied to many, indeed most, of the leading figures in the Cambodian protégé government. What is more, they are questions that continue to apply to the contemporary regime in Cambodia in 2017. Here is how I recorded his words at the time:

> Until 1976 the Pol Pot regime gave the impression that it would work through a parliament and Mat Ly was one of those elected to be a member of the parliament. His main duty, however, was to be in charge of economic development in his home district, Thbong Khmom in Kompong Cham province.
>
> He was called to Phnom Penh to hear Pol Pot nominated as the First Secretary of the Communist Party of Kampuchea.
>
> As he became aware of the system that Pol Pot presided over and of the massacres that were taking place he retreated to the forest in 1978 to oppose the Democratic Kampuchean regime. His wife, three children, some grandchildren, two daughters-in-law and all son-in-laws were killed.

The problem, then and now, is obvious and applies to a great many more Cambodians than just Mat Ly, not least to Heng Samrin, Hun Sen, Chea Sim and many others who held senior positions in the PRK government at the time I interviewed Mat Ly and for the successor administration in power in 2017. Mat Ly was telling me that he defected from the Khmer Rouge regime some time in 1978—he did not tell me the exact date when this occurred. Yet he was asking me to believe that he had been able to reconcile all he had known about the nature of the Pol Pot regime with remaining within it for more than two years.

It is quite possible to accept that by some time in 1978 there was an awareness of the nature of the government, leading to outright rebellion against the central authority in Phnom Penh, in the east of the country; and this issue has been studied at some length by students of modern Cambodian history long after my discussions in 1981. But even without the detailed knowledge that has subsequently accumulated, the new leadership in Phnom Penh installed by the Vietnamese, and consisting of people like Mat Ly, was asking us to believe that they either had nothing to do with what had happened under Pol Pot, or did not know what was taking place, or both. Yet the refugees I interviewed had a clear sense of what had been happening. My friend Ping Ling felt sure that when people were taken away from the barracks in which he lived in Phnom Penh were being taken to their deaths. And, as noted earlier, the refugees Henry Kamm interviewed and wrote about in July 1975 were already giving detailed accounts of the brutality of the Khmer Rouge regime, including executions.

Then, and now, I am sceptical about this remarkable national amnesia on the part of those who came to rule Cambodia after 1979. It's true that much effort had been put into a review of Hun Sen's life in Democratic Kampuchea before he defected to Vietnam in 1977 without any evidence ever being found of his personal involvement in the commission of atrocities. But it remains the fact that he worked within the Pol Pot regime for two years before his defection took place. As more and more observers cast a critical view on contemporary Cambodia, the more apparent it is that the kind of story Mat Ly was telling me could only be believed in part. Was he, and were others, really lacking in knowledge of what was happening until he figurative last moment, by which stage how many of the estimated 1.75 million Cambodians who died during those years had already perished?

It has frequently been said in relation to the occupied countries of Europe during the Second World War that those who did not experience occupation cannot understand what it was like to live through those times and the compromises that it would have been necessary to make – including collaboration with the regime in power. This surely was true of Cambodia in the short but terrible period the country was ruled by the Khmer Rouge. But to allow this awareness to remove the need for scepticism is surely a betrayal of historical standards. It is no wonder that Prime Minister Hun Sen does not want his compatriots, or the world, to look deeply into the history of Cambodia in the Pol Pot years and that he has called on the population to "dig a hole and bury the past". In this regard he has resisted attempts by the Khmer Rouge Tribunal, the Extraordinary Chambers in the Courts of Cambodia, to pursue new cases against alleged key figures in the Khmer Rouge regime, such as former Generals Meas Mut and Sou Met, who had acted as advisers to Pol Pot's Defence Ministry and who were accused of sending individuals to the Tuol Sleng extermination centre.

Envoi for Cambodia

Early in the afternoon of 1 September I flew out of Phnom Penh, as the only passenger, on an Indonesian cargo aircraft that had been chartered to fly aid supplies into Cambodia. It was a fine, clear day, unusually so for the time of the year, and I had my last view of Cambodia for thirteen years from the cockpit as we set our course for Singapore. I had spent nine days in Cambodia and felt gripped by a jumble of emotional reactions to what I had seen and heard. I had no sense at this time of how long it was going to be before I returned, but I was certain of one key point. Cambodia had been changed in a fundamental fashion from the country I had known in the 1960s and early 1970s. What had occurred in the years of war between 1970 and 1975, and then under Pol Pot, had meant that whatever parts of the past survived these would always be qualified by an experience of human tragedy that we outside observers would long struggle to understand.

As we flew over the Gulf of Thailand with the outlines of the Malaysian Peninsula coming into view I found myself thinking as much like an historian as an observer of contemporary politics. I reflected that it has been Cambodia's tragedy that for centuries others than Cambodians have felt that they knew what was best for the country. Historically the Thais and the Vietnamese, and then the French, exercised control over the state. Now, in 1981, I was convinced on the basis of what I had seen, Cambodia was firmly in Vietnam's orbit, however genuinely nationalist some, or eve all, of the members of the Phnom Penh regime might be at heart. For the moment, it seemed it seemed to me, the issue was intractable —the Vietnamese and the Cambodians said it was "irreversible". It was to be nearly ten years before this judgment needed revision.

* * *

Landing in Singapore and after the less than notable accommodation I had experienced in Phnom Penh and Battambang, I decided to treat myself to a night at the Goodwood Park Hotel, and to dinner in its Gordon Grill. I had failed to take account of how poorly I had eaten during my time in Cambodia and how unready I was for the indulgence I now craved. And so, to the dismay of the head waiter whom I had known from years before, "Captain" Wong, I could neither finish the steak I had ordered, let alone the bottle of Beaujolais I had chosen to accompany my meal. It was a notable waste and in itself a salutary reminder of where I had been.

Plus ça change, plus c'est la même chose – Soviet sailors surround a Vietnamese woman to be photographed in Saigon, August 1981.

Wrecked cars in Phnom Penh, close to the Psar Thmei or Grand Market, Phnom Penh, August 1981. The cars had been destroyed during the Pol Pot regime as symbols of Western decadence but were still to be cleared by the new regime.

20

1981

Was Not The End

Ending this this book in 1981 is a choice dictated by my personal circumstances, for at the beginning of 1982 I returned to work for the Commonwealth government at the Office of National Assessments as Head of the Office's Asia Branch. This employment meant that private travel to Vietnam and Cambodia and writing about those countries in any public fashion was no longer possible. I'm nonetheless tempted to pose the question: does the year 1981 have any significance as an end point in itself? The first and most obvious answer, it seems to me, is "no", anymore that any single date can be taken by itself as a terminal or a starting point without looking at what followed. And certainly for both Cambodia and Vietnam and their populations, including the refugees in Thailand, 1981 was a time of unresolved challenges with little sign that this would change. So perhaps this fact is what deserves attention in any longer view of history: the fact that so many issues in Southeast Asia remained unresolved in 1981.

In Cambodia in 1981 there was only a pretence that the country possessed an independent government. Although hindsight shows that

Hun Sen—then foreign minister in the protégé regime—was to become Southeast Asia's longest serving prime minister, in 1981 he and his colleagues in the government of the People's Republic of Kampuchea occupied their places at the pleasure of the Vietnamese. And, as recorded earlier, their Vietnamese mentors judged them as "below the standard required by their task". Cambodia's security was in the hands of the Vietnamese army and in 1981 that army had not yet begun to sustain the substantial costs that were, eventually, to make the occupation a matter of growing concern. In the longer term the Vietnamese occupation of Cambodia was to cost its army some 23,000 deaths, some from combat but many more from malaria and other tropical diseases.

For the Cambodian refugees who formed such a striking part of my Southeast Asian experiences in 1980 and 1981, there seemed no reason to believe that a resolution to their situation was in sight. They were caught between the determination of the Vietnamese regime and their Cambodian protégés, on the one hand, and the Thai government and its international supporters on the other, that resolving the refugee crisis could only be achieved by one or other of the opposed parties accepting the demands of their opponents: either the Thais recognised the PRK regime as a sovereign entity or the Vietnamese withdrew from Cambodia. It would nearly a decade, and a world-shattering series of events in the Soviet Union for this impasse to be broken.

Although Vietnam appeared in 1981 to be the regional winner, much of that country's apparent strength required serious qualification. Vietnam had won the war against the United States and its allies, had defeated the Pol Pot regime, and given the Chinese a bloody nose in the course of its northern neighbour's punitive invasion in 1979. But there was every reason in 1981 to ask whether the country's leaders were capable of waging peace as well as they had waged war. Nguyen Co Thach's confident presentation to me in 1981 was a masterly piece of political theatre, but it disguised existing and looming weaknesses. Most particularly it underplayed the potential power of China. Vietnam had every reason to be proud of the resistance of its forces to the Chinese invaders in 1979, but the coming decade in which Beijing played a decisive role in supporting anti-regime military forces in Cambodia—in fact the soldiers of the Khmer Rouge—was one of the key factors in the ultimate decision of the Vietnamese to withdraw their forces from Cambodia.

Yet if China's determination to bring Vietnam to heel was of great importance it was the collapse of the Soviet Union that, above all, opened the way for a resolution of the multiple problems that were associated with the post-Vietnam War political rivalries in what had once been French Indochina. What I was observing in Cambodia and Vietnam, and Thailand, in 1981 was as close as anything could be to political stasis in mainland Southeast Asia. It could not, and did not last. As the decade continued the cost to Vietnam's retaining its position in Cambodia grew, and even before the collapse of the Soviet Union Moscow had made clear to the leadership in Hanoi that it could not continue to maintain its flow of aid that was so essential at a time when Vietnam was not far from being an international pariah. And when the Soviet Union did finally fall apart China was poised to exert its will in a fashion that was fundamental to the settlement of "the Cambodia Refugee Problem": Vietnamese troops fully withdrawn; a United Nations temporary administration put in place in Cambodia with national elections held in 1993; and before that the return of the majority of Cambodian refugees from Thailand.

For a little more than two decades I had been an observer of tumultuous developments in mainland Southeast Asia. And I watched them with an awareness of the colonial experiences that had preceded the wars and revolutions that determined Vietnam's and Cambodia's future. When, in 1981, I flew out of Phnom Penh I could not possibly have predicted what I would find in Cambodia and Vietnam nearly three decades later. I could not imagine that Vietnam would be welcoming US Navy port visits at Cam Ranh Bay any more than I could envisage the bustling commercially-oriented city Saigon has become under its new name. I certainly had no sense that Hun Sen would emerge to dominate Cambodian politics, as wily and ruthless in his own way as Norodom Sihanouk. My inability to foresee these developments is a salutary comment on the limits of prediction. And as an historian as much as an observer of contemporary politics I am struck by the extent to which the political landscape of Vietnam and Cambodia today has diverged from that existing before the onset of French colonialism in the mid-nineteenth century.

Just as was the case in the 1850s Cambodia today is a relatively weak country sandwiched between two much larger and more powerful states, Thailand and Vietnam. While it can never been proven conclusively, France's colonial intervention preserved Cambodia's existence as Vietnam fell under the colonial power's control. But there is an element of the greatest importance present today that did not exist in the second half of the nineteenth century and much of the twentieth: a resurgent China determined and capable of exerting its influence over the countries of mainland Southeast Asia. Today its influence is profound. It looms as a constant presence over Vietnam, a historical tributary with which it has contemporary maritime disputes. And China is both Cambodia's largest aid donor and political supporter. It is as if the last stand of the French that ended with the Battle of Dien Bien Phu in 1954 and the subsequent involvement of the United States in the countries of Indochina that ended in 1975 has counted for nothing in history's longer perspective. Now that is a conclusion to ponder.

Exhumed skulls at Choeung Ek, 'The Killing Fields,' which were still being dug up in August 1981. The site then bore little resemblance to the 'tourist' location it has become today.

Vietnamese conscripts drilling at Kompong Chhnang, northwest of Phnom Penh in August 1981.

An Epilogue for Monsignor Tep Im

After I saw Monsignor Paulus Tep Im Sotha in Battambang for the last time in December 1970, and as the news from Cambodia became steadily worse, with the Khmer Rouge ultimately coming to power in April 1975, my thoughts often turned to this admirable man. It was not that I valued his friendship above the concerns I had for the other friends I had made in Phnom Penh. But it is correct to say that, from the time I first met him in 1966, his was the most deeply intellectual of all my Cambodian friendships. I think, too, I initially harboured a hope that what I thought of as his non-political position as a Catholic cleric might protect him from the dangers likely to affect my other friends. But I should have realised that this was an erroneous judgment, for as he had once pointed out to me Catholicism was thought of by Cambodians as *sassena barang*, a "foreign religion", and so as much a target for the Khmer Rouge as other Western influences.

When Phnom Penh fell to the Khmer Rouge, I had made the grim assumption that Colonel Kim Kosal's association with the government in the closing stages of the war against the Khmer Rouge meant that there was little reason to think he was still alive—the Khmer Rouge had made clear their intention to kill those linked to the government in Phnom Penh. Indeed, the scant evidence I have been able to gather subsequently suggests he was executed either immediately or very shortly after the Khmer Rouge seized Phnom Penh on 17 April 1975, possibly beheaded along with other senior officials in the grounds of the Cercle Sportif not far from the *Phnom*. As for Prince Entaravong, as a minor member of the royal family he seemed all too likely to be a target of the new regime. I learnt later that he and his wife simply disappeared after being driven out of Phnom Penh in the forced exodus that followed the Khmer Rouge victory. Prince Entaravong's son, my oldest and closest friend, Sisowath Phandaravong, or Ratsody to use his nickname, survived because he was working in Bangkok when Pol Pot's Khmer Rouge came to power in 1975. (I had learnt that his half-brother, Sisowath Dusseday, who had defected to the insurgents in the late 1960s, had apparently died at some point after 1975.) But in 1975 and 1976 I had absolutely no news of Tep Im. Of other friends, including Khao Song Beng, I could find no information at all.

Not knowing where else to turn for information, and at this stage living in Singapore, I wrote to a Jesuit acquaintance in the Philippines, Father John Carroll SJ, a fellow but older graduate from the Cornell Southeast Asia Program, whom I had met in both Ithaca, New York, and Manila. I sought his help in finding out what, if anything, might be known at the Vatican about Tep Im's fate. Within a remarkably short time I received a reply from Father Carroll which told me he had learnt from Rome that the understanding in the Vatican was that Tep Im was dead, having been executed by the Khmer Rouge shortly after the Pol Pot regime gained power.

Some considerable time later I found further information in a book by the French missionary priest, Father François Ponchaud. Best known for his book, *Cambodia: Year Zero* (*Cambodge: année zéro*), which provides an eye-witness account of the Khmer Rouge driving Phnom Penh's population out of the city, he had also published a much less well known history of the Catholic church in Cambodia, *The Cathedral of the Rice Paddy*, (originally published in French as *La Cathédrale de la rizière*). In this book Father Ponchaud writes of how Monsignor Tep Im celebrated his last mass on 13 April and gave general absolution to his parishoners. He was subsequently seized by the Khmer Rouge and later shot after being told he would be allowed to leave the country for Thailand. He also recounts but dismisses the existence of a rumour, which I heard repeated when I visited Battambang in 1981, that Tep Im's skeleton was later found, identified by its unusual height and by the presence of a silver pectoral cross and his monsignor's ring.

As the years passed, and despite further enquiries that I made on my visit to Cambodia in 1981 and many visits into the new century, I continued to wonder if in some fashion new and more detailed information about Tep Im's death might yet be available. Finally, in 2008, I decided to make one last effort and to go directly to the Vatican myself. The question was, how to do this? Eventually, and with the help of a Catholic friend, I was given the name of a figure to whom I could turn, Archbishop Claudio Maria Celli, President of the Vatican Commission for Social Communications, a cleric with Asian experience and said to be very approachable. And indeed he was, replying promptly by email to my letter asking for assistance in my search for details about Tep Im's death and saying that I should call on him when I visited Rome in December 2008.

I never did see Archbishop Celli, but instead was received by one of his clerical assistants, and not as I had hoped, with my attachment to history, within the confines of Vatican City itself, but rather in a modern building not far from St Peter's on the Via della Conciliazione. He could not help me in terms of information but undertook to put me in touch with someone at the Congregation for the Evangelisation of Peoples, once better known as the *Propaganda Fide*, who might be able to help me. And so, a day later, I found myself talking to Monsignor Phuong, a Vietnamese cleric with responsibilities for Cambodia at the Congregation's headquarters in the Via Propaganda, near the Spanish Steps. Sadly, as we talked about Tep Im in French, he could add nothing fundamentally new as the details the Congregation possessed confirmed those already recorded by Father Ponchaud. But Monsignor Phuong did show me the transcript, in English translation, of a letter written by a Cambodian Catholic from the village of Chomnon, where, as I note below, Tep Im and a Father Badré had sheltered for a short period in late April 1975. Writing to a priest whose name is not given, the author of the letter, one T. Romloeung, gives a brief account of Tep Im's death and notes that, "As for me, the father Badré told me to remain at Chomnon, saying to me, 'If I can leave [for Thailand], I will return to get you later.'" Of course, if Romloeung had accompanied the priests he would not have survived. And the letter concludes with a simple but poignant sentence from its author that reflects this fact: "That is why I am still living today."

So, as far as it is possible to be certain of what happened, the following is an account of Monsignor Tep Im's last days on the basis of the sadly limited evidence. As Father Ponchaud reords, he had celebrated mass for the last time on 13 April 1975 and given general absolution to his parishoners. He was still in Battambang when Khmer Rouge soldiers seized control of the town on 17 April. Although the bulk of the town's population was then driven out into the countryside almost immediately after, Tep Im remained until 25 April, by which time the Khmer Rouge had killed many officials and soldiers of the overthrown regime, both in and close to the town. For whatever reason, he had not been taken into custody at this stage. Deciding that he should try to reach Thailand, and accompanied by a Benedictine monk, Father Jean Badré, and two young catechists, Tep Im left Battambang on 25 April driving along back roads in Father Badré's Land Rover. They reached the Catholic village of Chomnom and remained there for about a week. At some point they were joined by a man named Arnaldo Marini, who has been variously identified as Italian and as Australian, and his Cambodian wife.

Some few days later, with the suggestion it was on 30 April, Tep Im, Father Badré, Arnaldo Marini and his wife were seen at Mongkol Borei, near Sisophon, and by this stage they were in Khmer Rouge custody. They were held there, or at Bat Trang nearby, for a further five days before being taken away in a "jeep" by a Khmer Rouge official or soldier, named Soy, who said he was leading them to the frontier with Thailand. Then, near Bat Trang, the four were ordered from the vehicle and told to climb down a river bank. At this point Soy shot them all in the back with an AK-47 and stripped their bodies of their clothes.

* * *

Tep Im's name is barely remembered in today's Cambodia, even among members of his own faith, with the exception of the small Catholic community in Battambang and by some of his fellow priests. The church at which I first met him, in 1966, the Eglise Hoalong, in Phnom Penh, was demolished by the Khmer Rouge and all that remains as a memory of its existence is a few *ex voto* tablets set in a rock that shelters a small image of the Virgin Mary.

An Epilogue for Norodom Sihanouk

Throughout this manuscript Norodom Sihanouk, king, prince and chief of state of Cambodia has been a persistent presence, sometimes front and centre, at other times lurking in the background. What follows is an obituary I wrote of him some years before his death at the request of Michael Hayes, the pioneering and courageous founder and editor of *The Phnom Penh Post*. It was finally published, with minor amendments in *The Phnom Penh Post* on 17 October 2012 after Sihanouk's death, and I express my sincere gratitude to that newspaper for waiving any copyright issues connected with the publication of the obituary. It is a matter of some surprise that to date I have written the only full-length biography of Sihanouk: *Sihanouk: Prince of Light, Prince of Darkness*, published in 1994. His life is a subject that surely demands a more up-to-date and detailed appreciation.

Norodom Sihanouk – King, Chief of State and Prime Minister of Cambodia Born 31 October 1922 died 15 October 2012.

By any standard, Norodom Sihanouk was one of the most remarkable political figures of the twentieth century. During the course of a lifetime that lasted eighty-nine years, he filled the roles of king, prime minister and chief of state of his country and in doing so took actions for good and bad that had profound effects on the course of Cambodia's modern history. In his early adult life he was by his own account a playboy, and, in his own words, "randy as a rabbit" (*un chaud lapin*). He was a musician of more than modest talent, but in his other artistic endeavours as a filmmaker his efforts were at best mediocre, even banal. In the late 1970s he was, for nearly three years, a prisoner of the murderous Khmer Rouge. It says much about this extraordinary man that such a listing only touches the surface of his many public and private roles.

Above all, and for those who have studied modern Cambodian history, Sihanouk was a subject of controversy. For some, the present writer included, he was a man of many but flawed talents whose personal weaknesses cost his country dearly. For others, he was the man who by his personal efforts transformed a sleepy kingdom from a French protectorate into a modern Southeast Asian state. According to this view, whatever faults he may have possessed were negated by his many positive contributions and by the fact, on which all can agree, that he always acted in the belief that he had the good of his country and its people in mind.

Sihanouk's installation as King of Cambodia in 1941 came as a surprise to most contemporary observers. Born in 1922, the only child of Prince Norodom Suramarit and of Princess Sisowath Kossamak, there was little reason in the early years of his life to think that Sihanouk might one day occupy the Cambodian throne. With a father who was an intelligent but rather lazy man and an amiable womaniser, and a mother who was strong-willed and a staunch supporter of Cambodian traditions, Sihanouk appeared to be just another of the many members of the sprawling royal family who might theoretically be eligible to mount the throne, but seemed, in fact, unlikely to do so. This was so because the reigning king at the time of his birth, King Sisowath, was a member of a different branch of the royal family from Sihanouk. And when Sisowath died in 1927, he was succeeded by one of his sons, King Monivong.

This succession seemed to accord with the prevailing view within the French administration in Cambodia that members of the Norodom branch of the royal family, to which Sihanouk belonged, were less reliable allies than their cousins, the Sisowaths. Indeed, the possibility of a Norodom ever being placed on the throne seemed unlikely to most observers. Sihanouk's own account of his early life makes clear that he was a lonely child. His parents had little to do with him as his mother followed the advice of an astrologer and handed control of the young prince over to an elderly female relative for the first five or six years of his life. She, in turn, delegated her responsibilities to a female servant, whom Sihanouk later described as being like one of the trusted house slaves in *Gone with the Wind*. As for his father, although he was not unkind to his only legitimate child, he simply spent little time in his company. Nevertheless, Sihanouk's parents did not neglect his education, sending him first to the Ecole François Baudoin in Phnom Penh, then enrolling him as a student at the Lycée Chasseloup-Laubat in Saigon, the best-regarded secondary school in French Indochina, where he embarked on a classic French education.

In a telling comment on this period which gives a sense of his previous loneliness, Sihanouk has stated that it was while he was living in Saigon, boarding with a French customs official of Indian descent, that he made his first friendships. These were with two fellow *lycéens*, one an ethnic Vietnamese, the other an ethnic Chinese. Overall, and despite maintaining links with the wider royal family in Phnom Penh during vacations, the picture that emerges of Sihanouk in his mid to late teens is of a vulnerable, even timid individual. Many years were to pass before there was a distinct change in his personality. It does not take deep psychological insight to judge that his later resentment of contrary opinions to his own had links with this earlier period when he was offered little if any support by his family and had, of necessity, to develop a sense of self-reliance that was mixed with a latent resentment of views contrary to his own.

Sihanouk's life was transformed by King Monivong's death in April 1941. Following Metropolitan France's defeat by Germany two months later the pro-Vichy colonial administration in Indochina only managed to maintain its control over Cambodia, Laos and Vietnam by allowing Japanese forces free access to and transit through its territories. Against this background, the French administration put its doubts about the Norodoms aside and chose Sihanouk to succeed to the throne. It did so in the confident conviction that he would be a pliable figurehead, one whose royal status could be used to France's advantage. His selection came as a total surprise to Sihanouk. As he later put it, "My first reaction was of fear, of fright, I broke down in tears." Five months after Monivong's death, Sihanouk was crowned king. Pictures of this event show a doleful Sihanouk staring wistfully at the camera. It is tempting to conclude that he was reacting to the predictions of the court astrologers that his would be a glorious reign but that, in the end, this would avail him nothing.

To a larger degree than Sihanouk was subsequently ready to admit, his first few years on the throne while the Pacific War was still in progress, justified French calculations. He took his place at official functions as the French required, presided over traditional court ceremonies, and indulged his passions for music and amateur dramatics. He took no part in a major demonstration against the French administration in Phnom Penh in 1942, and it is clear that in most matters that he was entirely ready to follow the guidance of his French mentors. Yet some hints of Sihanouk's later personality did begin to emerge in the early years of his reign. One was in the control he showed himself ready to exercise over the way in which the royal palace was run. For decades members of the royal family had treated it as a location where they could gather and if necessary live with their servants, making the palace compound something resembling a transit camp. He ended this practice and at the same time did away with the dispensing of opium to royal family members, a practice tolerated by his predecessors. He also opposed French plans to romanise the Cambodian script and to eliminate education in monastery schools, apparently recognising how deeply offensive these proposals were to most of his compatriots. Nevertheless, in a frank commentary on these war years, he admitted that most of his time was spent in "horse riding, the cinema, the theatre, water skiing, basketball, without speaking of my amorous adventures". His reference to the cinema in this catalogue is notable, since this was a pleasure that was to have political significance in later years.

The next major, dramatic change in Sihanouk's life came in March 1945, when the Japanese mounted a *coup de force* throughout the countries of Indochina overturning the French administration and orchestrating the declarations of "independence" in Cambodia, Laos and Vietnam. In the months between the Japanese action and the return of the French to reassert control over Cambodia, Sihanouk was swept up in events rather than playing a part to shape them. Advised and to a large extent controlled by older conservative Cambodians at this time, Sihanouk slowly came to recognise that his kingly status provided him with the opportunity to play a determining role in Cambodian politics. By the late 1940s he had concluded that most of those who were playing a part in his country's politics were either unable to separate policy from personal ambition or, even more seriously in his eyes, were ready to contemplate a Cambodia in which he had no place of power. With regard to this latter judgment, he was particularly concerned and suspicious of those who had embraced left-wing views. In his eyes, with a considerable degree of accuracy, he saw such men as inevitably linked with the Vietnamese communists who by this time were engaged in a bitter war against the French.

It was at the end of the 1940s that Sihanouk shook off the range of past constraints that had hindered his becoming the dominant political figure in the country. He showed himself increasingly ready to play an active role in Cambodia's political life and, most importantly of all, to take the lead in working for the country's independence from France. In embarking on a "Royal Crusade" for independence, an initiative which included appeals to international opinion, brief self-imposed exile from Phnom Penh, and suggestions that the alternative to his program was the likelihood of a communist takeover of Cambodia, Sihanouk both gained independence from France in 1953 and established himself as the leading political figure in the country. What is more, he was able through his success to marginalise the embryonic communist movement in Cambodia that, at this stage, was essentially working under the direction of the Vietnamese Communist Party. It was also during this period in the early 1950s that Sihanouk began his long association with Monique Izzi, (now referred to as Queen Monineath) a relationship that was to last to the end of his life as she stood by him throughout the many vicissitudes of his career and became his closest confidant and adviser.

Despite these successes, and to his increasing annoyance, he found that there were still some politicians who were not ready to accept that his voice alone should be the one that directed the affairs of the state. Faced with this fact and relying on a trusted group of conservative advisers Sihanouk, in March 1955, took the dramatic step of abdicating the throne in his father 's favour. Shortly after he founded and became head of the Sangkum Reastr Niyum, the People's Socialist Community, a broad based movement designed to be flexible enough to encompass a wide range of views, always provided it was accepted that Sihanouk's policies were those that were followed. Sihanouk's abdication was a masterstroke and the five or six years that followed were the most politically productive of his long career.

Concerned to transform Cambodia into a modern state, he supported the expansion of education and health services, using his apparently unflagging energy to push programs to completion. Some of these initiatives resulted in real achievements, but too often what resulted was more form than substance, or had consequences that were far different to those Sihanouk expected. In education, most significantly, he gave little thought to the results of pushing ever-larger numbers of students through secondary education when there were no jobs for them to fill once they left school. By the early 1960s there was a growing pool of discontented youth who were ready to listen to the views of the small but committed group of left-wing radicals who were working clandestinely in Phnom Penh. Among them was the man who went by the name of Saloth Sar, the later Pol Pot.

Sihanouk pursued his domestic agenda against a background of generally difficult, and often poisonous, relations with his neighbours in South Vietnam and Thailand, and the overt suspicion of the United States for his embrace of a "neutral" foreign policy that depended on warm relations with the People's Republic of China. As the target of two plots against him involving South Vietnam and Thailand in 1959, in one of which there was clear American involvement, Sihanouk was convinced that China alone could act as the ultimate guarantor of Cambodia's security. He saw this as a vital issue as he increasingly came to believe that the communist government in Hanoi would eventually control the whole of Vietnam. From 1960 onwards, and despite his readiness to act brutally against left-wing groups in Cambodia itself, he followed policies designed to appease Hanoi. In doing so he took the fatal step in 1963 of turning his back on American aid, which had propped up Cambodia's army, while striking a secret agreement the allowed Vietnamese communist forces to use Cambodian territory as a sanctuary. In 1965 he broke off diplomatic relations with the United States.

From 1966 onwards, the apparent promise of Sihanouk's early years political dominance had begun to fade. He still was the unquestioned leader of his country, at least in the world of open politics, by this stage wearing the mantle of Chief of State that he had assumed after his father's death in 1960. He had assumed this new position rather than allow any other royal figure to take the throne in case this could lead to a challenge to his position. But the country's economy was stagnant and there was growing concern among Cambodia largely conservative political class at the policy of appeasement towards Hanoi that Sihanouk was pursuing. What is more, Sihanouk was no longer showing his formidable energy in controlling domestic politics as he spent more and more time engaged in the production of full-length "feature films", which he claimed would show Cambodia's many beauties to the outside world. While it would be wrong to give too much emphasis to the negative impact that this film making activity had on political opinion, there is no doubt that many elite Cambodians saw Sihanouk's preoccupation with films as an important symbol of his failure to address more serious issues.

Against a background of external threats over which Sihanouk had little if any control, and as war raged next door in Vietnam, Sihanouk sought to achieve a balancing act both domestically and in foreign affairs. By opting out from the selection of candidates for election to the National Assembly in 1966, he insured that the government that came into power that year was of a deeply conservative cast and even ready to question some of his policies. And in the field of foreign policy, while still continuing to allow Vietnamese communist forces to make use of Cambodian territory, he sought to repair relations with the United States. Complicating matters for him by early 1967 was the outbreak of a series of rural revolts against Phnom Penh's authority. While the immediate cause of these revolts appears to have been local discontent with heavy-handed government actions associated with the forced collection of rice, the small Cambodian communist movement rapidly gained control of these insurrections that increasingly posed a threat to the authority of the state

From 1968 onwards Sihanouk alternated between frenetic activity in the political arena, including authorising the brutal suppression of the rural insurgences, and losing himself in the production of his feature films His devotion to the latter culminated in the mounting of two Phnom Penh International Film Festivals, in both of which the top award of the "Golden Apsara" went to Sihanouk himself. While little recognised by the outside world, Sihanouk's grip over the direction of the state was steadily slipping. Most particularly this was so because those who had previously been his closest allies—the conservative politicians and the members of the officer corps—no longer felt that his policies matched their own interests. From a very different point of view, a small but significant number of middle class Cambodians had come to the conclusion that only a revolution could solve Cambodia's entrenched social problems and do away with the corruption endemic in Sihanouk's regime. They joined the radical groups already active in the countryside who were making steady progress in recruiting peasant support as they contrasted the indulgent life of the Cambodian elite with the harsh realities of rural existence. Ironically, the radicals were able to point to the scenes of Phnom Penh high life depicted in Sihanouk's films to buttress their arguments that Cambodia had to be transformed through revolution.

In the event, it was Sihanouk's former allies rather than the growing left-wing movement in the countryside that overthrew him and his regime in March 1970. Debate still rages over the extent to which there was American involvement in the coup d'etat, but while it is certain that some American intelligence services were privy to the preparations that were being made to depose Sihanouk the best judgment remains that the coup was very much a Cambodian affair, with Sihanouk's cousin Prince Sirik Matak and an initially reluctant General Lon Nol as the principal plotters. Sihanouk's downfall was the start of a long period of terrible tragedy for his country. Consumed with a thirst for revenge against those who had removed him from office, Sihanouk joined forces with the Cambodian communist movement that was now working in tandem with the Vietnamese communists to fight the Lon Nol regime in Phnom Penh. While it is clear Sihanouk realised that he had little in common with the radicals who were now his allies, he appears to have thought that their victory would eventually lead to his being able to play some ill-defined leadership role in Cambodia. He certainly cannot be accused of associating with those whom he had earlier termed the Khmer Rouge with any recognition of the murderous policies that they would institute once they came to power.

Once the Khmer Rouge were in power, from April 1975, their leaders saw no reason to permit Sihanouk any role in the regime that transformed the country into a murderous tyranny leading to the death of nearly two million Cambodians. At the end of December 1975, after having visited a number of socialist countries that had recognised the new Democratic Kampuchean regime, Sihanouk returned to Phnom Penh and to three years of house arrest. While it is clear that the conditions of his detention were far from rigorous. He had every reason to fear for his life during this time. Yet when the Pol Pot regime was overthrown in January 1979 he was briefly ready to defend it at the United Nations in New York after having escaped in the company of senior Khmer Rouge officials just before the invading Vietnamese forces reached Phnom Penh. While still in New York, and angered that he would not be made head of the

Khmer Rouge delegation that remained accredited to the United Nations, Sihanouk engineered his escape from Khmer Rouge surveillance and began a long period of exile, mainly in Beijing, becoming in 1982 head of the Coalition Government of Democratic Kampuchea. In this role Sihanouk vacillated between long periods of distancing himself from the military and political activity designed to oust Vietnam from Cambodia and brief efforts to exert his control over the disparate elements of the coalition. When international events combined to bring a settlement of the Cambodia problem in 1991, Sihanouk played an important part in forging an agreement between the various Cambodian factions that enabled the United Nations to establish a position in Cambodia and to oversee the elections that took place in May 1993. Later that same year Sihanouk was once again reinstated as King of Cambodia in September 1993.

By the time he was once again recognised as Cambodia's monarch, Sihanouk was beset by a range of illnesses, including cancer. Partly because of this fact, which led to his spending long periods in China for medical treatment, but largely because control of his country's politics was now in the hands of others, most notably Prime Minister Hun Sen, Sihanouk was unable to play a pivotal role in Cambodia's politics in the closing years of his life. At best, he was able to exercise a degree of moral authority from time to time. But the reality of where political power lay meant that he had become a figurehead rather than a leader. After repeated verbal clashes with Hun Sen and with a clear fear that the monarchy might vanish as an institution if he remained as king, Sihanouk elected to abdicate in favour of his son, Prince Norodom Sihamoni, in 2004 and to assume the title of King Father.

Sihanouk was never Cambodia, as some foreign observers were inclined to say, but without question he was the most enduring and important figure in his country for over half a century. For all of the good things that he did, or tried to do, his greatest weakness was his inability to recognise that he was not the only person in Cambodia possessed of wisdom. In speaking of his people as children who had no right to their own ideas he crippled political development in the years before 1970 and contributed to the tragedies that followed his deposition in that year. As I have written previously, he was a 'prince of light and a prince of darkness'. In personalising politics while he held power he deserved praise for his achievements, but he insured that he would also be judged for the many failures of his long time as Cambodia's leader.

Acknowledgements

The list of those to whom I am indebted for this book stretches back over fifty years. Without the readiness of a wide range of people to talk to me in a frank fashion, often in times of national and international difficulty, I would never have been able to write the detailed daily journal on which much of the material in this book depends. In Cambodia, with one exception, all my close friends who were so forthcoming in the 1960s, into 1970, died as victims of Pol Pot's tyranny. Those about whom I write in relation to Vietnam in the 1960 and the beginning of the 1970s are also no longer alive. They include General Tran Van Don, the diplomat Phung Nhat Minh, and Senator Le Tan Buu. The last welcomed me as a house guest in his home on two occasions. He survived twelve years of detention after the communist victory in 1975 before remaking his life in the United States. Others, such as Gerald Hickey, whose deep understanding of Vietnam did not stop his American academic colleagues vilifying him for not joining in a rejection of the South Vietnamese regime, have also passed from the scene.

Throughout the years covered by this manuscript Australian officials and military personnel, both in Cambodia and in Vietnam, generously shared their views with me, leaving me to decide the extent to which I would reflect their comments in any of my then contemporary writing. In the present book I have chosen to record their views in more detail than ever before with the thought that the passage of more than fifty years is a sufficient time to have passed for frankness to prevail.

More immediately I have debts of a different kind to record. When I first contemplated writing this book I discussed its form and projected content with Jill Ker Conway, a dear and lifelong friend ever since we met as students at the University of Sydney. Her encouragement to turn my thoughts into a manuscript was central to my decision to go ahead with the task of writing.

As he has done on previous occasions David Chandler commented helpfully on a much earlier draft on of this manuscript. We first met in Phnom Penh in 1960 since when David has become the world's pre-eminent historian of Cambodia. I treasure the friendship we have maintained since that time. I am most grateful that Gerard Henderson, the Executive Director of the Sydney Institute, should have agreed to read the manuscript on which this book is based and to comment in detail on it. Given that I spent much of the 1960s and almost all of the 1970s living away from Australia his knowledge of domestic issues that bore on international concerns was extremely valuable as was his suggestion that Connor Court might be interested in publishing the manuscript. Alex Odum, Chief Executive Officer of The Phnom Penh Post, kindly waived copyright on the obituary of King Norodom Sihanouk that I published in that newspaper on 17 October 2012. My old friend Truong Buu Lam, whom I first met at Cornell in 1966, has kindly allowed me to quote from his translation of Nguyen Trai's 'Great Proclamation upon the Pacification of the Wu', the poem celebrating the defeat of the Ming invaders of Vietnam in the early fifteenth century. The full text of the poem is found in his monograph, Patterns of Vietnamese response to foreign intervention, 1858-1900, published by Yale Southeast Asia Studies in 1967.

As has been the case over many years I am grateful to Nicholas Pounder who was always ready to solve technical problems associated with producing the manuscript on which this book is based. His expertise in technical matters is only equalled by his helpful comment on the content of the book.

I am happy to record my thanks to Connor Court Publishing, and in particular to Anthony Cappello, for the great care they have exercised in bringing this book to publication.

As must always be the case, none of those to whom I owe thanks and gratitude are responsible for the facts as I present them and the conclusions I offer. For these I alone am responsible. This comment applies, most particularly, to those who were ready to put up with me at a domestic personal level as I pursued my growing fascination with a world that now exists only in memory.

Milton Osborne, Sydney,   2018

www.ingramcontent.com/pod-product-compliance
Lightning Source LLC
Chambersburg PA
CBHW071844270326
41929CB00013B/2094